Patriot Graves

Discovering a California Town's Civil War Heritage

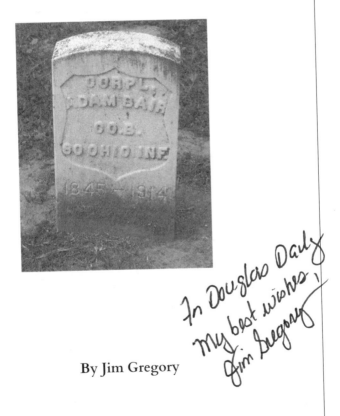

*In Douglas Daily
My best wishes,
Jim Gregory*

By Jim Gregory

Cover image: Grand Review, Washington D.C., May 1865. *Library of Congress.*

We are not enemies, but friends. We must not be enemies. Though passion may have strained it must not break our bonds of affection. The mystic chords of memory, stretching from every battlefield and patriot grave to every living heart and hearthstone all over this broad land, will yet swell the chorus of the Union, when again touched, as surely they will be, by the better angels of our nature.

–Abraham Lincoln,
First Inaugural Address
March 4, 1861

*For Thom Wade, teacher, mentor,
husband, father, inspiration.*

*For my sons, John and Thomas, who grew up
straight and tall, just the way I'd hoped.*

Table of Contents

Acknowledgements

The great Irish actor Daniel Day-Lewis is known for disappearing into every film role he's preparing, whether it's Hawkeye in *Last of the Mohicans*, Bill the Butcher in *Gangs of New York*, or Daniel Playview in *There Will Be Blood*. He disappeared so convincingly in Steven Spielberg's *Lincoln* that I instantly recognized on the screen the man I wanted all my life to meet. He gave me my Father Abraham.

Lincoln, about eight weeks before his death, in an Alexander Gardner photograph. *Library of Congress.*

And that is the one and only similarity between this actor and myself. When I was writing this book, I disappeared, as well: I was 150 years gone. I never realized how charged a topic the Civil War was for me and how much of it I had stored inside—fifty years' worth of study, or reading, or sorrow (Another Civil War film, *Glory*, brought me to tears). No college course ever touched me more than the University of Missouri's History of the Old South, taught by Charles B. Dew, because the lives slaves lived became so real to me, and in their endurance I found American bedrock. I learned to be immensely proud that their heritage is ours, too.

When I write, it is my wife, Elizabeth, who becomes the victim of my little trips in the time machine that is my laptop computer. While I was writing this book, she was almost as isolated as was Lincoln during much of his presidency. She was nonetheless understanding and constantly supportive.

With support like that, almost anyone can do what I did. It takes curiosity, tenacity, and superb teachers and writers who, in this case, include the late Bruce Catton, whose books I return to over and over again when life deals me scraped knees and dashed hopes. Catton's intimacy with his subject, the Union Army, allows him to talk about it and to us in a conversational and completely arresting way that reminds me that all good history, as I learned from my father, is good storytelling.

The book's focus is on Union veterans because of Catton's influence and the influence of a younger historian, Brian Matthew Jordan. Additionally, it is their burials that have been the most reliably recorded in Arroyo Grande. I decided, then, to start this telling of the Civil War when these soldiers' hopes were at low ebb, with the terrible casualties Lee inflicted on them at Antietam and then, the following spring, when the great general destroyed their new-found confidence at Chancellorsville.

Two Southern historians were of immense help in understanding Lee's successes and the ordeal of the war's last year. Shelby Foote's massive three volumes, *The Civil War: A Narrative,* are more detailed and analytical than Catton's work—I don't pretend to be a military historian—but just as invaluable. Even though this book addresses the Union Army, Douglas Southall Freeman's volumes, *Lee's Lieutenants,* are like three Sinai tablets, when Moses was issued only two, on the Army of Northern Virginia and they point endlessly to Lee's genius for inspiring younger men. Admittedly, I had a hard time forgiving Lee when I stood above Devil's Den at Gettysburg and actually cursed him under my breath for sending boys and men to take such an easily-defended position. I did the same for Ike at Omaha Beach, however, so I may not be not a reliable judge of military leadership.

Thomas, Jim and John Gregory at Gettysburg, 2001. *Photo by Elizabeth Gregory.*

I owe a debt of thanks to many people, including Michael Marsalek, the head guardian of my small town's cemetery, because the grounds he keeps so faithfully, maddening for a Californian like Mike in times of drought, were where I found my first clues. The book's title comes from Lincoln's reference to the generation of 1776, but the generation of patriots who fought the Civil War left researchers with invaluable starting points— their own tombstones—which record the regiments and even the companies in which they served.

That knowledge led me to the database maintained by the National Park Service and to one of my favorite ways to waste time, ancestry.com. Thanks to these websites, I was able to translate tombstones into regiments and so into battlefields, to trace our veterans to where they would have fought and what they would have seen unless, as I might have done, they chose July 1, 1863—the first day of Gettysburg—to go on their company's sick list. That's unlikely, since these men fought most of all for each other. The tombstones also led me to firsthand accounts from the men our veterans would have served with—from their officers' reports in *The War of the Rebellion* to vigorous first-hand accounts by private soldiers in wartime diaries and letters home. These are voices that deserve to be heard again.

Arroyo Grande native Jack English was incredibly generous in sharing the story of his ancestor Erastus Fouch, and holding Erastus's leather-bound wartime diaries in my hands was a life-changing experience. Tom Alcott was also helpful in researching his ancestor, John Henry, born on an immigrant ship from England in mid-Atlantic, and so was Blake Bristol in researching his ancestor, Charles. I would have known nothing about the postwar lives of local veterans without the help of Paul Provence of the South County Historical Society, who got me into the Branch Street meat locker where the old weekly *Herald-Recorders* are stored, some of them so aged now that they are as fragile as New Kingdom papyrus. Shirley Bennett Gibson and her mother, Manetta Bennett, were both sources of expert information on the history of Arroyo Grande and my most reliable morale-boosters. Don Barr of Paso Robles was a terrific source on the 58th Indiana at Chickamauga, and it was wonderful to find someone as enthralled by the Civil War and the history of the American West as I am.

And thanks, in division strength, to some superb English teachers: Amber Derbidge, my dear friend, fellow European traveler and chaperone for many student trips, and my longtime teaching partner in the integrated Advanced Placement European History/Pre-AP European Literature courses at Arroyo Grande High School. Thanks, as well, to former Arroyo Grande High School colleague John A. Silva, another good friend, now English Department Chair at

Ravenwood High School in Brentwood, Tennessee. St. Joseph High School's Paul Ontiveros gave the manuscript a final vetting, *and* during his vacation time, and his, expertise, too, is deeply appreciated. All contributed unselfishly and provided key insights in their editing of the book.

Judkins Intermediate School teacher Terry Handy is to be both thanked and praised for his annual Civil War encampment, in which his students learn the rudiments of Civil War soldiering and more—they have a feel for the war, I believe, that few young people share. Mr. Handy is a superb

Mr. Terry Handy and his troops of the "36th Ohio" at Judkins Intermediate School, Pismo Beach, California. *Author photo.*

teacher. While researching the book, I had the privilege of watching him turn a typically-restless group of eighth graders—more terrifying to this veteran high school teacher than Stonewall Jackson's corps—into a "battalion" of Ohio troops who learned to shift from rank and file to a marching column of fours in a little over forty minutes. Mr. Handy reminds me, as well, to send thanks to the young people I had the privilege to teach over the years at both Mission Prep and Arroyo Grande High School, and many of the latter are Mr. Handy's veterans.

I need to thank, too, the following friends who offered me financial, moral and editorial support and for their faith in me:

Cat Anderson, Madison Ansbro, Richard Awalt, Manetta Bennett, Chuck Brooner, Dana Bruce, Andrew Carroll, Beth Carroll, David Carroll, Joanne Carroll, Virginia Casey, Dominic Dal Bello, Chantal Deines, Ben Davis, Amber Derbidge, Catherine Donovan, Dona Fuchiwaki, Steven M. Frisby, Ellen Gaver, Shirley Gibson, Mary Giambalvo, Chris Grossi, Beverly Harben, Jack Harris, Alicia Hightower, Dami An Jones, Dan Krieger, Liz Krieger, Judy Leonard, Bonnie Len, Kaytlyn Leslie, Elizabeth Lobo, Deborah Love, Kevin McCarthy, Shari McCarthy, Donal McGuirk, Crystala Melea, Gwendolyn Melton, David Middlecamp, Kevin Mounts, Moyses Muguira, Mary O'Connor, Pat O'Connor, Kay Orrell, Connie Patterson, Patsy Phelan, Todd Pope, Paul Provence, Gerrie Quaresma, Kara Reid, Holly Russell, Susie Salmon, Jack San Filippo, Dan Sebby, John A. Silva, Julie Anne Silva, Marjorie Stinson, Eva Ulz, Laurie Waller, and Richard Waller.

Finally, I need to thank most of all three fine men, Sadly, Arroyo Grande High School English teacher Thom Wade, brilliant and beloved, always a friend and a moral support to me in my teaching, died unexpectedly as this book was deciding to finish itself, and he will be missed. I also want to recognize two young men who make me proud, John Bruce Gregory and Thomas James Gregory, my sons. I am indebted to you, John and Thomas. This book is small payment for the great happiness you have brought in the good place that is our home, Arroyo Grande, California.

Union Veteran Burials Recorded in Arroyo Grande, California

1. **Austin Abbot** unknown -1894 7th Michigan Infantry
2. **Seneca Abbot** unknown-1895 1st Regiment, Michigan Light Artillery
3. **Alexis Adams** unknown-1907 Co. D, 12th Maine Infantry
4. **Herbert D. Adams** unknown-1895 Co. K, 12th Maine Infantry
5. **John H. Alcott** 1829-1904 Co. G. 16th Wisconsin Infantry
6. **William John Ash** 1834-1892 Ordinary Seaman, United States Navy
7. **Adam Bair** 1845-1917 Cpl. Co. B. 60th Ohio Infantry
8. **Henry Bakeman** unknown-unknown Co F, 2nd Iowa Infantry
9. **Francis X. Belot** unknown-1906 Co. K, 4th Minnesota Infantry
10. **Henry Bouchard** 1842-1943 155th Illinois Infantry
11. **John William Brassfield** Co. M 11ᵗʰ Illinois Cavalry
12. **Joseph Brewer** unknown-1921 Co. C 11th New Jersey Infantry
13. **Charles E. Bristol** 1848-1916 Co. D. 87th Ohio Infantry; 8ᵗʰ Michigan Cavalry
14. **John D. Brown** 1842-1910 Co. H 34ᵗʰ Illinois Infantry
15. **Harrison Marion Bussell** 1835-1906 Co. G 1st Colorado Cavalry
16. **Charles S. Clark** 1848-1916 Co. F. 1st New Jersey Cavalry
17. **Francis A. Craig** unknown -1912 Co. F 73rd Illinois Infantry
18. **Jacob Davis** 1833-1895 Capt. Co. B 58ᵗʰ Indiana Infantry
19. **Morris Denham** 1833 -1916 Co A 12th Wisconsin Infantry
20. **James A. Dowell** 1832-1919 Co. M 16th Kansas Cavalry
21. **Erastus Fouch** 1844-1926 Co. I 75th Ohio Infantry
22. **Stephen Daniel Harding,** 1832-1907 Co. I, 73ʳᵈ Indiana Infantry
23. **Thomas Exley Hodges** 1846-1933 45th Missouri Infantry

24. **Lauretta H. Cutter Hoisington** 1826-1915 Union Army Nurse, Chattanooga, Tennessee (Halcyon Cemetery)
25. **Bela C. Ide** unknown-1922 Co. C 24th Michigan Infantry
26. **George A. John** unknown-unknown Co. H 73rd Indiana Infantry
27. **Otis M. Keesey** unknown-1917 Co. D. 98th Ohio Infantry
28. **Thomas H. Keown** 1846-1933 Co. F. 12th Missouri Cavalry
29. **Emery Knotts** unknown-1912 Co. A, 145th Indiana Infantry
30. **William Lane** 1835-1923 1st Lt Co. C 24th Iowa Infantry
31. **Samuel McBane** 1834-1901 Co. F 123rd Ohio Infantry
32. **Richard P. Merrill** 1844-1909 Cpl. Co. E 130th Pennsylvania Infantry
33. **Isaac Dennis Miller** 1843-1896 Co. D 24th Iowa Infantry
34. **Samuel B. Miller** Sgt. Co. G 24th Iowa
35. **George Monroe** unknown-1930 Co F 148th Ohio Infantry
36. **James Morgan** 1837-1915 2nd Lt. Co. E 80th Indiana Infantry
37. **Timothy Munger** 1838-1911 Cpl. Co. C 8th Ohio Cavalry
38. **George Henry Purdy** 1840-1913 Capt. Co. A 11th West Virginia Infantry
39. **Paul Riel** 1810-1906 Sgt. 6th U.S. Infantry
40. **John S. Rice** 1829-1910 Pvt. Co. F 10th Minnesota Infantry
41. **Irwin L. Ross** unknown-1898 Cpl. Co. B 13th Michigan Infantry
42. **Steven Vitalis Runels** 1845-1927 Co. C 47th Ohio Infantry
43. **Edward Stewart Shaw** 1843-1902 Cpl Co. B 74th Illinois Infantry
44. **Granville Shinn** unknown-1907 Co. C. 118th Illinois Infantry
45. **Otis W. Smith** 1844-1923 Co. G. 95th Ohio Infantry. Medal of Honor
46. **John W. Spears** 1833-unknown Co. M 3rd New York Cavalry

47. **James G. Stevenson** 1829-1910 Co C 74th Ohio Infantry/Co. I 154th Ohio Infantry
48. **William Haze Strobridge** unknown-1903 1st Michigan Cavalry
49. **Sylvanus Ullom** unknown-1914 Cpl. Co. C 25th Ohio Infantry
50. **Thomas Whiteley Sr.** unknown-1898 4th Massachusetts Militia
51. **George Wood,** 1832-1911 Co I 29th Missouri Infantry
52. **Jefferson Wright** unknown-1905 Co. A 55th Ohio Infantry

Note: This compilation was as complete as possible as of April 2016; there are likely other veterans who, for various reasons, do not appear in local records. Appendix II identifies the Confederate veterans who have been confirmed since the book's publication.

Samuel W. Doble was the drummer boy in Alexis Adams's Company D, 12th Maine Infantry. *Library of Congress.*

Wartime Leaders

Abraham Lincoln, President of the United States, Commander-in-Chief

Ulysses S. Grant, Union Army commander 1864-65

William Tecumseh Sherman, Commander, Army of the Tennessee, Army of Georgia

Philip Sheridan, Commander, Army of the Shenandoah

Joseph Hooker, Commander, Army of the Potomac, Spring 1863

George Thomas, Commander, Army of the Tennessee, 1864

John Schofield, Commander, Army of the Ohio, 1863-64

George McClellan, Commander, Army of the Potomac, 1861-62

George Gordon Meade, Commander, Army of the Potomac, 1863-65

George Armstrong Custer, Commander, Third Cavalry Division, Army of the Shenandoah

Jefferson Davis, President of the Confederate States

Robert E. Lee, Commander, Army of Northern Virginia

Thomas J. "Stonewall" Jackson, Commander, II Corps, Army of Northern Virginia, 1862-63

Richard Ewell, Commander, II Corps, Army of Northern Virginia, 1863-65

James Longstreet, Commander, I Corps, Army of Northern Virginia

Joseph Johnston, Commander, Army of Tennessee, 1865

John Bell Hood, Commander, Army of Tennessee, 1864

Jubal Early, Commander, Confederate Army of the Shenandoah Valley, 1864-65

John B. Gordon, Commander, II Corps, Army of Northern Virginia, 1865

Some of the Battles and Campaigns in which Arroyo Grande Veterans Fought

Fort Donelson

Feb 11, 1862

Glorieta Pass

March 26-28, 1862

Shiloh

April 6-7, 1862

Sioux Uprising, Minnesota

August 1862

Antietam

Sept. 17, 1862

Chancellorsville

May 1-2, 1863

Champion Hill

May 16, 1863

Gettysburg

July 1-3, 1863

Chickamauga

September 19-20, 1863

Missionary Ridge

November 25, 1863

Invasion of Georgia

May 1864

The Wilderness

May 5-7, 1864

Spotsylvania Court House

May 8-21, 186

Cold Harbor

May 31-June 12, 1864

Battles for Atlanta   July 22-Sept 2, 1864

Shenandoah Valley   August-October
Campaign   1864

March to the Sea   November-
                                       December 1864

Franklin   November 30, 1864

Nashville   December 15-16,
                                       1864

Siege of Petersburg   June 9, 1864-March
                                       25, 1865

Appomattox Campaign   April 2- 9, 1865

Powder River Expedition   July-October 1865

Union Army encampment, Nashville, December 1864. This is where Otis Smith, who would become an Arroyo Grande farmer, won the Medal of Honor. *Library of Congress*

Union Army Organization

Company	100 Men, Captain commanding
Regiment	8 Companies, 800 men, Colonel commanding
Brigade 2,600	2-5 Regiments, men, Brig. General commanding
Division	2-4 Brigades, 8,000 men, Maj. General commanding
Corps	2-3 Divisions, 26,000 men, Maj. General commanding
Army	3 corps, 80,000 men, Maj. General commanding

Prologue.
Brothers

THE SECOND BATTLE OF BULL RUN, FOUGHT AUG? 29TH 1862.

A Currier & Ives print of the Second Battle of Bull Run, which the Union lost. *Library of Congress.*

Before photography began to appear in newspapers, and long before television, Currier and Ives prints dominated the popular American visual imagination. Their Civil War battle scenes depict a unity of purpose that was neither in the national mood nor reflective of wartime reality. Currier and Ives soldiers galloped in lockstep into the enemy, a forward rank's bayonets leveled at the Southern foe at precisely the

1

same angle and every soldier's *kepi,* the service cap modeled on that of French soldiers, perfectly squared, every uniform pristine and unmuddied.

This wasn't reality. Like every Civil War soldier, Erastus Fouch knew mud intimately. He also knew body lice, thirst, diarrhea, blisters, cold and wet cold, hunger, soreness, terror, friendship, sweat, exultation, his Bible, mail call, coffee, homesickness, fury, and most of all he would know loss. Erastus's regiment came to the Shenandoah Valley from his Ohio home in 1862. He left us his diaries, where irregular spelling—spelling was not completely standardized in the 1860s and Civil War soldiers spelled in ways that made sense to them—does nothing to diminish a young man who, at sixteen, was obviously very bright, very observant, armed with both an Enfield rifle and a wry sense of humor. Erastus was fully aware that he was involved in a world-changing event that would be the greatest adventure of his life.

His brother Leonidas was part of the adventure. Brothers only two years apart have the chance to become friends as well as relations, and the two had, by May 1862, been soldiers for several months in the same regiment, the 75th Ohio, and in Company I, and whatever bond had impelled them to enlist together must have grown even stronger with the hardships they'd shared and the lessons they'd learned together.

Their commanding officer on May 8, 1862, was one of the most famous men in America. He was "The Pathfinder," John C. Fremont, maybe the most renowned Western explorer since Lewis and Clark and the commander of the ragtag "California Battalion" said to have camped, during its Mexican War adventures in 1846, along the Arroyo Grande Creek, no more than two miles from the farmhouse that Fouch would build in the 1880s.

But no more than two miles away from Fremont and the Fouch brothers that day in 1862 was a Confederate general whose fame would eventually eclipse Fremont's. He was Thomas J. "Stonewall" Jackson, a gifted Mexican War artillerist, a rigid, pedantic, and uninspiring math instructor at the Virginia Military Institute in the years between the wars, a man susceptible to the passions of Protestant revivalism and one noted for his eccentricities, like holding one arm straight up in the air, index finger extended, while riding with his staff, in order to restore the balance of unspecified bodily fluids. On May 8, 1862, he was also perhaps the best field commander in the world.

As it was for any Civil War general, Jackson's job was to kill young men, and as many young men as he could, in defense, in his case, of a cause he knew to be divinely ordained. So far in the Civil War, he'd proved a master at this pursuit, confounding Union generals with his army's elusiveness, with the power of the blows it landed in the Shenandoah Valley, and with the quality of the soldiers he commanded, lean men, men who were contemptuous of military decorum, like their World War II descendants would be, but, like those soldiers, they were superb fighters. Many of them were barefoot yet they could still outpace any Yankee infantry sent to pursue them, lose them, find them again, and fall on them without warning.

That day, Fremont found Jackson's Confederates. They were on a hill preparing for a battle, the Battle of McDowell, that would be a footnote when compared to an Antietam or a Cold Harbor. While Jackson considered leisure to be one of the gravest of sins, Fremont, at McDowell, moved with a slowness that afflicted the entire Union Army for most of the Civil War. He had his artillery bombard the Confederate hill for hours, with little visible effect, while his foot soldiers, like the Fouch brothers, watched, perhaps trying vainly to nap.

3

Finally, Fremont sent his men, including the 75th Ohio, in to take on Stonewall Jackson's infantry.

This is when the real killing began.

Generals persisted for much of the Civil War to fight a war—Napoleon's—that had ended nearly fifty years before. That meant constant formation drilling that taught men to fight in dense phalanxes where the firepower of their muskets would be most telling at short range. But Civil War soldiers, with few exceptions, no longer fought with muskets. Napoleon's men had used weapons that had an optimal range of only fifty yards. The American soldiers used rifles, like the British-made Enfields that Erastus and Leonidas had been issued, that were accurate at ten times that distance. Yet the 75th Ohio closed to within 200 yards of Jackson's men fought standing up in a style that typified the war. Civil War antagonists fought close enough to transform anonymous uniformed men in the enemy's firing line into individuals with unique mannerisms, fighting styles, and personalities. They fought close enough, too, to wither whole regiments away. The Fouch brothers' regiment began the Civil War with close to a thousand men but would end it with fewer than two hundred.

After what must have seemed like an eternity of firing and reloading, the 75th's battle ended with Stonewall Jackson's men driving Fremont's back. That may have been when, with the gunsmoke beginning to clear, Erastus began to look around, in increasing desperation, for his brother Leonidas. It wasn't long before he learned, perhaps from another man in the company who'd seen the moment happen, that he was now alone. Leonidas, Erastus wrote in his diary that night, "fell, to rise no more." This was a turning point in Erastus Fouch's life, and losing his brother so close and so young must have motivated the cause he adopted with such passion thirty years later.

By then, Erastus was a farmer in the Arroyo Grande Valley in California, and he became one of the most forceful advocates for the founding of the town's high school. The eighteen-year-olds who have graduated from the high school ever since the 1890s have done so unaware that this part of their education was a gift, in a way, from another eighteen-year-old who never knew he'd given it. He died a violent death in the Shenandoah Valley in Virginia in 1862, yet this school so far away from that battlefield testifies to the power of the love that one brother can have for another. This is something that never dies.

Alexander Gardner's Civil War photography would begin to depict war as Erastus Pouch would have seen it. Here, a Union soldier contemplates the grave of a comrade while a young Confederate awaits burial. *National Park Service.*

Introduction.
Confederates and Yankees

So we beat on, boats against the current, borne back ceaselessly into the past.

F. Scott Fitzgerald, *The Great Gatsby*

James H. McBride. *Courtesy Missouri State Historical Society.*

I grew up in Arroyo Grande, California, in San Luis Obispo County, a farm town near the sea about midway between San Francisco and Los Angeles. When I was nine, the nation was beginning to mark the centennial of the American Civil War, and I was the descendant of Confederates when, in 1961, the descendant of Irish immigrants, who spoke with broad Boston Yankee vowels that delighted impersonators, was the President of the United States. His ancestry was important because, in my home, John F. Kennedy, despite his reputation as a Cold Warrior, brought us peace in a kind of domestic Civil War.

My mother was a Republican, my father a Democrat, and their lively political discussions were memorable and educational, though one cost us a dessert when my mother ended it by dumping a colander of fresh strawberries upside-down on my father's head. But she, too, was a descendant of Irish immigrants—both her family and Kennedy's had left Ireland for the Americas (hers, to Quebec, Kennedy's, to Boston) in famine ships from New Ross, in Wexford, in Ireland's southeast. She could vote for *this* Democrat.

While their personal Civil War ended, ours, as kids, continued during the centennial. We played Confederates and Yankees—the latter were the bad guys—with the three Shannon boys. We outranked the three because our ancestor outranked theirs, but they had a better claim to being descended from "real" Confederates; in fact, the youngest Shannon, Cayce, had been named for a member of a notoriously hard-hitting unit, William Barksdale's Mississippi brigade. Mr. Shannon farmed the fields of row crops—peppers and cabbage, lettuce and Brussels sprouts, pole beans and peas—that carpeted the Upper Arroyo Grande Valley. He, with permission, I hope, provided the cannon, doubtless meant to resemble a Napoleon 12-pounder, that my older brother Bruce built along with Michael Shannon. It was sited in its gun position in the midst of my chicken pen and a distressingly Yankee flock of Plymouth Rock hens. The cannon was made of axle and wheels from an old cultivator, tongue from antique lengths of cut lumber, barrel from a sawed-off section of five-inch irrigation pipe. From a distance, it looked a little menacing.

Shannons and Gregorys share a meal about 1958. Clockwise, from top left: Patricia Keefe Gregory, Michael Shannon, Jim Gregory, Roberta Gregory, Jerry Shannon, Bruce Gregory, Cayce Shannon. *Author's collection.*

In my family, the Civil War had never been distant. In a cupboard in the den of our home, where my accountant father did taxes, there was a rolled-up Confederate battle flag from a veterans' reunion that had taken place just before

America entered another war, in 1917, that, like the Civil War, changed it irrevocably. My Civil War began with my birth. I was named for my great-great grandfather, James Haggin McBride (the flag was part of a reunion in his honor), a Missouri judge and brigadier general of Confederate militia who'd fought at the Battle of Wilson's Creek and at Lexington, Missouri, early in the war. My middle name, Douglass, comes from his son, a young Confederate staff officer killed in action in Arkansas. The elder McBride is a dim twinkle in the constellation of Confederate generals, if, indeed, he belongs there at all. He'd commanded a "division"—in reality, no more than a regiment—of rough-hewn, obdurate Ozark hill men, armed with hunting rifles, at Wilson's Creek, and his "command" wasn't all that commanding. Contemporaries recalled that McBride, an officer, like many Civil War citizen-soldiers, who had no military experience, ran his staff meetings like he did trials at the county courthouse, with junior officers acting as opposing counsel and private soldiers occasionally wandering into the tent as uncalled expert witnesses.

He helped to turn the tide at the 1861 Battle of Wilson's Creek, near Springfield, Missouri, which claimed the life of Union Gen. Nathaniel Lyon, shot from his horse in a way so many natural leaders died in Civil War battles. I used to think, as a history teacher, that tragedies like Lyon's helped to explain the lengthy list of White House mediocrities between Lincoln and Theodore Roosevelt. McBride's men attacked Lyon's on what is today called Bloody Hill. Their assault would prove decisive at Wilson's Creek, but the battle would prove to be, for Missouri rebels, a short-lived victory in a losing effort. The state remained tenuously part of the Union, and Missouri would go on to raise as many or more Union regiments, thanks in part to an intensely patriotic German immigrant population, in St. Louis and along the Missouri River Valley, as Confederate ones in the course of the war.

McBride's war ended with his death, from illness—two Civil War soldiers died from disease for every one killed in battle–while he was raising troops in Arkansas. A disagreement with a superior officer had led to his resignation from his command; meanwhile, his application for a regular brigadier's commission in the Confederate Army—he did secure a colonelcy– may have gotten entangled in the red tape that even governments devoted to states' rights can generate. The animosity that the war generated in Missouri, a border state, would persist for decades. My father remembered a Fourth of July picnic where he grew up, in Texas County, that was interrupted when an octogenarian Confederate veteran pounced on a former Union drummer boy with a Barlow knife. The two men hadn't spoken to each other in sixty years—if one saw the other coming down the street, he'd cross to the other side, if one went to the barbershop for a shave and saw, through the window, the other in the barber's chair, he'd get his shave another day. That day, when the old Confederate snapped (it might've been during the playing of "The Star Spangled Banner," my father remembered), it took several strong and young men to separate the two before the white-whiskered Confederate was taken to jail, in triumph. He'd sliced off the former drummer boy's ear.

McBride, also a Texas County man, did not look like someone who took disagreements lightly, either. That imperious set to his jaw, I realized many years later, was as familiar to me as the Gettysburg battlefield would be when my wife and I took our sons there when they were little boys. (We stayed overnight at the reliably haunted Cashtown Inn, where several Confederate officers had slept the night before the battle. We were disappointed by the scarcity of ghosts but immensely pleased with the generosity of the Inn's Belgian waffles.) I saw my own grandmother, Dora Gregory, the General's granddaughter, in the General's image. She was a grave, dignified woman, a rural schoolmarm and as tough as

10

cured leather—on her visits to our Arroyo Grande home, she would use a poke with her cane to "correct" her grandchildren—and it had perhaps been her pride in her own ancestry that led to the incident for which my father never completely forgave her. Her husband, my grandfather, John Gregory, was a courtly, Kentucky-born Missouri farmer— a kindly man, he was such a graceful waltzer that barn dances meant that the entire teenaged female population of Texas County arrived with Mr. Gregory's name already penciled onto their dance cards. My grandmother was not amused.

My grandmother, Dora Gregory, ca. 1910. *Author's collection.*

One day when he was elderly and edging into deafness, he never heard the Ford roadster that struck him, breaking his legs, as he was crossing the county road in front of his farmhouse. My teenaged father had been walking with him, but Dora Gregory called her son back to the house because he was barefoot, and no descendant of the General's was going to pay a visit barefoot, not even to Mr. Dixon's across the road. So the Civil War, in an odd way, killed my grandfather: born in the war's second year, he died in a Springfield hospital in 1933.

That was the year that two of Arroyo Grande's Union veterans died, at about the same time Franklin Roosevelt delivered the most memorable Inaugural since Lincoln's two: "The only thing we have to fear is fear itself." Like Lincoln, FDR would be called a tyrant for assuming so much political power, but, like Lincoln, his powers were wartime powers (during the New Deal, government spending peaked at about

11% of the national GDP; it reached 48% during World War II[1]), so World War II was another transformative war—this war made America the world superpower, albeit one poised on the edge of nuclear disaster, that I grew up with in part during John F. Kennedy's presidency.

I wrote a book about World War II's connections to Arroyo Grande, and they were connections made easily, with two of our young men killed on *Arizona* and twenty-five of the high school's 58-member Class of 1942 banished to internment camps in the Arizona desert because of the accident of their ancestry. It would seem implausible to try to make similar connections to the Civil War, fought so far away and so long ago. Yet feelings here were strong: as county historian Daniel Krieger notes, San Luis Obispo postmaster Alexander Murray was instrumental in rallying "unconditional Union men" and in raising money for the Union cause, but his efforts were compromised by a strong pro-Confederate sentiment that was palpable locally and even more pervasive in Southern California.[2]

However, the population of all of San Luis Obispo County at the time of Fort Sumter was under 1,800—even in 1869, Arroyo Grande consisted of one smithy, one small school and one store[3]— and so precluded a large military involvement with the war back east. Company A of the 1st Battalion of the Native California Cavalry, in an effort to provide soldiers for the Union, recruited here, but the unit saw only limited action in 1863-65, fighting an array of Indian people in Humboldt County and later, fighting

---

[1] Nate Silver, "What is Driving Growth in Government Spending?" New York *Times*, January 16, 2013, http://fivethirtyeight.blogs.nytimes.com/2013/01/16/what-is-driving-growth-in-government-spending/?_r=0

[2] Daniel Krieger, "Times Past: Civil War-era postmaster helped keep California in the Union," San Luis Obispo *Tribune*, October 6, 2012, http://www.sanluisobispo.com/news/local/news-columns-blogs/times-past/article39425256.html

[3] "Mrs. Isabelle Ballagh Is One of Oldest Pioneers in This Valley," Arroyo Grande *Herald-Recorder Golden Anniversary Edition: 1887-1937*

Apaches in the Arizona Territory. And rather than the superb local *Californio* horsemen that the 1ˢᵗ California's founders had envisioned, Mexican, Chilean, and Yankee newcomers made up most of the recruits for Company A, and many of them proved to be habitual deserters.[4] The company roster identifies one cavalryman, Joaquin Baldes, who can be definitively linked to the area; Baldes joined in San Luis Obispo in 1863 and died of disease in the Arizona Territory two years later.

Arroyo Grande in the early 1900s. *Courtesy Blake Bristol.*

So while battles like Antietam and Chickamauga raged elsewhere in America, the crisis central to life in Arroyo Grande were the dry years of 1862-1864. Drought, not the war, was a more appreciable disaster: it decimated the cattle on local pioneer Francis Branch's Rancho Santa Manuela and nearly destroyed his fortune, the aggregate of twenty-five years of self-creation in the kind of hard work twenty-first century Americans can't begin to imagine. But Branch, by birth, was a New Yorker and, in temperament, a Yankee,

---

[4]Tom Prezelski, "California and the Civil War: 1st Battalion of Native Cavalry, California Volunteers," California State Military Museum, http://californiamilitaryhistory.org/1stNatCavCV.html

practical and tough and forward-looking, and even as he watched one fortune die on the hillsides of the Upper Valley, he was beginning to build a second in cultivating crops, in milling flour, and in dairy farming. Meanwhile, he was laying out the street plan for what would become Arroyo Grande.

And it was at this point when the connections to the war can be found, for among the men who built the town Branch had put down on paper down were the Union veterans who would be buried here, one of them a Medal of Honor winner, and they would begin to make their marks in the years after Branch's death in 1874.

When I found the list of these veterans compiled by researcher James Henkel, I was astounded both by their numbers and by their varied states of origin: New Jersey, Illinois, Ohio, Pennsylvania, Wisconsin, Minnesota, Iowa, Missouri, and Kansas. Because each man's tombstone includes the regiment and the company in which he served, I was able to connect them to a litany of places made famous by violence: to Chancellorsville and Gettysburg, Franklin and Atlanta, to Sheridan's Valley Campaign and to Grant's final campaign in 1864-65, the series of battles that presaged the trench warfare and attrition tactics of the Somme or Verdun in the First World War.

For me, a cemetery can sometimes be inspirational. The starting point for the World War II book had been the grave of a nearby Corbett Canyon farmer's son killed over 5,000 miles away, on Iwo Jima, two days before he would have turned twenty-one. That terrible timing, recorded on the young Marine's tombstone, represented a tragedy that struck a deep emotional chord inside me, but more often, cemeteries lead me to imagine what the lives of these people must have been like.

So I was able to begin, at least, to imagine our veterans in the places where they'd fought when some of them were as

14

young as sixteen. What would they have seen and heard? What generals commanded them? What orders did their division or brigade or regiment receive on the day of battle, and how well did they and their comrades carry those orders out? What were their lives as soldiers like? This book will attempt to answer some of those questions, using both secondary sources and primary sources—whenever possible, the words of men who served in the same regiments as the Arroyo Grande veterans— and so tell the stories of these men and tell them from the vantage point of someone who has spent a lifetime studying and teaching their war, someone who lives in the same town where, one hopes, these men found a measure of peace. Any mistakes I make in the telling are purely my own.

The fact that these soldiers would grow old in in southern San Luis Obispo County, so far away from the battlefields of their youth, is another part of the story, and the impetus for telling that part comes from a remarkable book, *Marching Home*, written by a young Yale-trained history professor, Brian Matthew Jordan. Jordan's book breaks new ground in Civil War history in that he addresses the lives of Union soldiers after Appomattox. In many respects, Jordan finds, the experiences of their youth would haunt veterans like ours for the rest of their lives. They were experiences that only they themselves could understand from a war that the rest of the country, swept up in the dynamism of Gilded Age industrialization and in Horatio Alger's success fables, wanted to leave behind.

Remarkably, Jordan argues, despite the devastation of the South, the end of the war was more emotionally satisfying for its losers. For the Confederate veteran there was immense comfort in the tradition of the "Lost Cause," which perhaps had its unconscious inception with the mourning that marked the passing of the South's great martyr, Stonewall Jackson, who died of complications from his wounding at Chancellorsville in 1863. Jackson's stark Calvinism only enhanced his martyrdom, and the Southern cause had implicit but powerful Christian overtones, woven even into the fabric of the Confederate battle flag, with its blue cross of St. Andrew evocative of both white Southerners' faith and the Scots Lowland origins of many of the South's people. In Missouri, in 1861, the Confederates who fought for leaders like James H. McBride went into battle behind a navy blue battle flag dominated by a white Christian cross.

So a kind of Romantic mythology about the war dominated Southern perceptions of it, and this included the mythology that the war was fought over "states' rights." Admittedly South Carolina's "Declaration of Causes" for secession (South Carolina was the first state to secede) both champions state sovereignty but then contradicts itself by explicitly *condemning* states' rights in a passage on Northern states who claimed the right to harbor runaway slaves; the Palmetto State drafters of the Declaration in fact excoriate the federal government for failing to use federal power to coerce obedience to the Fugitive Slave Act. Slavery, its preservation, and even its expansion are the overriding causes, according to the Declarations of states like Georgia, Mississippi, and Texas, for the break with the North.[5] Most Southern soldiers were not slaveowners, yet for them it was the possibility of acquiring slaves that would provide them with the foundation for social and economic betterment. Just as important, slavery was the institution that ensured social control over the slaves themselves. The memories of Nat Turner's slave rebellion in 1832 South Carolina remained vivid, and John Brown's raid on Harpers Ferry in 1859 generated the hysteria that so characterized the election of 1860, when Lincoln was variously portrayed as an abolitionist, a miscegenationist, and a complicit slave

---

[5] "Why did the South Secede?" (Declaration of causes for South Carolina, Georgia, Mississippi and Texas)
http://www.digitalhistory.uh.edu/active_learning/explorations/south_secede/

insurrectionist. Southern politicians and propagandists were just as skilled then as similar figures are today in persuading poor and working-class white men to support a social order that in reality worked against them and for those at the apex of society. The Civil War, as many soldiers would learn bitterly, "was a rich man's war and a poor man's fight." Yet Southern mythology would make leaders like Jackson and Lee Olympians. At war's end, for white Southerners, their returning soldiers were Homeric. They were heroes and would be celebrated as such to the ends of their days.

Union veterans faced more complex postwar lives. They came home changed men, as all veterans do, but they were often feared as much as they were welcomed: they were hardened, coarse-talking and strangely detached. They'd become strangers to their own families. The veterans, meanwhile, had formed surrogate families within their wartime regiments. They missed the friendships of their comrades, living and dead, that had been the most powerful emotional attachments many of them would ever have. Some of them came home maimed from field hospitals. Soldiers marching toward the sound of musketry had to confront, outside medical tents, tubs full of amputated arms and legs, the detritus of surgical tables. The men who had survived those surgeries were the most visible reminders of the war and so, for most Americans, may have been the most unwelcome veterans of all.

Jordan's scholarship reveals that, unlike their Southern counterparts in 1865, Union veterans faced disenchantment in many different ways. They endured homecoming parades, flowers, lisping poetry recited by grave little schoolgirls, but afterward they endured alone. Their contributions, in many cases, faded into obscurity, not into myth. The nation was building railroads, steel mills, and oil refineries in a forced march forward into modernity. Americans, for the most part, had no desire to look backward to a past so dark that it lacked the benefit of electrical lighting and back to a war that was too psychologically painful to contemplate. The memories of the war were briefly revived and communally mourned when one of the heroes of that war, George Armstrong Custer, sent to the West to erase the culture that represented America's indigenous past, was himself erased at the Little Bighorn nine days before the nation's 100ᵗʰ birthday. For veterans, there were other news stories were even more painful: race riots, lynchings, and the rise of the Klan led them to question whether they'd won anything at all.

Arroyo Grande veteran Otis Smith at the Sawtelle Home for Disabled Veterans in Los Angeles. *Courtesy Debbie Gragg.*

Almost no soldier escaped the war without psychic wounds, and some of the Union veterans of Antietam or Lookout Mountain or Cold Harbor turned to alcohol to dull the memories of what they'd seen in combat. In veterans' homes nationwide, like the Sawtelle Home for Disabled Veterans in West Los Angeles, alcohol abuse led to petty theft, physical violence and sometimes to institutionalization in mental hospitals. It ended lives, too: Jordan's book tells the story of one veteran who committed suicide by lying down on the railroad track; he left a bottle of whiskey close by as a kind of symbolic suicide note. The same demons that took this man's life doubtlessly haunted the men, and the one woman, an army nurse, who would live their postwar lives in Arroyo Grande. The chance that they were haunted by the war is implicit in their very mobility: most of them had left New Jersey, Illinois or Kansas and moved at least once more before they arrived in Arroyo Grande; these were restless men. Sometimes their health was precarious. Admissions and discharge records show that some, many suffering from wartime diseases or possibly from psychological trauma, checked in and out of the Sawtelle home more than once. For a few, their lives would draw to their close in Sawtelle hospital wards.

But what is remarkable about the old soldiers buried here are the lives they'd lived. They had, as young men, been swept up into what was the world's first large-scale industrial war. Because of the technology that made battlefield slaughter so efficient, they'd had their Victorian notions of glory and gallantry shattered. This was the war captured best by a Realist writer, Stephen Crane, yet it was fought by boys and men who'd anticipated the kind of war of a depicted by a Romantic poet, in the doomed charge of Tennyson's Light Brigade. Despite the trauma of Civil War combat, something the war conferred on nearly every participant, it was Civil War veterans who in their maturity, as farmers, businessmen, professionals, and as citizens, built Arroyo Grande, a farm town on the Pacific coast. That was only part of the greater inheritance they left behind. These were men who had saved the United States of America.

Chapter 1.
War without End

Robert Hicks, in his vivid novel *The Widow of the South,* describes the windows of the homes in Franklin, Tennessee, rattling in their panes in 1864 as thousands of Confederate troops, many of them barefoot, marched into town to smash the Union army waiting for them there. This is what happened instead: The Confederates smashed themselves upon the Federals, who, because they had gotten to Franklin first, went to work with picks and shovels. They'd thrown up earthworks beyond a two-mile stretch of bare field that was punctuated only by islets of scrub not big enough to hide a dog, let alone a man. Once they came into Franklin, the Confederates were ordered to cross that field and take the earthworks. This was in part because their commander's audacity had won him promotion after promotion in fighting the war that had whittled him half away. John Bell Hood's reputation for bravery grew even as he'd lost a leg and the use of an arm in validating it; at Antietam, in 1862, he'd lost even more when he sent his Texans shrieking like Comanches into the cornfield beyond the Dunker Church. They'd gone into the cornstalks and disappeared in a hail of canister fired from a Union artillery battery. Hood was asked later where his division was. "Dead on the field," he'd replied.

Now, in 1864, Hood, so diminished that he had to be strapped into his saddle, had been sent south to replace a general, Joseph Johnston, with too much finesse and not enough deference for the taste of the Confederate commander-in-chief, President Jefferson Davis. Hood was a smasher. In truth, he had been promoted this time beyond his capabilities. But now, in the late fall and early winter, even the smasher was playing, strategically, at least, with finesse. If he could raise enough hell in Tennessee—enough, maybe, to get in between the two Union armies there and then replicate Napoleon at Austerlitz, or Hood's breathing hero, Lee, at Chancellorsville—he could take on one army, bloody it, and then turn and knock aside the second on a fighting march north into Kentucky. And that feat, if Hood could accomplish it, would force Sherman to double back on the path he was burning across Georgia. Sherman would have no choice but to come to the rescue of the wreckage John Bell Hood had left for him in Tennessee.

Hood wasn't impressed with the material he'd been given to fight the campaign he'd so artfully designed. He was convinced his army was made up of diggers. Like the Yankees two miles away, they fought only behind earthworks or stout stone walls. They didn't have the drive or the killer instinct of the Texans Hood once commanded, and a few days before, at Spring Hill, they had allowed one of the armies that Hood had wanted to maul a free march, screened by trees, past their encampment, so close that a few Yankees had come up to the Confederate campfires to light their pipes, where they were taken prisoner instead.[6] That was a few Yankees. The rest of the army—the Army of the Ohio, led by Union Gen. John Schofield—had slipped away in the night as noiseless as Lee's had at Antietam in 1862, and in the morning an enraged Hood discovered they were gone.

On November 30, he found Schofield's army again. They waited behind their entrenchments, two miles away across ground bare enough for Hood to put his entire Army of Tennessee on parade. And this, essentially, was what Hood intended to do. This would be an assault to remember; Hood would teach his 26,000 Confederates a lesson. They would *take* entrenchments, not hide behind them. He was going to put some salt into the Army of Tennessee and they would earn some glory.[7] What happened next was, of course, murder.

Prunes again. Otis W. Smith weighed only a little more now than he had when his Ohio regiment arrived at Franklin in 1864, almost sixty years before. It was the diet, or the lack of a diet, at the Sawtelle National Home for Disabled

---

[6] Shelby Foote, *The Civil War, A Narrative. Vol. III: Red River to Appomattox*, Vintage Books, New York: 1986, p. 661
[7] Foote, p. 662

Veterans in Los Angeles, California, which allowed Smith, even while confined to a wheelchair with wire wheels big enough to drive a motorcar, to remain lean. He didn't want to eat now; he didn't want to eat then. Smith had seen dead men before—he'd enlisted in 1861, at sixteen—but never on the scale that John Bell Hood had arranged. Smith's 95th Ohio regiment came up the day after Hood's assault,[8] so he had seen the Confederate dead strewn in driblets across the field and packed in dense clumps against the face of the Union earthworks. Some were shapeless, torn by artillery shells, not men, but sacks of men. He may have helped burial details dig the long, shallow trenches into which the bodies, or the assembled fragments of bodies, were rolled by the dozens. *Forty Confederates buried here,* a penciled epitaph might read on a tombstone no more substantial than the lid from a crate of hardtack.

The Confederates, being dead, couldn't complain about their lot, but neither could the living graybeards who were Smith's friends at Sawtelle. If the "inmates," as the papers called them, complained about the food or an attendant's cruelty, they'd be "shown the gate." One Sawtelle veteran, suffering from old battlefield wounds, taught them an object lesson about what life was like beyond the gate: he'd been burned alive, paralyzed, according to the newspapers, because of the morphine to which he was addicted, when his little Santa Monica apartment caught fire after he'd overturned a lamp. Once another had wandered off the grounds, tumbled into a ditch, and hadn't been found for hours—he was lucky enough to go to a hospital, where the food might be marginally better and the staff's attitude marginally softer. A third wasn't nearly as lucky. He was on furlough from Sawtelle when he disappeared—in fact, he'd been granted an extension to his furlough—and what that extra time away

---

[8] "95th Regiment Ohio Volunteer Infantry," Ohio Civil War Central, 2016, Ohio Civil War Central. 12 Feb 2016
<http://www.www.ohiocivilwarcentral.com/entry.php?rec=890>

from the veterans' home had brought him was a lonely death in the Mojave Desert. Two field workers found what was left of him with only a Sawtelle postcard to identify him.[9]

Sawtelle, near what is today the UCLA campus, Los Angeles, *California State Historical Society.*

Sawtelle had been investigated twice and exonerated twice, in 1893 and in 1912, for allegations of mistreating veterans. Several of them maintained they were fed a substandard diet; one told a reporter in 1909: "I know exactly what we'll have for dinner tonight. It will be prunes or applesauce, tea or bread, costing about three cents." [10] There were charges that policemen beat a veteran nearly to death,

[9] Los Angeles *Herald,* Feb. 28, 1908, p. 7; Sept. 24, 1906, p. 10; Oct. 15, 1905, p. 7
[10] Los Angeles *Herald,* June 19, 1909, p. 1.

and, during one inquiry, rumors of shoddy building materials were confirmed when several pounds of plaster fell on a stenographer and government investigators.[11]

From the old photographs, Sawtelle, all Victorian turrets and gingerbread, belies the newspaper stories. It looks beautiful, as do the grounds, shaded by cypresses and palm trees. Otis Smith liked a dappled spot next to a little Spanish fountain, built in a style typical of California. It was in California where Smith had made a life for himself, when he'd had his health, as a farmer in the Huasna Valley, east of Arroyo Grande. But apparently none of the Sawtelle veterans, none of his friends in Arroyo Grande, and not even Smith's family, knew the secret he'd hidden about the war.[12] In combat against John Bell Hood's Army of Tennessee in December 1864, Otis Smith had won the Medal of Honor.

A month after the Battle of Franklin, outside Nashville, Gen. John Schofield was stalling. Perhaps it was the memory of what he and Otis Smith had seen at Franklin in the tangled mounds of Confederate dead. Now, in December, Schofield was in the same place Hood had been at Franklin. The Union general was about to lead an assault on an enemy that was well dug in. There was one difference between Schofield's situation and Hood's. He was a subordinate officer, not in command. Maj. Gen. George Thomas was Schofield's superior, and Thomas was ordering him, in the second day of fighting at Nashville, to attack a hillside held by entrenched Confederates. So it would be Hood's men who would be waiting for Schofield's this time, not the other way around, and they would be eager to return the favor of Franklin. Earlier that afternoon, December 16, three regiments of U.S.

---

[11] San Francisco *Chronicle*, Dec. 12, 1912, p. 50
[12] David Middlecamp, "Photos from the Vault," San Luis Obispo *Tribune*, May 8, 2001.

Colored Troops had attacked the Confederate right and were repulsed with forty percent of them dead or wounded—the Confederate officer commanding the troops that had inflicted this destruction noted the African Americans' bravery in his official report.[13]

The state capitol steps at Nashville, protected by an artillery battery, 1864. *Library of Congress.*

Now, on the Confederate left, Schofield was to duplicate that costly effort and send his men up the steep slopes of Shy's Hill. So he hesitated. He asked General Thomas for reinforcements. Thomas studied the hill for a moment and the decision was suddenly made for him: there were Union troops *already* attacking the entrenchments there. They were Brig. Gen. John MacArthur's men. MacArthur, an aggressive and, on December 16, an insubordinate Scot, born in a town

---

[13] Greg Brigg, "The Battle of Nashville: The Crushing Blow of a Forlorn Hope," *Hallowed Ground* Magazine, Winter 2014, http://www.civilwar.org/hallowed-ground-magazine/winter-2014/the-battle-of-nashville.html

on the River Clyde, had grown tired of waiting. Thomas ordered Schofield to follow MacArthur's lead and send in the rest of his men.[14]

Otis Smith's 95th Ohio Infantry was on the right of the impetuous Scot's attack when MacArthur let it go at 3:30 p.m. The 95th advanced silently, with fixed bayonets, and began to clamber up the hill, ironically, up hillsides so steep that they protected Smith and his comrades from the enemy entrenched unwisely on the summit, rather than below it, where they would have enjoyed a shallower and so more punishing field of fire. The men atop Shy's Hill included a depleted Florida brigade; in fact, they could manage to field only enough troops that day to make up a regiment. Their position had been further weakened by Hood, who'd transferred troops from the hill to other points in his line. The Floridians had worked all night digging trenches, had been soaked all day by a cold rain, and so they were exhausted. Suddenly, the 95th Ohio, after advancing without a cheer and without firing a shot, were in the Floridians' entrenchments, Otis Smith among them, killing the Southerners with their bayonets.

The Confederate position collapsed and Hood watched, dismayed, as his army's left dissolved. Those left behind were now surrounded by the Union brigade that included Smith. One Floridian started to tear his regimental flag into pieces to keep the victors from having it. For the 6th Florida, it was too late: during the assault, Otis Smith had seized their regimental colors. After the capture of Shy's Hill, the rest of Hood's men followed their comrades who were retreating on the left. Hood later wrote that he had never seen a Confederate army retreat in such confusion.[15] His army was finished. Less than a month after their rout at Nashville, Hood resigned his command, and Otis Smith would be awarded the Medal of

---

[14] Shelby Foote, p. 701.
[15] Foote, 702.

27

Honor that he never talked about, perhaps because it was tarnished.

A replica of the battle flag captured by Otis W. Smith at the Battle of Nashville. *Courtesy Matthew J. Sterman.*

This is why. The officer commanding the Floridians on Shy's Hill, Gen. Thomas Benton Smith, was being conducted to the rear when he was confronted by Otis Smith's regimental commander, a peacetime physician, Lt. Col. William Linn McMillen. Words were exchanged. McMillen may have been drunk. He suddenly drew his saber and began striking the disarmed Gen. Smith on the head; one blow was so deep that Smith's brain was exposed.[16] McMillen's own men intervened to disarm their enraged commander. No charges were ever brought against him. He was later promoted, grew cotton in Louisiana after the war, was a state senator, and won patronage jobs from two presidents as postmaster and then port inspector for New Orleans.

---

[16] Mike West, "CSA scout Dewitt Jobe died horrible death," *Murfreesboro Post*, October 7, 2007 http://www.murfreesboropost.com/csa-scout-dewitt-jobe-died-horrible-death-cms-6850

In 1886, his victim at Nashville, Thomas Benton Smith, was admitted to an insane asylum where he would spend most of the rest of his life, crippled by the depression that doctors said was a result of his injuries that day below Shy's Hill. He was temporarily released in 1910 to attend a veterans' reunion. Out of kindness, he was allowed to conduct close-order drill with some of his old soldiers, and the moment transformed him. An observer wrote that the old general was "as full of the animation of the old days as could be imagined" as he put his little command through its paces.[17] Gen. Smith died on May 21, 1923, ten weeks after Medal of Honor winner Smith died at the Sawtelle Home in Los Angeles.

🦅

A man like Otis Smith was unique. So was an army like William Sherman's. In the Grand Review that marked the end of the war in May 1865—mourning bunting still draped official Washington's buildings, since only a little more than five weeks had passed since Lincoln's assassination—hundreds of regiments paraded down Pennsylvania Avenue for what was intended to be a public farewell. Grant's Army of the Potomac, buttons polished and formations precise, led the review. The second day was marked by Sherman's Westerners, in company-strength phalanxes wide enough to brush each curb, each company a component segment of a column of soldiers fifteen miles long. This was an army that had lived off the land for nearly a year. They were lean as wolves and rough-edged and they marched with a loose, swinging stride, with pride that resembled a kind of casual insolence. The people of Washington immediately loved them. Among Sherman's soldiers was another future Arroyo Grande resident, Morris Denham, who'd served with the 12th

---

[17]Ibid

Wisconsin in Georgia and the Carolinas. One of the 12th's officers wrote home to his parents about their turn in the Review:

> That day we all fell in, and it seemed the minute the order was given, our boys took on an appearance of glory and holiness, and they marched, oh how they marched, never before did they stride like that. Just imagine the scene, Mother and Father, if you can! Men marching in their old worn-out uniforms, some with new pants that stood out like sore thumbs, scuffed shoes, the guns seeming to speak out "we have seen better days," our flags tattered and torn, and all along the way, crowds upon crowds of people, cheering so loudly they deafened our ears. own Pennsylvannia [sic] Avenue we proceeded, and I fancied myself a "little Napolean" [sic] on my horse — and she lived up to qualifications by prancing as if she had been trained purposely for this type of duty and performance.[18]

It was a glorious day for young officers on horseback, but it may have been less so for the private soldiers in their formations, their shoes making a continuous, sibilant hiss during the six hours it took them to pass the official viewing stand with its braided generals, senators, ladies and their parasols, and Andrew Johnson, who, in March, had been visibly drunk when he'd appeared for his swearing-in as vice president. Lincoln had stared intently at his own shoetips while Johnson, without warning, launched into a speech that was not required nor requested. It was a rambling tribute to his own rise above his humble Tennessee origins. So Johnson, who had come close to robbing Lincoln's inauguration of its dignity, was one of the factors that robbed the review of its joy. The soldiers who filed past Johnson saw only a counterfeit. They missed their rightful leader, Abraham Lincoln. They had been cheated of him, and the bitterness of Lincoln's taking rankled. If they somehow had the chance go

---

[18] "1865 May 29: Edwin Levings on The Grand Review — 'The moments of that day will long linger in the memories of our boys,'" *The Civil War and Northwest Wisconsin*, May 29, 2015. https://thecivilwarandnorthwestwisconsin.wordpress.com/

into battle again, one soldier remarked after the assassination, they would take no rebel prisoners.[19]

Arroyo Grande settler Morris Denham was part of Francis Blair Jr.'s XVII Corps, which had fought with William Sherman. Blair and his staff are leading the corps during the May 1865 Grand Review. *Nationai Archives.*

But they would not go into battle again, and, as irksome as the Grand Review seemed to many, an unwelcome interruption between themselves and home, the gathering of the great armies from the Eastern and Western theaters reminded the soldiers, too, of how many friends they had lost,

---

[19] Brian Matthew Jordan, *Marching Home: Union Veterans and their Unending Civil War,* Liveright Publishing, New York: 2014, p. 19.

and that personal accounting sobered them. Another emotional moment awaited: for many, mustering out would take weeks or even months, but for others this was the day that marked the breaking up of their regiments, and now, even as the memories of dead comrades filled their minds, it was time to say goodbye to the living as well, to men they might never see again. "The thing was over," wrote Irving Bronson, an officer in the 107th New York. "We had said goodbye and shaken hands, some of us for the last time. It was like breaking up a family, and about as cheerful as a funeral."[20]

For some of these soldiers, the trip home was so seamless as to be anti-climactic. Leander Stillwell left home as a newly-mustered private in 1861 and came home a mustered-out lieutenant in 1865. He felt "profound contentment" at seeing his parents again at their Illinois farm, and wrote that the day after his homecoming, "I doffed my uniform of first lieutenant, put on some of father's old clothes, armed myself with a corn knife, proceeded to wage war on the standing corn." [21] Stillwell's wry metaphor suggests he was acutely aware of how mundane his life would be after four years of war. Never again would he encounter the chaos, the fear—and the exhilaration —of combat.

On the third day of Gettysburg, massed Confederate artillery unleashed a cannonade that made both the men and the earth they clung to tremble. For all the intensity of their cannon fire, the Confederates were firing high and long. A cringing Union soldier on Cemetery Ridge unwise enough

[20] Jordan, *Marching Home*, p. 25.
[21] Leander Stillwell, *The Story of a Common Soldier of Army Life in the Civil War, 1861-1865*. Project Gutenberg, September 8, 2008, p. 278.
http://www.gutenberg.org/files/26561/26561-h/26561-h.htm

to open his eyes and look to the rear might see a shell descending on an artillery caisson of a sister unit and watch it detonate to send wheels, gun crew and horses high into the sky. Meanwhile, the massed artillery fire was so loud that the good citizens of Harrisburg and Philadelphia, of Baltimore and Washington City, as safe as were the "gentlemen in England now abed" in *Henry V's* Agincourt speech, glanced idly skyward to look for the thunderheads that should have been there, but weren't. A Minnesota soldier described what happened next:

> On our immediate right a three years' Philadelphia regiment, the 72nd Pennsylvania, was ordered to charge. They advanced a short distance wavered, fell back, and could not be got forward. On our immediate left a regiment of nine month's men from Vermont Green Mountain boys, numbering between three and four hundred men more than our whole brigade, when ordered to charge, advanced across the field into that fire with as much apparent coolness, as much steadiness and with as perfect a line as I ever saw a regiment of veterans pass in review on a gala day. Vermont stock suddenly rose, while Pennsylvania went down below zero.

> But the Rebs were driven and the field won, the old 2nd Corps reduced to 7,000, taking 22 stands of color, and our division some 2,000 prisoners. 1st Minnesota's color staff was shot away, but capturing a Rebel color, we spliced the Rebel staff to the Union colors, and thus we carry what is left of our flag.

> For two hours we had fought desperately. The men seemed inspired and fought with a determination unconquerable. I believe they would have died or taken on the spot before yielding. Men fell about us unheeded, unnoticed; we scarcely knew they were falling, so great was the intensity of attention to approaching foe. Our muskets became so heated we could no longer handle them. We dropped them and picked up those of the wounded. Our cartridges gave out. We rifled the boxes of the dead. Artillerymen from the disabled pieces in our rear sprang forward, and seizing guns and cartridges from the wounded, fought by our side as infantrymen. Many of the men became deaf, and did not recover their hearing for a day or two. It was

a grand and terrible scene. I wish I could paint it to you as I was and felt it.[22]

A soldier who had endured the third day of Gettysburg and emerged unhurt, and who had then seen his own boys in their counterattack destroy Pickett's Charge (12,500 Confederates participated in the famed assault on July 3, the last day of the battle. Only half of them made it safely back to their own lines.) and so destroy the myth of Robert Lee's invincibility, had already passed the zenith of his life. Nothing like this would ever happen to him again, and what had happened to them brought them, ironically, great joy.

So, for a generation enmeshed in the ethical web spun tightly by mid-Victorian Protestantism—these were Christian soldiers who fought in armies, on both sides, marked by intense waves of wartime revivalism within their camps—the excitement of battle generated a profound moral contradiction. In *This Republic of Suffering,* a superb account of coming to terms with the scale of death the Civil War generated, Harvard president and historian Drew Gilpin Faust describes the experience of a stunned Confederate who, during a firefight, came to the aid of a shrieking comrade, only to find out that he was "executing a species of war dance," exulting over the body of the Union soldier he'd just killed. In another battle in 1862, Union soldiers on the firing line called their shots, as if combat were billiards: "Watch me drop that fellow," one said to his comrades; battle was, indeed, like a game.[23]

The killing didn't end when the war did. Violent crime rose at three times the rate of population growth in the decades following the war, and perhaps as many as two-thirds

---

[22] Alfred Carpenter, "Letter on the Battle of Gettysburg," *A Civil War Journal: Company K, 1st Minnesota Volunteer Infantry Regiment at Gettysburg, July 1-4 1863.* Winona County Historical Society, 1998.
[23] Drew Gilpin Faust, *This Republic of Suffering: Death and the American Civil War.* Vintage Books: New York, 2008, pp. 37-38.

of the nation's convicted felons were veterans.[24] Soldiers understood, on some level, that combat had changed them irrevocably and some worried about it. Society, one Vermont soldier wrote his sister, "will not own the rude soldier when he comes back, but turn a cold shoulder to him, because he has become hardened by scenes of bloodshed and carnage."[25] He was, in many respects, right: some of the soldiers who came home to Vermont, New Jersey or Iowa brought with them a measure of fear—they had become, in the Civil War novelist Michael Shaara's term, "Killer Angels."

Many Union soldiers had demonized themselves and by extension all of their comrades by celebrating their mustering out with epic alcohol binges and episodic violence throughout the demobilization summer of 1865.[26] A Chicago civilian's insulting comment about William Sherman set off a saloon brawl that cascaded into a riot that police were helpless to put down. Only the fortuitous appearance of the legendarily hard-drinking Gen. Joseph Hooker, who had the credibility to intervene with combat veterans, brought the violence to an end.

But for even the most sober of veterans that was precisely the problem with homecoming: it brought them little peace. Professor Jordan describes a sense of what, at its mildest, could be called disorientation. Home wasn't home anymore. Even little farm towns had changed so much in four years that, for some veterans, they didn't feel like home at all. Soldiers from the hard-fighting regiments of the Old Northwest, states like Iowa and Minnesota, couldn't reconcile themselves to the cold winters they'd forgotten while fighting in Mississippi or Georgia. There was a more sinister change

---

[24] Michael C.C. Adams, *Living Hell: The Dark Side of the Civil War*, Johns Hopkins University Press, Baltimore: 2014, p. 198.
[25] Edward Alexander, "Life of the Civil War Soldier in Battle: And Then We Kill," *Hallowed Ground* Magazine, Winter 2013, http://www.civilwar.org/hallowed-ground-magazine/winter-2013/life-of-the-civil-war-soldier-battle.html?referrer=https://www.google.com/
[26] Jordan, pp. 46-47.

to which they couldn't adjust: Union veterans resembled the little boys who'd survived the 1918 influenza epidemic and were finally let out to play, only to find there was no playmate on their city block left alive. The survivors of "Pals" Battalions who'd joined the Great War's British Army together went home to neighborhoods empty of the young men with whom they'd grown up. Their pals were gone, swallowed up by the Western Front.

Gone too, in 1865, were whole towns of young men in New York or Vermont or Indiana, dead and buried on Southern farmland that had been poisoned by violence, land still studded with spent bullets. Other young men had vanished without a trace in dark, dense woodlots or fetid swamps. Soldiers came home, then, ostensibly alive and whole and strong but with unseen dead spaces inside where their comrades had once lived. Missing them, or the trauma of seeing them killed, figured in the chronic depression with which so many veterans struggled. Now that the war was done, they still were caught in its aftermath like swimmers in an undertow, struggling to break surface, to find light and cool air, to breathe again.

They recognized, too, that what they had fought for—for the rededication of the democracy Lincoln had described at Gettysburg in November 1863—was fast slipping away. Union veterans remained intensely suspicious of and hostile toward the defeated South; Lincoln's assassination had been one impetus for their rancor but their anger only intensified when they read the newspaper accounts of the postwar emergence of the old Slave Codes, now called Black Codes. They read, too, of the defiance and the terrorism of the Ku Klux Klan, co-founded by a cavalryman, Nathan Bedford Forrest, who had bedeviled some of them in the Deep South. When Reconstruction ended in 1877, Jim Crow laws revived white supremacy in a way that rivaled the days of slavery. The Union veterans' hostility was exacerbated because the

other side refused to admit—significantly, on a moral level—
that they'd lost the war. Typical, in 1894, were the dedicatory
remarks that accompanied the unveiling of a Confederate
memorial in Richmond, when newspapers noted that the
clouds parted and the sun emerged when the speaker, the
Rev. R.C. Cave, began an oration that included passages like
this:

> But brute force cannot settle questions of right and wrong.
> Thinking men do not judge the merits of a cause by the measure of its
> success; and I believe
>> The world shall yet decide
>> In truth's clear, far-off light,
> that the South was in the right; that her cause was just; that the men
> who took up arms in her defence were patriots who had even better
> reason for what they did than had the men who fought at Concord,
> Lexington, and Bunker Hill; and that her coercion, whatever good
> may have resulted or may hereafter result from it, was an outrage on
> liberty.[27]

Similar remarks by Southern speakers invited to a
Gettysburg reunion in 1913, Professor Jordan notes, rankled
the same Union veterans who had protested another
unveiling, in 1909, in the Capitol's Statuary Hall: a sculpture
of Robert E. Lee. No matter how chivalrous Lee had been
(He never, for example, uttered the word "Yankees," using
instead, in his verbal orders to his subordinates, the term
"those people."), he was a killer, and he had harvested
thousands of solders' lives. The survivors of what they saw as
Lee's war would protest again at the rapturous reception, one
that included the Southern-bred President Woodrow Wilson,
awarded the 1915 D.W. Griffith film *Birth of a Nation,* which
depicts Klansmen, too, as chivalric heroes who reassert
Southern white supremacy over rapacious carpetbaggers and
predatory African Americans. "It is like writing history with

---

[27] R.C. Cave, "Dedicatory Remarks, Soldiers' and Sailors' Monument, May 30, 1894,"
Southern Historical Society Papers, Volume 22. Reverend J. William Jones, Ed.
http://www.perseus.tufts.edu/hopper/text?doc=Perseus%3Atext%3A2001.05.0280%3
Achapter%3D1.27%3Asection%3Dc.1.27.198

lightning," the president said, "and my only regret is that it is all so terribly true."[28] The most enduring image of the 1913 Gettysburg reunion is that of Confederate survivors of Pickett's Charge reaching across the stone wall–fifty years before, it had been their objective–to shake the hands of Pennsylvania veterans. What goes unmentioned is the fistfight at the same event that sent seven aged Yankees and Confederates to the hospital.[29]

At least two veterans seem to have worked out a truce at the 1913 Gettysburg Reunion. *Library of Congress.*

Even as Southern whites reasserted their social and political primacy, American democracy in the North was no

---

[28] "D.W. Griffith's *Birth of a Nation*," *The Rise and Fall of Jim Crow*, PBS., http://www.pbs.org/wnet/jimcrow/stories_events_birth.html
[29] Jordan, p. 197.

tribute to the sacrifice of Civil War veterans, either. The Radical Republican Congress and Andrew Johnson finished what should have been Lincoln's second term in what resembled the political equivalent of a Western range war. Johnson escaped conviction on impeachment charges by one Senate vote. Grant's relentlessness and drive had served him well in the struggle against Lee, but another aspect of his personal character—an almost childlike credulity—ate his presidency alive in a series of scandals perpetrated by subordinates who betrayed Grant as surely as Warren G. Harding would be betrayed by his "Ohio Gang" in the 1920s.

The corruption penetrated to state houses, where the lobbyist for the Santa Fe Railroad kept a slush fund in his office safe for the frequent lubrication of Kansas legislators about to vote on regulatory bills; the monopoly that railroads enjoyed in their American fiefdoms and the freight rates they demanded were so egregious that it cost a farmer more to ship a bushel of wheat from Topeka to Chicago, by rail, than it did to ship that bushel from Chicago to Liverpool, mostly by water. Machine politics dominated cities from New York to San Francisco, where Irish-American voters really *did* vote early and often, and deceased. In New York, the most famous political machine was Tammany Hall, and it was Tammany Hall's Boss Tweed who disbursed the equivalent of $4 million to a Tammany-contracted plasterer for two days' work on City Hall.

In both their disillusionment and in their restlessness, the Civil War generation seems to resemble the generation that came of age during the First World War. After that war, they would become expatriates—Ernest Hemingway, F. Scott Fitzgerald, John Dos Passos among them—young men, many of them veterans, and young women, who no longer recognized or understood the America they'd known as children. They were among the members of Gertrude Stein's "Lost Generation." During the 1920s, they were always on the move: Ernest and Hadley Hemingway, for example, lived in Paris, a Paris captivated by American musicians like Sidney Bechet and entertainers like Josephine Baker (Parisians were also captivated by Chiquita, Baker's pet cheetah, whom the dancer walked on leash.), fished mountain streams and watched matadors at their work in Spain, and put up in little Italian *penziones*. In fact, the couple moved so frequently that on one trip they left behind a steamer trunk that contained everything young Hemingway had ever written. It was never found.

Charles Bristol typifies the restlessness of his generation. After his service--he's seen holding his wartime 8th Michigan Cavalry saber here—he lived in Missouri and Kansas before moving to Nipomo, just south of Arroyo Grande, in 1892. His descendants still live in the area. *Photo Courtesy of Blake Bristol.*

So, like the young people of the 1920s, Civil War veterans were members of a generation on the move. In postwar America, veterans, according to a 2010 study by Seoul University economist Chulhee Lee, were 54% more likely to move to a different state and 36% more likely to move to a different region than non-veterans.[30] Lee posits several reasons for this phenomenon: a central one is the idea that veterans had been exposed to the concept of a wider nation, one beyond their rural farms or row tenements, by campaigns in the South. Westerners, too, fought along the Atlantic seaboard, and some Easterners saw combat or garrison duty during the 1860s Indian Wars on the frontier. Lee's point is a key one: Americans had been so isolated and disparate before the war that an outbreak of measles that would make a New York regiment sick would kill soldiers in the Iowa regiment bivouacked alongside, soldiers that, before the war, were so geographically isolated that they lacked the immunity to that particular strain of measles—measles, in fact, killed 11,000 soldiers during the war.[31] The war had begun to break that isolation down, and the troop movements necessary to fighting it had opened young soldiers' minds to the vastness of their nation and to the possibility of starting over somewhere else.

This pattern of increased mobility was a key factor in the lives of Arroyo Grande's Union veterans. Over fifty would settle the Arroyo Grande Valley and nearby Nipomo. Enough census data exists to follow twenty-three of them, in the course of their lives. After the war, seven of them moved once from the state they'd served as soldiers; seven moved twice. Nine moved three times or more before they came to the Arroyo Grande area. So the men who came here had come as far as they could—like Jody's grandfather in the Steinbeck novella *The Red Pony,* they had to stop because

---

[30] Chulhee Lee, "Military Service and Economic Mobility: Evidence from the American Civil War," February 2010.
http://www.sciencedirect.com/science/article/pii/S0014449831200046
[31] "Civil War Diseases," http://www.civilwaracademy.com/civil-war-diseases.html

they'd arrived at the Pacific: their days of "Westering" were over.

Most of them were farmers—census data show them living in the Huasna Valley, the Branch Tract of the Upper Arroyo Grande Valley, Los Berros, Oak Park, the Arroyo Grande Township, Pismo Beach, and Oceano or in Nipomo.[32] They'd arrived here when the area was being touted as a kind of agricultural paradise, marked by dairy farming and by the truck gardening of vegetables, tree crops, and seed flowers.

Most Arroyo Grande veterans were farmers, and one important crop was flowers. Here, a Waller Seed Company employee tills a field in the Lower Arroyo Grande Valley. *Photo courtesy Richard Waller.*

---

[32] Census figures were taken from the website ancestry.com

Most of the veterans had arrived in the Valley earlier, but nearly all of them were established by 1900, when Arroyo Grande's population was approaching 1,000. Thirty-eight years before, in a single day's combat, Antietam had claimed the equivalent of twenty-two Arroyo Grandes in killed and wounded men. Whatever wounds these men still carried inside, they made a decision to move their lives forward; here, they had work to do in planting pumpkins and onions, peas and tomatoes, squash and beans. They were still, in their mature years, building a nation that had come perilously close to disappearing in the darkest months of the Civil War, in the long casualty lists produced by Antietam and the humiliation of the defeat inflicted at Chancellorsville.

Chapter 2.
Between Hammer and Anvil
Lee, 1862-63

Early in the war, Robert E. Lee's reputation was as a "king of spades," a man who was fond of having his troops dig trenches. He would become the Lee history knows best when, in 1862, the commander of the main Confederate army in Virginia, Joseph Johnston, was seriously wounded and President Jefferson Davis put Lee in his place in command of what would become known as the Army of

Northern Virginia. Lee quickly established a new reputation. The aggressiveness he showed in fighting the June 1862 Seven Days Battles and turning back the meticulous, pompous Union commander, George B. McClellan, who was attempting to seize the Confederate capital of Richmond, revealed that Lee was the master and McClellan the arrogant student, one who thought he knew the subject. He didn't. Lee had sent the Army of the Potomac limping back to Washington. Now, in the late summer of 1862, it was Lee who was on the move: he would invade the North and teach McClellan, dubbed by Northern newspapers the "Young Napoleon," a new lesson. Lee and President Jefferson Davis hoped, in the process of defeating the Army of the Potomac on northern soil, that the success of the Army of Northern Virginia would win diplomatic recognition and material and financial aid for the Confederacy from two cotton-hungry European powers, Great Britain and France.

Lee's army crossed into Maryland—capturing, in the process, future Arroyo Grande area settler Charles E. Bristol, then a teenaged member of the 87th Ohio, and with him the entire garrison defending the indefensible arsenal at Harpers Ferry. (On an exposed peninsula at the junction of the Shenandoah and Potomac rivers, tucked beneath mountains, Harpers Ferry offers everything short of a welcome mat to an invading army.) Bristol, a determined young man, wouldn't allow his war to finish this way; he was paroled, joined the 8th Michigan Cavalry, fought in Tennessee and in an 1864 raid on Macon under Gen. George Stoneman during Sherman's Atlanta campaign. Stoneman and most of his command were captured[33]—including Stoneman's aide, the Irish officer Myles Keogh, who would be killed at the Little Bighorn—but Bristol and the surrounded 8th Michigan fought their way free, only to be recaptured two days later.

---

[33] "Stoneman's Raid," *New York Times*, Aug. 9, 1864, http://www.nytimes.com/1864/08/15/news/stoneman-s-raid-raid-capture-gen-stoneman-campaign-atlanta-tennessee-copperheads.html?pagewanted=all

McClellan showed little of this kind of aggressiveness. He followed Lee, in his typical fashion, both distantly and cautiously. McClellan's "slows" infuriated Lincoln: "If General McClellan isn't going to use my army," he once remarked, "I'd like to borrow it." Fortune smiled benignly on McClellan when some of his soldiers found a small treasure: cigars wrapped in a piece of paper. The wrapper, turned over to the soldiers' superior officer (the fate of the cigars is not known) contained Lee's campaign plans, dropped by some distracted Confederate staffer. Even with this intelligence coup, McClellan trailed after Lee almost timidly. Two armies, nearly 120,000 men, were on the march, one seeking the other, along the turnpikes and country roads of Maryland.

A remarkably candid photograph shows Lee's army on the march through Frederick, Maryland, during the Antietam Campaign, 1862. *Library of Congress.*

Historian Bruce Catton wrote that for Union soldiers on a march like this one, coffee was their addiction and their reward. Because of the Union blockade, Confederates had to make do with weak substitutes, and when two armies were camped close together, pickets did a brisk trade in swapping Southern tobacco for Northern coffee. Union soldiers drank it, like Arroyo Grande Valley farmers do today in local coffee shops, strong and black—lattes and cappuccinos are something both those farmers and the veterans who'd preceded them in cultivating the Valley would snort at. When an army was on the march and broke for a rest, little knots of soldiers, tent mates, immediately began building fires to set water to boil. They'd pull their precious supply of coffee beans out of a haversack, smash them with the rifle butts of their Springfields or Enfields, toss the grounds into the boiling water and brew the coffee long enough to straighten the hair of the curliest-headed private soldier. And then they would savor it, drinking out of metal cups, seated, if they were lucky, beneath the shade of roadside trees.

If they weren't lucky, a soulless regimental commander would order the march resumed with the coffee not yet brewed. A soldier in the ranks might forgive officers a lot of things, but interrupting their coffee break was unforgivable. Indeed, Massachusetts historian Jon Grinspan writes that a Union soldier released from a prisoner of war camp was enjoying his first cup of coffee in over a year when he wondered if he would ever forgive "those Confederate thieves for robbing [him] of so many precious doses" of his favorite beverage.[34]

During cross-country marches, the better-supplied Union soldier might be burdened with sixty pounds of equipment, while his relatively impoverished Confederate counterpart traveled light, with all his possessions tightly

---

[34] Jon Grinspan, "How Coffee Fueled the Civil War," New York *Times*, July 9, 2014, http://opinionator.blogs.nytimes.com/2014/07/09/how-coffee-fueled-the-civil-war/?_r=0

rolled in a blanket slung across his torso. A contemporary newspaper reporter described how a regiment on the move behaved, and it was with less than military precision:

> When these marches commenced, the men would be in regular military order, four abreast; but the first half-mile usually broke up all regularity. The men before they had walked that distance would become dispersed all over the road, some walking along the banks and others in the ditches: a squad straggling along the centre would be all the orderly part of the regiment. Some ran down into gullies to search for water, and others started off to see curiosities. Many on long marches became exhausted by fatigue, and lay down under the trees to rest. In warm weather these marches--if prolonged to six or eight miles--were most trying. The suffering for water was usually the greatest trouble --men carrying such heavy burdens as the soldiers requiring a great deal, and good water in any quantity being rarely discovered.[35]

Learning to march in the first place was an ordeal for many recruits; drill sergeants soon discovered that farm boys didn't know left from right. They did know the difference between straw and hay, so calling "straw foot, hay foot" at drill helped them. Civil War shoes— heavy brogans, and durable if a soldier took care of them—were assembled on straight lasts, and so had no left or right. Breaking in new shoes would have left blister on top of blister, and this was probably the case for the men of the 130th Pennsylvania Infantry, one of the units in pursuit of Lee in September 1862. The regiment had just been formed in August, so a rookie regiment on the march would be marked by footsore stragglers. It would have been the job of a newly-promoted corporal like Richard P. Merrill to help keep his company closed up.

Merrill would survive the fighting of the Civil War but, as was the case for many veterans, its effects would contribute

---

[35] "How the Civil War Soldiers Marched,"
http://www.civilwarhome.com/soldiersmarch.html
http://opinionator.blogs.nytimes.com/2014/07/09/how-coffee-fueled-the-civil-war/?_r=0

to his death, in Merrill's case, in 1909 Arroyo Grande. A blog on the 130th Pennsylvania reveals a soldier with a complex and mysterious life: "Richard P. Merrill" was born "Richard Best" on February 19, 1844, in Newville, Cumberland County, Pennsylvania, the son of Henry and Catherine Best. In 1860, he was a student living in Newville and stood 5' 8" tall with brown hair and brown eyes. He pursued a variety of trades during his life—prospector, hotel manager, peace officer and, of course, soldier.

He was mustered into federal service at Harrisburg on August 12, 1862, in Company E as a private. He used "Merrill" at his enlistment and kept it after moving to Cambria, California, in 1872 (via Missouri, Montana, and Arizona). His brother, William, never understood why he'd changed his name, and none of his friends knew it was an assumed name until after his death. He remained closed-mouthed to everyone about his pre-California history and never joined the local veterans' organization, the G.A.R. He married his boss's daughter, Mary Ann Lingo, on December 29, 1880, in Santa Margarita, San Luis Obispo County, and Mary Ann Merrill didn't learn his real name until 23 years into their marriage. He broke up his time in California by living one year in a town called Total Wreck in Pima County, Arizona, working as night watchman for a silver mine. He also served several years as a San Luis Obispo deputy sheriff and as Cambria's town constable. He was "a great sufferer," according to a family historian, with recurring spells of dysentery that followed him all his life.[36]

The 130th would also suffer greatly. On September 16, 1862, McClellan finally found Lee's army near the little town of Sharpsburg, Maryland, along Antietam Creek. The battle that ensued the next day would claim the largest number of Americans killed and wounded in a day's combat

---

[36] "Richard P. Merrill," http://opinionator.blogs.nytimes.com/2014/07/09/how-coffee-fueled-the-civil-war/?_r=0

It was the sight of a field gun and its caisson, like these from the 2nd U.S. Artillery, that so enthralled Merrill's comrade, Edward Spangler, at Antietam. *Library of Congress.*

in the nation's history. On September 17, as Merrill's regiment arrived on the battlefield, one soldier, a 16-year-old Company K private, Edward W. Spangler, was enthralled by the sight of caissons with their bouncing artillery pieces going into action at breakneck speed, their gun crews unlimbering and opening fire just as rapidly on the Confederate positions in front of Sharpsburg. He was also afraid, especially so when a Confederate bullet whizzed just over his head as he climbed a wood rail fence. Then his mood changed, as it did for so many soldiers caught up in combat:

The moment I discharged my rifle, all my previous scare was gone. The excitement of the battle made me fearless and oblivious of danger; the screeching and exploding shells, whistling bullets and the awful carnage all around me were hardly noticed. Nothing but positive orders would have induced me to cease firing.[37]

The objective of the assault that included both Merrill and Spangler was an old farm road, sunken by years of traffic and so a natural trench for the Confederate defenders, who had taken down fence rails and piled them to their front as an effective parapet. The 130th would go up against two North Carolina regiments, the 2nd and the 14th, who would greet them with withering rifle fire from what would be aptly called "Bloody Lane." The Union regiment got into position at 8 a.m. to take its part in a general attack on the sunken road at 9:30. The Confederates, outnumbered by at least two to one, would hold on desperately for four hours.

The colonel commanding the Confederate defense, John B. Gordon, marveled at the precision and the beauty of the advance of the Federal troops—what a pity, he thought, to kill them. Gordon, an untrained but intuitive combat commander, ordered his men to hold their fire until the last possible moment. The effect was terrible. A junior officer told Gordon later that a man could walk across the field beyond Bloody Lane on a carpet of Union bodies. But the federal troops' return fire proved just as lethal: "The first volley from the Union lines in my front," Gordon later wrote, "sent a ball through the brain of the chivalric Colonel Tew, of North Carolina, to whom I was talking, and another ball through the calf of my right leg."[38] Gordon was in fact shot five times that day; the last bullet hit him in the face, just below his left eye, and sent him to a field hospital.

---

[37] Edward W. Spangler, *My Little War Experience.* York Daily Publishing Co., York PA: 1904, pp. 34-35.
[38] "John B. Gordon," http://www.brotherswar.com/Antietam-Gordon.htm

Two soldiers who faced each other at Antietam: an almost impossibly young Pvt. Edward W. Spangler, 1863. From *My Little War Experience;* Col. John B. Gordon, whose left cheek shows evidence of his Antietam wounding. *National Archives.*

The 130th would fail to carry the North Carolinians' position but kept up their galling fire. Private Spangler fired his entire eighty-cartridge issue and more, taking spares from the cartridge box of a dead comrade when it registered briefly that a bullet had sheared off the top of the man's skull. The barrel of Spangler's rifle was too hot to touch by the time the regiment was called off the line to regroup and replenish its ammunition. At about that time, the weight of numbers finally told, and Union forces broke the Confederate line. The sunken road was packed with the North Carolinians' bodies. Lee's center was shattered, and Lincoln would agonize when he learned that his commander, McClellan, failed to finish off the breakthrough. Although he had thousands of troops in reserve, the Young Napoleon refused to send them in to exploit the collapsed Confederate center. McClellan was convinced, perhaps by the Pinkerton agents he retained for intelligence-gathering, that he was outnumbered by two to one. In fact, it was the Union men who had that advantage.

The position that John B. Gordon's men defended, "Bloody Lane," after the battle. Fence rails are stacked at the road's lip to provide cover. A burial party, likely from Merrill's 130th Pennsylvania, assigned that duty after the battle, prepares to go to work. *National Park Service.*

The Battle of Antietam would continue until dusk; Lee was close to defeat when a division under Gen. A.P. Hill came up after a rapid march from Harpers Ferry and checked the final Union attack of the day. McClellan again refused to send in the reserves that would have sent Hill's tough but understrength division flying.

When darkness fell, Richard P. Merrill and his comrades would have seen the twinkling of thousands of Confederate campfires across Antietam Creek as the 130th prepared itself for another day of battle. But Sept. 18 was quiet as the two armies nursed their wounds and eyed each other warily. That night, Lee ordered the Confederate campfires lit again, but they were a decoy. The Army of Northern Virginia slipped away in the night, headed south for the Potomac crossings. When dawn broke, there were no Confederates for the 130th Pennsylvania to fight. The assault on Bloody Lane had killed or wounded about a third of the men in Merrill's regiment,[39] and in return for their sacrifice, McClellan had allowed Lee to escape.

Silvanus Ullom was nineteen when he joined the army. He had already lived a far harder life than his peers; a notation on his family tree notes that he was "living with the Lynches" at the time of the war. This is because these things, excerpted from his family's history, happened when Sylvanus was in his early teens:

- Death of sister Sarah Catharine Ullom, January 27, 1855.
- Death of father William W. Ullom, July 29, 1855.
- Death of brother George Ullom, Nov. 9, 1855.
- Death of mother Judith Smith Ullom, November 12, 1855.
- Death of brother William Ullom June 25, 1856.

And then

- June 10, 1861. Enlistment, Pvt Co B, 25th Ohio Infantry Regiment[40]

Ullom was a resilient young man. Despite a young life so disrupted by both familial and wartime death, he would learn

---

[39] 130th Pennsylvania Volunteer Infantry Monument.
http://www.nps.gov/anti/learn/historyculture/mnt-pa-130.htm
[40] "Sylvanus Ullom," ancestry.com.,
http://person.ancestry.com/tree/7953517/person/24031195449/facts

a trade—as a carpenter—and, in the 1880s, would live on Third Street in Oakland, in a little neighborhood, not far from the waterline, where he would recognize some of the houses that still stand there today. He and his wife, Rebecca, would raise four boys and four girls, leaving the city by 1900 and farming first in Pozo and then in Arroyo Grande; by the time he died in 1914, Ullom had obviously lived a full life. He was a survivor. And, because he had joined the 25th Ohio, he would need to be.

Union troops at drill about three weeks before the May 1863 Chancellorsville campaign. *Library of Congress.*

That was because the 25th Ohio and the rest of the Army of the Potomac had to endure poor leadership. By the fall of 1862, Abraham Lincoln could abide George McClellan no more. "Little Mac" looked every bit the soldier; he had organized, instructed and inspired the largest army ever fielded in North America. But the man was a curious amalgam of arrogance—once, when Lincoln paid a call on the McClellans, the general was out, and, on returning, walked past the waiting president and upstairs to his bedroom without saying a word—diluted by a deep and perverse timidity. McClellan, who declared in melodramatic letters to his wife that it was he, and not the bumpkin president, who would save the nation, failed to do so when that was his duty. He would compound his failure as a military leader by losing the 1864 presidential election to the man who did save the nation. The one enduring legacy he left the United States was a saddle that he'd designed, named, of course, after himself.

The tension between McClellan, left, and Lincoln is transparent in this photograph, taken after the Battle of Antietam. *National Archives.*

So Lincoln fired McClellan, although the general was still popular with his men, and replaced him with Gen. Ambrose Burnside, known for his whiskers rather than his leadership. Burnside launched a winter attack on entrenched Confederates at Fredericksburg, Virginia, that was foolish—as foolish as John Bell Hood's assault at Franklin—and costly.

Now Lincoln turned to Joseph Hooker, a man who had a reputation for admiring fine cigars, good whiskey and Joseph Hooker. But Hooker was at least industrious. He and his staff, in the spring of 1863, rebuilt the army and put together a campaign that would slip a retrained and renewed Army of the Potomac across the Rapidan and Rappahannock Rivers and pitch it into the Confederates before they knew what hit them. "If the enemy does not run," Hooker crowed, "God help him."[41]

Maj. Gen. Joseph Hooker. *National Archives*

Lee and his subordinates, like John Gordon, had already taught George McClellan a lesson on leadership at Antietam, where Lee's men in Bloody Lane had shown unparalleled stubbornness in holding a static defensive position. The lesson

---

[41] James Harrison Wilson, *The Campaign of Chancellorsville, April 27-May 5, 1863.* Charles L. Story, Printer: Wilmington, Delaware, 1911, p. 16.

that Lee and his most valued subordinate, Thomas "Stonewall" Jackson, would teach Hooker now would be one on how to fight a war of movement, because Hooker was right. The enemy *would* run. They would run completely around the Army of the Potomac and fall like a sledgehammer–Stonewall Jackson's hammer on Lee's anvil–where they were least expected. God would not help Joe Hooker.

✖

Venn I come from der Deutsche Countree,
I vorks somedimes at baking;
Den I keeps a lager beer saloon,
Und den I goes shoe-making;
But now I was a sojer been
To save der Yankee Eagle,
To schlauch dem tam secession volks,
I goes to fight mit Sigel.

–A Civil War marching song

Many of Hooker's men were immigrants and had come to America because hunger stalked Europe in the 1840s. It was most visible in Ireland's Famine, when just-harvested potatoes turned to tar overnight in their cellars, and mothers were reduced to gathering nettles to make soup where they grew best, in graveyards. Cold winters and poor crop yields marked life throughout Europe as well in 1848. The Continent that year mirrored France on the eve of revolution in 1789, when poor harvests meant that the price of scarce bread in Paris ate the wages of an urban worker even as the worker ate his bread. And so revolutions erupted throughout Europe in 1848. In "The Communist Manifesto," Marx proclaimed the birth of *the* Revolution. He was wrong, of

58

course: the one common thread to 1848 was that every European revolution was crushed.

Germany—or, rather, the collection of north European states that would someday become Germany—endured a failed revolution, as well, one led by idealistic intellectuals. At the Frankfurt Assembly, they sought the formation of a modern liberal democracy, modeled on England's constitutional monarchy, and a united Fatherland. When they offered the crown of their Germany-on-paper to the King of Prussia, he refused to accept it, since it came, as he put it, "from the gutter."

When their 1848 revolution collapsed, thousands of disillusioned Germans—the largest single national immigrant group in our history—emigrated to America. Called "The Forty-Eighters," they would bring their innate liberalism to Lincoln's Republican Party: they were anti-slavery, pro-union and when Fort Sumter signaled the opening of the war, they became soldiers, "mit Sigel." They brought their language, too, in everyday words from "kindergarten" to "angst." They settled in dense neighborhoods in Milwaukee, St. Louis, and Chicago; settled, too, in lonely places like the Hill Country in Texas, where some of them died at the hands of Comanches. In Oklahoma, many walked behind the plows that broke the Plains, only to find two generations later that the topsoil they'd shattered was just a crust and that, once disturbed, great winds would carry it away to darken the East Coast or to fall on ships in mid-Atlantic. With the justice that is too infrequent in history, many of them, with names like Eisenhower and Nimitz, Eichelberger and Spaatz, would be instrumental in the destruction of the Nazis and their allies. Another, earlier, military man, Franz Sigel, was a Forty-Eighter who had commanded Union troops with some distinction in Missouri and Arkansas early in the war. In 1862, he became commander of the XI Corps, largely made up of German immigrants with a portion of "native" units like those of three future Arroyo Grande residents: Sylvanus

Ullom's 25th Ohio, Jefferson Wright's 55th Ohio, and Erastus Fouch's 75th Ohio.

Sigel, inspirational to his foreign-born soldiers, was liked far less by his superior officers: The Eleventh was the smallest corps in the Army of the Potomac, and his repeated appeals to enlarge his command were turned down. So he resigned and XI Corps passed to Gen. Oliver O. Howard shortly before Hooker's spring 1863 Chancellorsville campaign. This would be a critical command change and one that would have a decisive impact on the battle to come. Sigel's departure demoralized his German-born and German-American soldiers and Howard, a Mainer and a man whose Christianity resembled that of an implacable Nathaniel Hawthorne Puritan, was, as historian Stephen Sears puts it, "the wrong general in the wrong place with the wrong troops" at Chancellorsville.[42]

Two commanders of the XI Corps "Dutchmen:" Franz Sigel (left) and O. O. Howard. *National Archives.*

---

[42] Stephen W. Sears, *Chancellorsville*, Mariner Books, New York: 1996, p.263.

Once Virginia's roads had dried from the spring rains, Howard's commander, Joseph Hooker, put the Army of the Potomac in motion for his offensive against Lee. In late April, 1863, he left 28,000 men under Gen. John Sedgwick at Fredericksburg, essentially as a decoy, while he took command of the remainder of the Army of the Potomac. At nearly 100,000 men, he had twice Lee's numbers, and Lee was short a corps, having sent Gen. James Longstreet and his men to deal with threats in coastal and southern Virginia.

Hooker got his army safely across the Rapidan and Rappahannock Rivers; on the other side, he would turn to the work of destroying the Confederates. On May 1, Hooker's army met Lee's: the Union forces drove the Confederates and seized the high ground near a tiny crossroads hamlet marked by the Chancellorsville Tavern. But then they got a further order from Hooker: return to your original positions. Hooker would later admit that he'd simply lost his nerve. Even private soldiers like the 130th Pennsylvania's Edward Spangler were stunned that Hooker had:

> ...directed the army to return to Chancellorsville and vicinity where the country was densely wooded with tangled undergrowth, with neither perspective nor eminence, in which it was impossible to manoeuvre an army to advantage, and in the absence of unremitting vigilance liable to surprises. Gen. Couch [the 130th Pennsylvania's corps commander] and other officers vainly endeavored to have this fatal order rescinded but Hooker was obstinate and seemed to have lost both his head and his courage. The day following, instead of correcting the error by selecting a suitable battle ground, the army remained stationary and inert awaiting developments of the enemy. They came from an unexpected quarter about 6 P. M.[43]

Gen. Howard's XI Corps was on the far right of Hooker's "inert" lines, on the edge of dense, tangled woods called The Wilderness, where, a year later, gunfire would set the brush ablaze to consume wounded soldiers alive. His line was "in

---

[43] Spangler, p. 91

the air"—it wasn't anchored, on his own right, by contact with another unit or with some kind of natural barrier, like a river. Hooker pointed that out to Howard the morning of May 2. He also pointed out that Howard had neglected to dig entrenchments for XI Corps, something other corps commanders had begun to do.

Hooker was unhappy when he returned to his headquarters; he then received word of movement in the woods, which he passed on to his corps commanders, including Howard. Throughout the day, the commanders of the 55th, 107th, and 25th Ohio regiments also sent word to their divisional headquarters that they believed a large body of Confederates was moving through the woods, possibly headed for XI Corps' right. At 2:45, another XI Corps regimental commander requested reinforcements, alarmed by the size of the columns of marching men that he could see only fitfully through the undergrowth to his front. None of these messages appears to have reached Howard, and neither did Howard order trenches and rifle-pits dug for his corps, facing south, toward Lee's army.

Gen. Thomas J. "Stonewall" Jackson; Lee called him "my right arm." *Library of Congress.*

But the rebel troops to the south of Hooker's men represented only half of Lee's army. Like the troops Hooker had left at Fredericksburg, they were a decoy. The other half was on the move: it was Stonewall Jackson and 30,000 Confederates, including men who'd marched so fast under Jackson's command in the Shenandoah Valley that they'd earned the nickname "the foot cavalry." They were, in 1863, the finest combat troops in the world, led by perhaps the finest combat commander in the world: the eccentric, flinty, devoutly Calvinist Jackson. His men called him "Old Blue Light" for the way his eyes lit up in anticipation of battle, which, for Jackson, was his way of doing the Lord's work. But even he, habitually taciturn, had asked once how any commander could possibly fail "with troops such as these." It was these hungry men, many of them barefoot and wearing patchwork uniforms, who were moving through the woods along a hidden road in a 12-mile flanking movement aimed at XI Corps, at exactly the spot that had so concerned Hooker. As Howard's men were preparing or eating supper in the twilight, one of the most electric moments of the war became part of the life stories of the survivors.

Suddenly, in the clearing where they were bivouacked, some XI Corps soldiers began to laugh as jackrabbits darted out of the woods and through their camp. But the jackrabbits were followed by foxes and then by deer. The animals were followed by 30,000 Confederates, shrieking their rebel yell, who fell on the south-facing XI Corps from the west, from woods so dense that Gen. Howard believed that they should have prevented the passage of a body of troops the size of the one now shooting and bayoneting his men at their suppers.

The surprise was complete: Hooker's right turned to powder as XI Corps men tried to escape with their lives. Some of their officers hit the runners in the backs with the flats of their sabers to shame them, but many officers joined what was becoming a stampede. Not all of XI Corps ran.

Sylvanus Ullom's 25th Ohio pivoted to the right and formed a firing line to meet the Confederates, firing three volleys into Jackson's men, buying time for other units to escape. An officer nearby described the 25th's conduct that evening as it covered another regiment:

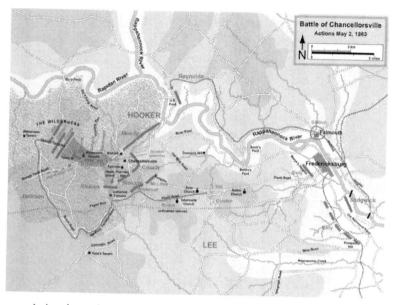

Jackson's attack on Hooker's right, through The Wilderness. *Map by Hal Jespersen www.posix.com/CW.*

That gallant regiment, the Twenty-fifth Ohio Volunteer Infantry, having deployed and presented a front to the advancing attack, with its left resting near the road, under the command of Lieut.-Col. Bambee, the companies successively from the right withdrew from the rifle-pit and formed line in rear of the Twenty-fifth, where the fighting was maintained until both the regiments were swept from their position by the overwhelming force of the attack. As a regiment it could not again rally.[44]

---

[44] Mike Mangus, "The Fifty-Fifth Ohio Volunteer Infantry," January 17, 2014. http://www.ohiocivilwarcentral.com/entry.php?rec=1183

Not far away, Erastus Fouch's 75th Ohio also was making a stand. But the force and the depth of the blow Jackson was delivering was too much, so the 75th broke and fled, as well. A third Arroyo Grande settler, Jefferson Wright, fought with a third Ohio regiment, the 55th, which also attempted to make a stand but had difficulty getting clear targets in the face of fleeing Union soldiers. The 55th began to retreat with the rest. For a time, the only resistance on Hooker's right seemed to be coming from a single cannon, also in retreat, but manned by a crew that would pause periodically to load and fire a canister charge, essentially, the artillery version of a shotgun shell, loaded with deadly steel balls, into their pursuers. The defiant artillery crew was directed by a German immigrant, Captain Hubert Dilger. A Southern artillerist described Dilger's actions that day as "superhuman," and the young Union officer would win the Medal of Honor.[45]

Dilger and the Ohio units had at least slowed Jackson's attack, which ultimately would be stopped by darkness rather than by Union resistance. The next morning, Richard P. Merrill's 130th Pennsylvania would renew the battle, when Merrill's regimental comrade Edward Spangler recorded indelible moments—a divisional commander, Gen. Hiram Berry, walked over to Spangler's K Company, raised his field glass, and was immediately shot dead; panicked horses were screaming and struggling in their traces with their artillery caisson wedged against a tree, and they, too, were shot down in his company's front; gunfire set a nearby forest on fire and Spangler marveled as a wounded soldier, one arm missing, walked calmly out of the flames.[46]

It was the beginning of the end for Joseph Hooker's command of the Army of the Potomac. On May 5, the Union army, so superior in both numbers and material, slinked back across the same rivers it had forded with so

[45] Robert K. Krick, "Like Chaff Before the Wind: Stonewall Jackson's Mighty Flank Attack at Chancellorsville," The Civil War Trust.
[46] Spangler, 110-13.

much hope only a week before. Because Lincoln lacked a viable alternative, Hooker would retain his command into late June, when Lee's Army of Northern Virginia launched a second invasion of the north, one that would end at a little crossroads town, populated largely by German immigrants, called Gettysburg. Chancellorsville had been a rout: Lee had the audacity to divide his outnumbered army into three; he'd held in place, with a small detachment, the men that Joseph Hooker had left at Fredericksburg, held Hooker's attention with part of his army along the Union front at Chancellorsville, and had sent Jackson with 30,000 men to fall on the poorly-led XI Corps men, blamed for the disaster and derisively called "The Flying Dutchmen," on Hooker's right.

It may have been Lee's greatest victory, but Lee had lost Stonewall Jackson, accidentally shot in the darkness of May 2 by his own men, as the price for Chancellorsville. When Lee sought another victory eight weeks later at Gettysburg, he would sorely miss Jackson's audacity and aggressiveness, absent in July in his subordinates, who seemed to be afflicted with a mysterious, paralyzing malaise. Among the troops facing Lee were four soldiers who would settle in Arroyo Grande; two of them, from XI Corps, would be among the great battle's casualties, one man wounded, the second taken prisoner.

For Richard P. Merrill of the 130th Pennsylvania, the war was over. He was invalided out of the army after Chancellorsville. Sickly for the rest of what would be a restless life, when Merrill died he seemed to have a found a home at last and there is evidence that he was, despite his compromised health, a remarkable man. His last job was as the janitor for the Arroyo Grande grammar school. Despite all that he had seen and all he'd endured, there is a revelatory line that reveals Merrill's truest character in his obituary, in a 1909 Arroyo Grande *Herald-Recorder*. Classes were dismissed at noon the day of this veteran's funeral so that students could have the chance to attend. "Mr. Merrill was a great favorite with the children," the article notes.

Richard P. Merrill worked as a custodian at this elementary school, on the site of what is today a Ford automobile agency at Fair Oaks and Traffic Way in Arroyo Grande. *Photo courtesy Randy Spoeneman.*

Chapter 3.
The Dead Boy with the Reins in his Hands
Grant 1862-63

Like the "Dutchmen" of Howard's XI Corps, Henry Bakeman was a German, born in Hanover, but by the time he'd established himself Arroyo Grande after the war, he'd become so completely American that he'd registered his own cattle brand for the stock he ran on thirty acres a mile outside town.[47]

Bakeman and his 2nd Iowa Infantry did not run at Shiloh when, at dawn on April 6, 1862, Confederates launched a surprise attack that rivaled Stonewall Jackson's at Chancellorsville. But many Union soldiers did break and run for the bluffs along the Tennessee River where they stood useless, disorganized, most unarmed, all of them thoroughly whipped. It must have seemed to Bakeman, in the thick of the fighting, as if his adopted nation didn't have much of a future. But the difference between the panic at Shiloh in 1862 and that at Chancellorsville in 1863 was in the character of commanders. Somewhere above the rabble of terrified Union soldiers, wishing fervently that the Tennessee River was *between* themselves and the Confederates, rather than *behind* them, was their general, calmly whittling and puffing on a cigar. It was Grant.

Ulysses S. Grant's story, of course, has to be one of the most compelling of the war. After serving capably in the Mexican War, loneliness, when he was stationed at a remote Oregon army post far from his wife, Julia, led to heavy drinking and ultimately to the West Pointer's resignation from the army in 1854. He had failed at his chosen career. He then failed as a farmer, lost an election to be a county engineer, and finally returned to his home in Galena, Illinois, to clerk in the leather shop owned by his family. This is when the war saved Grant, who became a volunteer officer and rose quickly: he turned three successive regiments from undisciplined and insubordinate civilians into real soldiers.

---

[47] Patricia Loomis and Mary Mueller, *The Settlers of Arroyo Grande, California*, CreateSpace Publishing, 2014, p. 71.

The war presented him, as well, with a perfect professional partnership with the perfect subordinate in William Tecumseh Sherman, a mercurial, driven, restless officer. Both men shared a kind of ruthless single-mindedness, but Sherman was the ideal match for imperturbable, stoic Grant.

Grant didn't know it, but young Pvt. Henry Bakeman was another ideal match. After the war, Bakeman, the cattle rancher, would move to Cholame and then to the Arroyo Grande Valley. When he died in 1895, he left 146 acres and a son who would turn to crop farming; the family left its name in the modern town's Bakeman Lane.[48] What Bakeman seems to have brought to both the battlefield and later, as a California settler, was a certain steeliness of character.

An 1897 illustration shows Gen. Charles Ferguson Smith leading Henry Bakeman's 2nd Iowa in the attack on Fort Donelson. *New York Public Library.*

His regiment had first shown that quality at one of Grant's first noted victories, at Fort Donelson, Tennessee, in

---

[48] Ibid.

February 1862. Grant had charged one of his West Point instructors, Gen. Charles Ferguson Smith, with taking Donelson's fortifications, and Smith had in turn entrusted Bakeman's 2nd Iowa with leading the assault. Smith led with style: "This is your chance!" he bellowed to the Iowans. "You volunteered to be killed for love of country and now you can be!" Unhappily, the 2nd's color bearer immediately obliged, collapsing when hit by four bullets. Smith then led the attack on horseback and leaped the Confederate earthworks with howling Iowans, bayonets fixed, right behind him. Once inside, they fired a volley into the defenders, who fled, then returned, trying but failing to dislodge Smith and his men from the trenches they'd occupied.

The next day, the Confederate commander of Donelson, Simon Bolivar Buckner (his son and namesake was to be the commander of American Marines and soldiers during the invasion of Okinawa, and the younger Buckner was killed in action there), pinned between Grant's men inside his fortifications and federal gunboats on the Cumberland River to his rear, asked for surrender terms. He got this reply:

Sir:

   Yours of this date proposing Armistice, and appointment of Commissioners, to settle terms of Capitulation is just received. No terms except unconditional and immediate surrender can be accepted. I propose to move immediately upon your works.

   I am Sir: very respectfully
   Your obt. sevt.
   U.S. Grant
   Brig. Gen.

It was a stunning victory, and one for which it was suggested that the "U.S." in Grant's name stood for "Unconditional Surrender." Only eight weeks later, a Confederate army commanded by Albert Sidney Johnston came close to negating everything Grant had done to right his life. Part of what saved Grant and doomed Johnston, who would die at this battle, the Battle of Shiloh, was the fact that Henry Bakeman and the 2nd Iowa demonstrated that they could fight as well defensively as they could in an attack like the one at Fort Donelson.

The problem at Shiloh, named for a little log church on the battlefield near Pittsburg Landing on the Tennessee River, was that the commander of the encampment near the church, William T. Sherman, had prepared no defense. It was like a foretelling of Chancellorsville; Sherman's blunder paralleled that of O. O. Howard. Sherman failed to dig the earthworks and trenches that, later in the war, would become automatic. Wherever a federal army stopped in Grant's overland campaign against Lee in 1864, for example, soldiers would begin digging entrenchments with bayonets or mess kits until picks and shovels came up from the supply train. But this was early in the war, and Sherman thought entrenchments sapped an army's morale. To prepare defensive works would unman soldiers who should always be ready to go on the attack. That was, of course, foolish, quaintly Napoleonic, but even worse was Sherman's dismissal of reports that there was a large body of troops in the woods beyond the tent city under his command.

Johnston's Confederates began nipping at Federal skirmishers at about 5 a.m. on April 6, but the seriousness of the situation became more apparent two hours later when 35,000 Confederates appeared and began to stampede Sherman's men, who had been placidly preparing their breakfasts. Sherman didn't realize his error in dismissing the earlier reports until he rode up to the encampment and had a staff officer beside him shot out of the saddle; Sherman, wounded slightly in the hand, turned his mount and began sounding the alarm: "My God, we are attacked!" The overall commander, Grant, was miles away when he heard the sound of firing and quickly boarded a steamboat that began puffing its way toward Pittsburg Landing. The morning promised to be the undoing of both generals.[49]

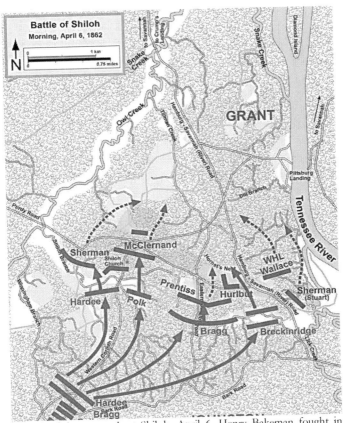

The Confederate attack at Shiloh, April 6. Henry Bakeman fought in W.H.L. Wallace's division; his commander was killed. *Map by Hal Jespersen www.posix.com/CW.*

Fortunately for Grant and Sherman, the Confederate attack was arrested by the smell of frying bacon; Johnston's hungry men began finishing the Union soldiers' meals and looting their tents of rifles, blankets, and shoes. Men who should have been clearing the field of the enemy were instead

---

[49] "My God! We are attacked! Disorganized surprise at Shiloh Church," *Civil War Daily Gazette*, April 6, 2012, http://civilwardailygazette.com/my-god-we-are-attacked-disorganized-surprise-at-shiloh-church/

frantically trying on Yankee footwear as if they were clearance sale shoppers. That gave Generals Benjamin Prentiss and W.H.L. Wallace—Henry Bakeman's divisional commander—enough time to form a defense, even as hundreds of panic-stricken soldiers bolted for the illusory protection of the bluffs near the landing on the river. They were done for the day.

Bakeman and the 2nd Iowa had just started. They were part of the defensive line formed along a sunken road, like the one that John B. Gordon's Confederates had occupied at Antietam, and their line, made up mostly of Iowa men from five different regiments, held most of the day. Their firepower began to take a toll, as one Confederate soldier recorded. The eyewitness was Henry Stanley, who would become famous as the journalist who found the missionary David Livingston in Africa a decade later:

> I marveled, as I heard the unintermitting patter, snip, thud, and hum of the bullets, how anyone could live under this raining death. I could hear the balls beating a merciless tattoo on the outer surface of the log, pinging vivaciously as they flew off at a tangent from it, and thudding into something or other, at the rate of a hundred a second. One, here and there, found its way under the log, and buried itself in a comrade's body. One man raised his chest, as if to yawn, and jostled me. I turned to him, and saw that a bullet had gored his whole face, and penetrated into his chest. Another ball struck a man a deadly rap on the head, and he turned on his back and showed his ghastly white face to the sky.[50]

The noise the bullets made gave this part of the battlefield its name: "The Hornet's Nest." One of the bullets took the life of the Confederate commander, Johnston, and as the day wore on, the morning's assault began to fray; what had once been a fairly coordinated attack dissolved into isolated and deadly firefights, including the one in the Hornet's Nest. By the time the Iowans' defense of that position collapsed—their

---

[50] "The Battle of Shiloh, 1862" Eyewitness to History, www.eyewitnesstohistory.com, 2004.

divisional commander, Wallace, was dead and three Iowa regiments were captured, with the 2nd escaping[51]— Grant had set up an ironclad defensive line, bristling with artillery, above Pittsburg Landing.

The Hornet's Nest, Shiloh, by Civil War artist Thure de Thulstrup, 1887. *Library of Congress.*

At the end of the day, an exhausted Sherman, who had rallied both himself and the Union right, walked up to Grant, who was pensively whittling a piece of wood. "Well, Grant," Sherman said, "we've had the devil's own day, haven't we?"

"Yes. Lick 'em tomorrow, though," Grant murmured.

That would be exactly what happened. On April 7, Grant and Sherman, reinforced by fresh troops led by Gen. Don Carlos Buell, would send the Confederates into

---

51 "The Battle of Shiloh: An Iowa Perspective," http://www.iowacivilwarhistory.com/uploads/1/3/0/6/13062452/item_6_-_shiloh_-_an_iowa_perspective_meyer_with_study_questions.pdf

retreat after a second day of hard fighting. Bakeman and the 2nd Iowa were on the far left of the counterattack that gave Grant the victory.

Grant as a lieutenant general, 1864. *National Archives.*

By the time the Battle of Shiloh was over, more Americans had been killed in two days of fighting than had been killed in all the wars the nation had fought since 1776.[52] If this struggle on the Tennessee River was a turning point

---

[52] http://blogs.ancestry.com/cm/2014/05/21/12-stunning-civil-war-facts/

for Ulysses S. Grant, his victory on the Mississippi a year later was a turning point for the Civil War. Arroyo Grande veterans would play a role, as well, in the Vicksburg Campaign.

🦅

In 1870, Francis Xavier Belot's France would go to war with the North German Confederation—one that included Henry Bakeman's Hanover—in the Franco-Prussian war, which would end in humiliation for the French; the new German emperor would, in fact, be crowned at Louis XIV's Versailles Palace. For the next forty years, the motto of the French army was *revanche!* and what had happened in France's nineteenth-century loss to the Germans would rebound with the terrible war of 1914-18, the war that still shapes international politics in the 21st century.

But Belot, who would farm Arroyo Grande's Huasna Valley, and Bakeman, the future cattle rancher, were American soldiers serving under Grant in the decade before Franco-Prussian War; that experience must have made the politics and the battles of their birth nations seem distant and irrelevant. By the spring of 1863, Bakeman's 2nd Iowa had earned relatively restful garrison duty, but Belot's 4th Minnesota—along with another Iowa regiment, the 24th, which included future Arroyo Grande settlers William Lane and Isaac Dennis Miller—would play key roles in a battle at Champion Hill, Mississippi, that decided Grant's Vicksburg campaign.

Vicksburg, a town set on bluffs high above the Mississippi River, was militarily, economically, and psychologically vital to the South. By the spring of 1863, the Union had control of the upper Mississippi and of New Orleans at the river's mouth, but Vicksburg's artillery emplacements denied them the lower Mississippi. Rail lines that connected at Vicksburg supplied, among other commodities, the Texas beef that helped to feed Confederate armies in the field and, if Vicksburg fell, Texas, Arkansas, and Louisiana were separated from the rest of the Confederacy.

Vicksburg's Confederate defender was by birth a Yankee, a Philadelphian. Gen. John Pemberton had elected to join the Confederate army thanks to his marriage to a Virginia woman and to years of duty in the South. Pemberton, well-intentioned yet somewhat inept, was trusted neither by his subordinate officers nor by his commanding officer, Joseph Johnston. In May 1863, as Grant approached Vicksburg from the south, Johnston ordered Pemberton to attack the invading army in the rear and break up the threat Grant posed. Pemberton thought Johnston's orders intemperate and decided instead to attack a Union supply train, more vulnerable than Grant's fighting columns and just as likely, once captured or destroyed, to force Grant to turn back. Instead it was Pemberton who was forced to turn back: Johnston heard of the junior general's unilateral decision to change the objective of his attack, was furious, and sent a dispatch rider to turn Pemberton and his 26,000-man army around and link up with Johnston's forces. A mortified Pemberton changed his army's direction and in the process blundered into a Union army corps, on the move in the Mississippi countryside, which included the 24th Iowa.[53]

William Lane, who would someday raise cattle and a herd of Lane children in the Huasna Valley, was a lieutenant in the 24th Iowa's Company C when the regiment, on the morning of May 16, 1863, confronted the Confederates, who were busily digging in on plantation property atop Champion Hill, whose slopes were covered with tangled

---

[53] Jon Stephenson, "Battle of Champion's Hill," *America's Civil War*, Sept. 1999, http://www.civilwar.org/battlefields/championhill/champion-hill-history-articles/battle-of-champions-hill.htm

scrub and cut by deep gullies. It would be a difficult position to take, but at 10:30, Grant arrived and ordered the division that included the 24th up the hill. Typically, the regiment shook out skirmishers—a thin line of advance troops whose assignment it was to probe the enemy's positions—and the skirmishers were followed by dense lines of attackers. It was the job of lieutenants, perhaps even more expendable than skirmishers, to order the maneuvers that would transform a company from a marching column into an attack formation. It was also a lieutenant's job to lead from the front, to keep his men closed up, and to wave his sword in an attempt to project ferocity. It might be understandable if, given his duties that day, twenty-eight-year-old William Lane was feeling as if every Confederate atop Champion Hill was aiming at him.

The men he was leading were confident, if the account left by a corporal in Company H, James Oxley, is any indication. Oxley succinctly and in his own spelling recounted what happened next:

> ...a short hault was ordered and we was informed that in a fiew hundred yards wer the Rebs. Strongly posted they had a battery which was for us to charge and capture it...The enemy was fast massing his forces more left when the [24th] Iowa was ordered to charge a six gun battery which was only a fiew hundred yards in our front.
>
> No sooner had the gallent sons of Iowa received the orders to charge till they went not willing that the fare fame of Iowa soldiers deminished rushed like wild and enraged tigers upon the men & batteries. Giving at the same time one of those furious yells which startled fear...dinging the Rebs and they wer driven like chaf before the wind.[54]

The 24th was savoring its capture of the guns and a few satisfactory moments of Reb-dinging—they'd shot or bayoneted most of the artillery crews—when they were confronted by a counterattack; after a fifteen-minute

---

[54] James Oxley, "A History of Company H 24th Iowa Volunteer Infantry" http://battleofchampionhill.org/oxley.htm

firefight, they were driven back down the hill and the Confederates re-took their guns. During the retreat, Major Edward Wright of the 24th, badly wounded, still managed, with the help of his revolver, to capture a burly Confederate who carried the wounded officer downhill and out of harm's way. The tide of the battle seemed to be turning when a brigade that included Francis X. Belot and the 4th Minnesota bowled into the surging Confederates' flank. The Fourth galloped up to, into, and over the other side of a ravine, arrested the Confederate counterattack, and captured 118 prisoners. They then confronted a sight so vividly described by Alonzo Brown, a corporal in Company B, that it must have haunted many in the regiment for the rest of their lives:

> When the fighting ceased we walked along the wooded, hill and examined the artillery captured from the enemy, and, unless mistaken, counted twenty-eight pieces which had been captured and which the enemy bad abandoned in the road after taking away the horses. We saw one battery upon the brow of the hill. Some of the horses had been killed, and upon one of them sat its rider, - dead. The animal lay on the side of a sharp little slope so that the right leg of the rider was under its body while the other was extended naturally, with the foot in the stirrup. He held the bridle rein in his right band and with eyes wide open, as if looking to the front, sat upright in the saddle as naturally as if still alive. His features looked like marble, and he was apparently not over seventeen years of age.[55]

By 4:00 p.m., Pemberton's fight was ending, and the general was both disheartened and furious at a recalcitrant division commander who had failed to move up in time to support the defenders on Champion Hill. He ordered a general retreat toward Vicksburg. Grant now had Pemberton where he wanted him, trapped in the town on the Mississippi bluffs. He attempted to attack Pemberton's fortifications there—the Fourth lost twelve killed and 42 wounded in an assault a week after Champion Hill —but then decided to besiege the city and starve it into surrender. The surrender

---

[55] Alonzo Brown, "Battle of Champion's Hill," *History of the Fourth Regiment of Minnesota Infantry Volunteers During the Great Rebellion, 1861-1865*, St. Paul, Minn., The Pioneer Press Company, 1892, http://battleofchampionhill.org/brown.htm

came, appropriately, on the Fourth of July, 1863, the bookend in the West to the great victory of the day before in the East, at Gettysburg. The first regiment to enter the conquered city was Francis X. Belot's 4th Minnesota.

The Confederacy was now severed at the Mississippi. "The drums of Champion Hill," the British military historian J F. C. Fuller intoned, "sounded the doom of Richmond."[56] Unfortunately for Ulysses Grant and for the Union cause, the sound of those drums hadn't carried to Chattanooga, Tennessee.

That was where, in the weeks after Grant's victory at Vicksburg, Gen. William Rosecrans was just as trapped as Pemberton's men had been. If anything, Rosecrans had gotten himself into a worse fix. If the terrain around Chattanooga can be compared to a soup bowl, then Rosecrans and his Army of the Cumberland were in the bottom of the bowl and the Confederates of Gen.

Gen. Braxton Bragg. *Library of Congress.*

Braxton Bragg were arrayed partway around the bowl's lip, on mountaintops that overlook Chattanooga—after Richmond and Atlanta, it was one of the most important industrial and rail centers of the Confederacy.

---

[56] Rebecca Blackwell Drake, "The Battle of Champion Hill," http://battleofraymond.org/history/chill1.htm

Patriot Graves

Rosecrans was, with the exception of his Chattanooga predicament, at least a capable general handicapped by a kind of serene bluntness—the man had no power to edit the words that came out of his mouth—that sometimes offended his superiors. Grant detested him. Opposing him was Bragg, a man who appeared, from his portraiture, to have suffered from perpetual indigestion and who made the firing squad a staple of his disciplinary style[57]. Rosecrans had driven Bragg out of Chattanooga the day before Vicksburg fell. His laxity in following up this victory, reminiscent of George McClellan's leisurely pace in the East, further irritated Grant.

In the fall of 1863, Rosecrans would finally find Bragg's army again, just across the Tennessee border at Chickamauga, Georgia, and there the Union general would commit the blunder that would be his undoing. This time—September 19-20, 1863–it was Bragg who would attack Rosecrans and the Confederate had the extra weight of the Army of Northern Virginia's James Longstreet. Longstreet's corps had been transferred, during a lull in the fighting in Virginia, to Bragg's army on a series of rickety rail connections— "rickety" because another victim of the prewar cotton economy and states' rights was railway transport. Southern rail lines were intended for short hauls to river or ocean ports, were not updated or well-maintained, and railroads in Virginia and Tennessee marked their respective states' sovereignty by using different gauges of track. Despite that deficiency, it was Longstreet's men, and specifically the division led by the ill-fated John B. Hood, the future commander of Confederate forces in Tennessee, that overwhelmed the Union troops that included Jacob Davis's 58th Indiana on September 20. After the war, Davis, who rose from private to captain during his service, would typify the

---

[57] Michael Haskew, "Bragg versus Rosecrans: Profiles in Generalship at Stones River," *America's Civil War Magazine*, January 1997, http://www.civilwar.org/battlefields/stonesriver/stones-river-history/bragg-rosecrans.html

restlessness of Union veterans. After marrying America McCrary in 1875 Indiana, the couple would move to Kansas, where the younger two of their four children were born, before settling in Arroyo Grande, where Davis was buried in 1895; three Davis children would settle just to the north, in San Luis Obispo.

Newspaper artist Alfred Waud's depiction of Confederates on the attack at Chickamauga *Library of Congress.*

At Chickamauga, Davis's misfortunes began two hours after the day's fighting had begun on September 20. Rosecrans, fearful of having his army's left turned, shifted troops that way. His command came at the precise moment that Hood's division, newly arrived by train, was preparing its assault.[58] Hood found, to what must have been his delight, that in place of the Union division opposite his there was nothing but farmland. At the edge of this gap was the 58th Indiana, and the retreat of a panicked artillery battery further

---

[58] "General William Rosecrans' Report at the Battle of Chickamauga," https://historyengine.richmond.edu/episodes/view/5179

weakened the regiment when its horse-drawn caissons galloped into the infantrymen's midst and created a second gap—three of the regiment's companies were separated by the battery's stampede at the moment when Hood's men fell on them.[59] An officer in Company E dutifully, and with an accountant's eye, recorded afterward what his overwhelmed enlisted men had left behind:

> 7 Enfield rifle muskets. Cal. 58
> 1 French rifle musket. " 69
> 8 Inft. Cartridge boxes & plates
> 8 Inft. Cartridge box belt & plates
> 8 Inft. Waist belts & plates
> 8 cap pouches & picks
> 8 ball screws
> 15 Tompions [gun muzzle guards]
> 4 Non Com officers swords[60]

The Federal right, including the 58th Indiana, collapsed. The left, over which Rosecrans was so fretful, had never been in trouble. It was commanded by the always stolid Gen. George Thomas, and the Union soldiers there held. While Thomas led a solid defense, it was his commander, Rosecrans, who led the panicked retreat of the rest of the army to Chattanooga. Once there, they would be trapped by Bragg's army positioned on the heights that overlooked the city. Rosecrans was relieved of command by Grant, who graciously noted his subordinate's helpful suggestions for the defense of the city. The junior general was banished to the relative backwater of the Department of the Missouri. Now it was up to Grant to find a way out of Chattanooga. He ultimately would see his soldiers find a way out for him, on November 25, but they did so in defiance of their commanding general's orders.

---

[59] "Death of Captain Charles H. Bruce," *Montgomery County, Indiana, Civil War History*, June 12, 2015, https://mccw.wordpress.com/category/58th-indiana-infantry/
[60] Matthew Rector, "Lost by Co E 58th Indiana at Chickamauga," Aug 7, 2009, http://www.authentic-campaigner.com/forum/archive/index.php/t-24215.html

A group of officers poses atop Lookout Mountain after the end of the Chattanooga campaign. *Library of Congress.*

There had to be very few Civil War reunions in Arroyo Grande where the Battle of Missionary Ridge didn't come up in the conversation. Seven veterans participated in this battle, at the end of the campaign that would drive Bragg and his Confederates off the mountaintops above Chattanooga. After firing Rosecrans, Grant busied himself with securing a thin line of supply into the city, called the "Cracker Line," after the hardtack that was the enamel-cracking staple of the soldier's field diet. In November, Grant moved decisively: on

85

November 23, George Thomas, the "Rock of Chickamauga," who had succeeded Rosecrans, attacked the Confederates at their position on a hill called Orchard Knob, found the defense there softer than expected, and drove the enemy up Missionary Ridge.

With that accomplished, Thomas's men, still stung by their defeat at Chickamauga, were to keep the center of the Confederate line on the ridge busy and hold them in place, making noises but not much else. The heavy fighting would be done by Grant's subordinates. Sherman was to assault the enemy's right. At the same time, an Eastern general, the onetime commander of Union forces at Chancellorsville, Joseph Hooker, and his veterans were to drive in the Confederate left on the slopes of the forbidding and fog-shrouded Lookout Mountain. Lookout Mountain's sheer cliffs and dramatic rock formations provided commercial photographers with hundreds of what we would today call "photo ops"—glass-plate images abound of victorious Union soldiers posing nonchalantly above sheer drops to sudden death—including, in one instance, the horn section of a regimental band, either tooting away or doing so in pantomime.

On November 24, Hooker began the job of clearing Lookout Mountain—more thinly defended than had been thought—when darkness fell. It fell even more heavily than usual. A total eclipse of the moon that night was interpreted, correctly, as a bad omen for Braxton Bragg. Hooker, meanwhile, was to finish his task the next day. So Thomas's men, including Francis Craig of the 73rd Illinois, Edward Shaw of the 74th Illinois, and Jacob Davis of the 58th Indiana, all future Arroyo Grande residents, had the night of the 24th and all morning of November 25 to seethe. They were seething because the glory was going to Hooker and his Easterners, whom the seemingly rustic Westerners resented for their crisp uniforms and crisp close-order drill; they were dudes, "paper-collar soldiers."[61] Among them was Jefferson Wright, a private in the 55th Ohio who had survived far worse insults, namely Stonewall Jackson's ambush at Chancellorsville. But while Wright and his like were assigned a mountain, Thomas's men had to be satisfied with a knob.

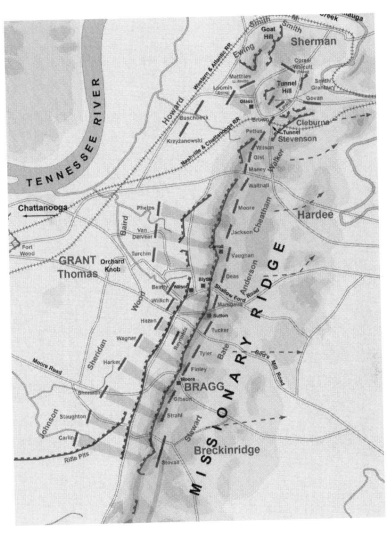

Thomas's troops attack Missionary Ridge. Francis Craig and Edward Shaw fought under corps commander Philip Sheridan. *Map by Hal Jespersen www.posix.com/CW.*

---

61 Shelby Foote, p. 843.

And on the other side of the battlefield, Grant's pet, Sherman, launched the attack on the Confederate right at Tunnel Hill. So George Thomas's men watched and waited, resentful, on November 25 as events unfolded to their left and to their right. Grant was watching, too, and in the afternoon, after lunch, he noticed some of Sherman's men retreating from their attack. He finally ordered Thomas forward, to draw some attention away from Sherman's assault, which was obviously running into difficulty. They were to advance on the enemy center, take his forward rifle pits, and stop. He repeated that order twice for clarity.[62]

A postwar McCormick Harvester promotional poster depicts Union troops beginning to overwhelm Confederate defenders, foreground, atop Missionary Ridge. Lookout Mountain looms in the background. *Library of Congress.*

---

[62] "Reconstructed comparative time table for the day of 25 Nov. 1863," The Battles for Chattanooga 23, 24, and 25 Nov. 1863, http://www.aotc.net/Chattanooga.htm#timetable

It was an order that was disobeyed with great gusto. Gen. Thomas's men stormed the rifle pits, took them, and kept going. Grant raged, then turned philosophical: "It will be all right if it turns out all right," he remarked ruefully.[63] Among the attackers were Francis Craig and Edward Shaw, under their brigade commander, Francis T. Sherman; two brigades to their left was the 58th Indiana and Jacob Davis. It may have been a spontaneous moment—perhaps Thomas's Westerners wanted to show paper-collar Easterners how real soldiers fought—but the spontaneity was contagious.

Even divisional commanders like Gen. Thomas J. Wood were carried away in the excitement:

> ...the enthusiasm and impetuosity of the troops were such that those who first reached the intrenchments at the base of the Ridge bounded over them, and pressed on up the ascent, after the flying enemy, without orders from any commander. The rank and file took in the exigencies of the situation, and quickly adopted the only way out of the danger with which they were environed, namely, to assault and carry the crest of the Ridge. The barricades at the base of the Ridge were no protection against the artillery on the summit. To remain at the base would be destruction; to retire would be both expensive of life and disgraceful. Officers and men all seemed impressed with this truth. In addition, the example of those who first bounded over the intrenchments and began the ascent was contagious. Without waiting for orders, the vast mass pressed onward up the rugged ascent, in the race for glory, each man apparently eager to be the first on the summit.

> Speaking for myself, individually, I frankly confess I was simply one of the boys on that occasion. I was infected with the contagion of the prevailing enthusiasm. The enemy's artillery and musketry could not check the impetuous assault. The troops did not halt to fire to have done so, would have been ruinous. Little more was left to the immediate commanders of the troops than to cheer on the foremost, to encourage the weaker of limb, and to sustain the very few who seemed to be faint-hearted. To the eternal honor of the troops, it should be recorded that the laggards were, indeed, few in number. Upward, upward, steadily went the standard of the Nation, borne

---

[63] "Civil War Quotes," http://www.21stmichigan.us/quotes.htm

onward by strong arms, upheld by brave hearts, and soon it was seen flying on the crest of Missionary Ridge![64]

20,000 men went up the steep slopes of Missionary Ridge. The regiment in the lead may well have been Edward Shaw's 74th Illinois, men from Winnebago County. They'd seen enough action in the war so far so that a plea went home for a battle flag to replace the 74th's tattered original. To the regiment's delight, the new regimental colors arrived eleven days before the assault on Missionary Ridge. It was the first flag to reach the summit, placed there after three color bearers in succession had been shot; the new flag itself had its baptism of fire formalized by no fewer than fifteen bullet holes.[65] Bragg's army dissolved: Chattanooga was free of him and his Confederates.

A view of Missionary Ridge after the battle. *National Archives.*

---

[64] Thomas J. Wood, "The Battle of Missionary Ridge," Oct. 1, 1890,
http://www.aotc.net/TJ%20Wood.htm
[65] Alex Gary, "Military 'miracle' part of history of 74th Illinois," Rockford *Register Star,*
Sept. 20, 2009, http://www.rrstar.com/article/20090920/News/309209925

In the surreal contrast between war and peace that so troubled Union veterans, that journey up Missionary Ridge, under Confederate rifle fire, should have been Edward Shaw's last. His life would end instead thirty-nine years later, after he rose from the kitchen table of his Los Berros farmhouse, walked a few steps, and collapsed.[66] If Shaw's death was mundane, his life wasn't: he was a successful farmer and father who had experienced an exhilarating and incomparable moment. On November 25, 1863, his struggle up the slopes of Missionary Ridge was part of one of the most improbable victories of the war. He had helped to erase the humiliation of Chickamauga.

The paper-collar soldiers would be given a chance, as well, to redeem their dismal performance at Chancellorsville when they confronted Lee's second invasion of the North at Gettysburg.

---

[66] "Death of E.S. Shaw," San Luis Obispo *Breeze*, Feb. 4, 1902.

Chapter 5.
The Turning Point
Gettysburg, July 1863

Lee's second invasion of the North in 1863 was blunted after three days of battle marked by both great courage and costly mistakes at Gettysburg, a little German farm town in southern Pennsylvania. Here, the great Southern commander lost, once and forever, his aura of invincibility. Four Arroyo Grande veterans fought in this, the war's most famous battle.

It was a battle, according to one participant, that began partly because of shoes. Confederate General Henry Heth blundered into Union General John Buford's cavalry outside Gettysburg on the morning of July 1, and in his 1877 memoirs, Heth wrote that the confrontation had come about because he'd heard a rumor that there was a shoe factory in the little town and sent a detachment forward to investigate.[67] As many as a third of Lee's soldiers in his Army of Northern Virginia were barefoot, which was yet another reminder that the South's industrial base was insufficient in waging a modern war. Instead of bringing back shoes, Heth's men brought on a battle with Buford's dismounted cavalry troopers, whose firing line blocked the way into town. The Confederate general then sent up more men to push the Federal cavalry aside, but Buford's men put up a stubborn defense that allowed Gen. John Reynolds to bring up his I Corps infantry and temporarily check Heth and his Confederates.

One of the I Corps units whose work it was to stop them was the 24th Michigan Infantry, which included a young man, Bela Clinton Ide, who would someday give his name to the street in Old Arroyo Grande where he would build his family's home. Ide's regiment was part of one of the most famous and hard-fighting units in the Civil War, the "Iron Brigade," made up of what were then Westerners, men from Wisconsin, Michigan and Indiana, who were noted for their headgear as well as their ability to absorb and mete out punishment. The brigade wore the 1855-issue broad-brimmed, high-crowned black hat, and the Confederates were said to have groaned when they saw them, "Here come those damn black hats again!"

Just as Buford's cavalrymen had put up all the fight they could, and then some—their carbines had nowhere near the

---

[67] "Did the Battle of Gettysburg really begin as a search for shoes?" www.todayifoundout.com. March 9, 2015.

range or hitting power of infantry rifles, and every fourth cavalry trooper had to be pulled off the firing line to hold the reins of his comrades' mounts–Reynolds sent the Iron Brigade's 2nd Wisconsin in as a counterweight. As Ide and the 24th Michigan followed the Wisconsin men, at about 10:45 a.m., Reynolds, a popular and talented officer, destined, some said, to command the Army of the Potomac, was hit; he toppled from his horse, dead. Meanwhile, the 24th, now joined by the 19th Indiana, hit the flanks of some Alabama troops, shattering their advance and capturing 200 prisoners, including Confederate brigade commander James Archer. After crossing a little creek, Willoughby's Run, the brigade was recalled and took up a defensive position, with Ide and the 24th in the center, in anticipation of a counterattack.

They weren't disappointed. The Confederates had been driving the Union forces until the Iron Brigade arrived, and now, as the morning gave way to afternoon, Gen. Heth wanted to regain the momentum. Leading his next assault was a rarity in the Civil War: a regiment, the 26th North Carolina, at full strength, with some 843 men. The 26th crossed Willoughby's Run and got within 40 yards of Ide and his regiment when the Michigan men opened fire. The first volley was devastating, but Ide and his comrades slowed the North Carolinians only momentarily before they returned a volley of their own.

The two units stood their ground and continued firing at each other at murderously short range—the North Carolinians' commanding officer died holding the regimental colors, and his second-in-command was then killed almost immediately by a bullet to the head. But the Confederate regiment hung on and the 24th Michigan, outnumbered and, with the 19th Indiana beginning to collapse, outflanked, withdrew to a second defensive line and then to a third, with the North Carolinians stalking them relentlessly. The 24th would eventually retreat, with the rest of I Corps and the newly-arrived XI Corps, through the streets of Gettysburg to Cemetery Ridge, just beyond the town. The damage that the two regiments had done to each other was staggering: 687 of the 26th North Carolina's 843 soldiers and 363 of the 24th Michigan's 496 soldiers were killed or wounded.[68]

This Gettysburg monument honors Bela Clinton Ide's 24th Michigan Infantry. *Photograph by Robert Swanson/Wikimedia Commons.*

After General Reynolds' death, command had passed to Gen. O. O. Howard, the commander of the much-maligned XI Corps and the next senior officer on the scene. One of

---

[68] "No Man Can Take Those Colors and Live," The Civil War Trust, http://www.civilwar.org/battlefields/gettysburg/gettysburg-2011/the-battle-for-herbst-woods.html

Howard's soldiers, coming onto the battlefield while the 24th Michigan was locked in its deadly fight with the North Carolinians, was Erastus Fouch. Fouch was the eighteen-year-old veteran of two years of combat in the Shenandoah Valley and Virginia, including Chancellorsville. Fouch's regiment, the 75h Ohio, showed the same inexorable attrition rate common to Civil War regiments, demonstrated so dramatically by the 24th Michigan that day. 984 men made up Fouch's regiment when it was formed near Cincinnati in the summer of 1861, only about 260 remained to fight at Gettysburg.[69] Among those who'd been killed along the way was Leonidas, Erastus's older brother, with whom he'd enlisted when he was himself only sixteen.[70] (Two more Fouches would die in another regiment fighting in Tennessee: Erastus's father and another brother.) When he'd joined, Erastus might have used the same dodge other underage recruits had used to avoid lying about their ages: a prospective soldier would write the number "18" on a slip of paper and tuck it into his shoe to allow himself to truthfully tell the recruiting officer that he was "over eighteen, sir."

Two years later, Fouch and the 75th Ohio were blameless members of the hard-luck XI Corps, the "Flying Dutchmen" blamed for the rout at Chancellorsville. But the corps was tough on the march that July 1, and even some of these Union soldiers were barefoot as the battle began because they'd walked through their worn shoes as they moved at a killing pace from Emmitsburg toward the sounds of battle in Gettysburg.[71] Once they got there, they would be vulnerable—100 officers and men had been detached from the regiment for scout duty, so only 160 men[72]—not enough to

---

[69] "75th OVI Notes," http://www.cwrumblings.info/Articles/75OVINotes.pdf
[70] "Private Erastus Fouch," http://www.findagrave.com/cgi-bin/fg.cgi?page=gr&GRid=55097035&ref=acom. July 18, 2010.
[71] Bruce Catton, *The Army of the Potomac: Glory Road.* Doubleday & Co., Garden City, New York: 1952. p. 276.
[72] "75th Regiment Ohio Volunteer Infantry, 1861-65," Ohio Civil War Central, http://www.ohiocivilwarcentral.com/entry.php?rec=1142

fill two infantry companies—would be sent into action as they marched through town, along the Emmitsburg Road, toward the sound of rolling musketry to the northwest.

Fouch's 75th Ohio would have passed the Codori family's farm, along the Emmitsburg Road, on its way to the battlefield. Two days later, this would be a staging area for Pickett's Charge. *Steven C. Berger photograph, Wikimedia Commons.*

Fouch's divisional commander, Francis Barlow, was an anomaly among Civil War generals. He was beardless and even more youthful-looking than his 28 years. One colleague described his appearance on the battlefield as that of "a highly independent newsboy." His appointment to the command of the XI Corps' 1st Division was a direct response to the corps' performance at Chancellorsville, because Barlow was a disciplinarian who liked to use his heavy enlisted man's saber, when his division was on the march, to whack the backsides of stragglers. His aim was intended to restore backbone to Howard's corps.[73]

As his division arrived on the battlefield, Barlow and Gen. Howard rode together to the objective the senior officer

---

[73] Chuck Teague, "Barlow's Knoll Revisited," http://www.militaryhistoryonline.com/gettysburg/articles/barlowsknoll.aspx. 2001

wanted Barlow to hold. It was north of the little town, and in the face of new arrivals from Lee's army, Richard Ewell's corps, double-timing from the north on the Harrisburg Road and a threat to flank the Union forces. What had begun that morning as a skirmish was cascading into a general engagement that pulled men from both sides, brigade after brigade, into what would become the turning point of the war.

Francis Barlow (left) with a group of generals that includes Winfield Scott Hancock (seated), who would assume command of the battlefield on July 1. *Library of Congress.*

But Barlow's immediate concern—while his mind was working, he at least noticed the discomfort of some of his men, taking fire from Confederate artillery[74]—was to stop Ewell's approaching forces to prevent them from outflanking the bulk of the army already engaged, still facing westward in

---

[74] Teague, "Barlow's Knoll."

response to the main Confederate assault. Barlow ordered the waiting division forward, to their relief, and got his men onto high ground on what locals called Blocher's Knoll. Here, he placed Erastus Fouch and the 75th Ohio in position alongside the 17th Connecticut. Barlow's decision did nothing to sweeten the luck of XI Corps. He had made a mistake in placing his men.

Blocher's Knoll was high ground, but it also was slightly in front of the troops who might have provided Barlow support on his flanks. When Ewell's men arrived, they lost little time in surrounding and then cutting off the soldiers in Barlow's salient, who faced intense rifle fire from multiple directions. Three Georgia regiments under the command of the indefatigable John B. Gordon, the general who'd been shot five times at Antietam but had somehow survived, sent both the 75th Ohio and the 17th Connecticut into retreat. The 75th left behind several prisoners, one of them Pvt. Erastus Fouch, but they had one more dramatic role to play at Gettysburg. Nearby, another of Barlow's regiments, the 25th Ohio, on the western slope of Blocher's Knoll, broke at about the same time. One of the 25th's wounded, who would be lucky enough to escape with his life, was Pvt. Sylvanus Ullom, only a few yards from Fouch, the orphan and Chancellorsville veteran who would someday join Erastus as a farmer in the Arroyo Grande Valley.[75]

Before his capture, Fouch must have seen a 19-year-old officer, mounted and under heavy fire, only a few yards from his regiment. Lt. Bayard Wilkeson commanded a battery from the 4th U.S. Artillery—his father, a war correspondent for the New York *Times,* was on his way to the battlefield at the time—and was calmly directing the removal of his guns, with their decimated crews and horses, when a shell killed his horse and mangled his leg. Wilkeson cut the remains of his

---

[75] "25th Ohio, Company B."
http://freepages.history.rootsweb.ancestry.com/~cemeteryproject/25th/CoB.html

leg away with a pocket knife and tied the wound off with a tourniquet; four of his men carried him to the farmhouse where, in the chaos that followed, the heroic young officer bled to death.[76]

Nineteen-year-old Bayard Wilkeson directs his artillery battery near Erastus Fouch's position on July 1, 1863. *Library of Congress.*

Meanwhile, Gen. Barlow was wounded and presumed dead, but after the Confederates had overrun the knoll, it was their commander, Gen. Gordon, who noticed that the Union officer was still alive. Gordon ordered that Barlow be taken immediately to a Confederate field hospital and so saved the life of Fouch's commanding officer. By the time Barlow went down, the pressure on Howard's XI Corps, facing north, and

---

[76] "Gettysburg: The Correspondence from the Famous Story of Lieutenant Bayard Wilkeson, Killed at Gettysburg." http://www.raabcollection.com/civil-war-autograph/civil-war-signed-gettysburg-correspondence-famous-story-lieutenant-bayard#sthash.y7l08iUv.dpuf

the late John Reynolds' I Corps, now commanded by Abner Doubleday, facing west, was too much to withstand. Both elements of the army collapsed and a jumbled retreat through the streets of Gettysburg followed—one that must have reminded the unfortunate soldiers of XI Corps of Chancellorsville.

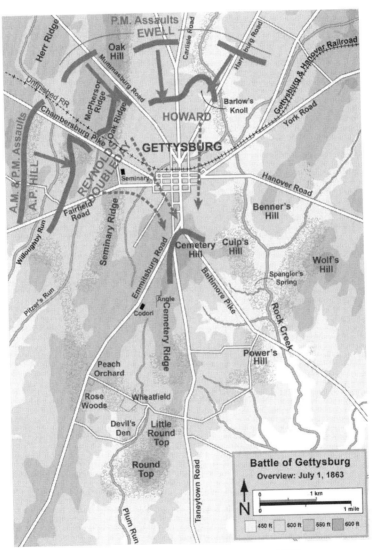

Day 1, Gettysburg. *Map by Hal Jespersen www.posix.com/CW.*

101

At the other end of the retreat, O. O. Howard was trying to rally men on Cemetery Hill, where soldiers were now firing at their pursuers from behind tombstones. Confederate General Richard Ewell, whose infantry had sent Barlow's division running, accidentally gave Howard the time he needed when he pulled up his Confederates, nearly as disorganized in pursuit as the Union soldiers had been in retreat, to regather them. The Confederate corps commander realized also that they had gone into action against Barlow's position after a forced march and were practically panting in exhaustion. But Ewell's halt came in the face of desperate pleas from more aggressive junior officers, and most notably from Gen. Isaac Trimble, who begged Ewell to let him continue the assault on Cemetery Hill before the Northerners themselves could reorganize. Long after the battle, armchair generals would wonder if the loss of a leg and the winning of a pretty young wife—Lizinka, born in St. Petersburg and named for her mother's friend, Tsarina Elizabeth Alexeievna, the empress and wife of Alexander I—might have robbed Ewell of the fighting spirit he'd shown earlier in the war.

The 61-year-old Trimble was one of the most spirited officers on either side that day, even if he was also one of the oldest. He'd been a particular favorite of the man who had preceded Ewell in command of the corps, Stonewall Jackson. It was his experience with the aggressive Jackson that compelled Trimble to demand that Ewell follow up on their success that afternoon. "Give me a division, General," he is said to Ewell, "and I will endeavor to take that hill." He got no response. He made the same plea twice again: he would take Cemetery Hill, if Ewell allowed it, with a brigade. He would take the hill, if Ewell allowed it, with a *regiment*.[77] Ewell put Trimble off, then snapped at him. He would *ask* his junior officers, Ewell said sharply, if he wanted their advice.

---

[77] Douglas Southall Freeman, *Lee's Lieutenants, Volume 3: Gettysburg to Appomattox.* Charles Scribner's Sons: New York: 1972, p. 95.

Trimble bristled, threw down his sword, and stamped away from the commanding officer who, in his eyes, could never hope to match Stonewall Jackson.

Trimble may have been right: what seemed like a decisive victory for Lee on July 1 was incomplete and it would lead to his ultimate defeat. In occupying the ridge marked at its high point by the town cemetery, XI Corps

George Gordon Meade, standing at left center, holds a council of war in a Gettysburg farmhouse in the early morning of July 2. Meade was in a difficult position: he'd only in been command of the Army of the Potomac for three days. Here, he solicited his subordinate generals' advice and they affirmed their commander's instincts: Gettysburg was a place where the Union Army should take a stand and where they had the chance to finally defeat Lee. *U.S Army Historical Institute.*

commander Howard had provided what proved to be a natural defensive position where the retreating Union troops could rally. This may have been the one sound military decision Howard made during the war—if indeed, he was the man who made it. Many historians credit just-arrived II Corps commander Winfield Hancock with choosing the high ground. Meade, still trying to catch up to the battle, had messaged Hancock that he was to take control of the battlefield until Meade arrived, which would take him until 3 a.m. on July 2. Howard was incensed at relinquishing command to Hancock, his junior, but in truth Hancock was the better choice. Howard would forever be known less as a soldier and more as an ardent abolitionist and a muscular Christian—as the man his soldiers nicknamed "Old Prayer Book."[78] Whether the architect of the Union defense was Howard or Hancock, whose nickname was the more soldierly "Hancock the Superb," is less relevant than the fact that Lee's attempts to dislodge the men on Cemetery Hill would be so terribly destructive to his Army of Northern Virginia.

Lee nearly won a victory the next afternoon, on July 2, but he would have owed it to a Union officer, Daniel Sickles, who commanded Meade's III Corps. Sickles was a political appointee, not a professional soldier, and his reputation had been built on both a stellar law career and the notoriety of a love triangle. In 1859, in broad daylight and in Lafayette Square, just outside the White House, Sickles had shot and killed his wife's lover, Philip Barton Key II, the son of the composer of "The Star-Spangled Banner" and the District Attorney for the District of Columbia. Sickles promptly turned himself in, retained a brilliant lawyer of his own, Edwin Stanton, who would become Lincoln's Secretary of

---

[78] Stephen W. Sears, *Gettysburg*. Houghton-Mifflin Co., Boston and New York: 2003, p. 189.

War, and acquitted thanks to the then-novel defense of "temporary insanity."[79]

Sickles might well have used the same defense to excuse his conduct at Gettysburg on July 2. Among his III Corps was the 11th New Jersey Infantry, and one member of the 11th was Joseph Brewer, like Erastus Fouch, a veteran soldier, and, like Fouch, a man who would eventually settle in Arroyo Grande.[80] Brewer's July 2 at Gettysburg would be harrowing, thanks to a still-controversial order from Sickles.

As troops continued to pour onto the battlefield during the evening and overnight, Meade assigned III Corps to the left of the Union line that he was forming along the spine of Cemetery Ridge. The Union position now resembled that of a fishhook, with the 75h Ohio at the top, near the barb, and III Corps, including Brewer's 11th New Jersey, near the bottom, along the hook's neck. Just to their south lay the two mountains called the Round Tops.

Sickles thought his corps had been placed unwisely. Just ahead of his assigned position, he saw higher ground on farmland marked by a peach orchard. He advanced his corps, placing the 11th New Jersey along the north-south line of the Emmitsburg Road, the same road Fouch's 75th Ohio had taken on its way to the battlefield the day before, but in so doing Sickles had lost contact with the corps on his right and with the troops scrambling to establish a position on Little Round Top to his left. Even worse, the corps commander had moved forward without orders. When word of Sickles's advance reached the general in command, he was furious. Gen. Meade, who looked irritated in the best of times (he was once described as a "goggle-eyed old snapping turtle") rode to the front to demand an explanation from Sickles who,

[79] "Dan Sickles's Temporary Insanity," http://www.murderbygaslight.com/2009/10/dan-sickless-temporary-insanity.html. November 2009
[80] "Joseph S. Brewer," *Register of Officers and Men of New Jersey in the Civil War 1861-65.*

unusual for an experienced lawyer, could not give one. He offered to withdraw his troops. It was at that moment that the Confederates' artillery opened fire: it was too late. The bombardment was preparing the way for an infantry attack.[81] Meade told Sickles to hold until he could bring up other troops to support him.

It would be Confederates under the command of James Longstreet who attacked Sickles's new position. Joseph Brewer's 11th New Jersey was hit particularly hard by tough Mississippians led by William Barksdale, on horseback and conspicuous by the red fez he chose to wear that day. Company E of the 11th was ordered to direct their fire on Barksdale and, hit by at least five bullets, he tumbled from his horse. Barksdale's men would exact a frightful price for the loss of their commanding officer, described in this passage from *New Jersey Troops in the Gettysburg Campaign*:

> The change of front to meet Barksdale's charge brought the Eleventh to the foot of the slope in rear of the Smith house, and there occurred its greatest loss, the casualties among the officers being unusually large. Colonel McAllister fell severely wounded just as he gave the command. Major Philip Kearney, the next in command, soon received a shot in the knee, and spinning around like a top fell, ten paces away. Captain Luther Martin, of Company D, the senior officer, was notified to take the command, but before he had time to realize the responsibility of his position, was killed. Captain D. B. Logan of Company H, who succeeded him, also fell severely wounded, and four men who were taking him to the rear were all shot down before they could reach a place of safety and Captain Logan killed. Captain Andrew H. Ackerman, of Company C, then assumed command and he, too, soon fell dead.[82]

The 11th eventually withdrew to safety, but more than half the regiment had been killed or wounded in the Peach Orchard. The most prominent of the wounded in III Corps that day was Gen. Sickles. His leg was shattered by an

---

[81] Sears, p. 263.
[82] Samuel Toombs, *New Jersey Troops in the Gettysburg Campaign from June 5 to July 31, 1863.* The Evening Mail Publishing House, Orange, NJ: 1888, p. 240.

artillery shot (the bone was preserved for posterity at the Smithsonian Institution and the general, on crutches the rest of his life, would occasionally visit it), but it was his decision to advance his troops, and not his wound, that effectively ended his command career. Brewer survived the terrible Peach Orchard fight, farmed in Oklahoma, and, by the early 1900s, was raising vegetables in the Oak Park area of Arroyo Grande with his wife, Effie, a stepson, and two daughters.[83]

On the 25th anniversary of Gettysburg, Daniel Sickles and two brother officers tour the battlefield near the site of the Peach Orchard fight of July 2. *Library of Congress.*

Meanwhile, a man who would become a neighbor of Brewer's, Jefferson Wright, went into action that day with another one of the XI Corps' regiments that had stood and fought at Chancellorsville. His 55th Ohio was to the north, deployed along the Taneytown Pike. Their monument today is just across Steinwehr Avenue from the site for Lincoln's Gettysburg Address, delivered to dedicate the military

---

[83] "Joseph S. Brewer," 1910 United States Census.

cemetery in November 1863. Any speeches made at that spot on July 2 would be unprintable today because the dominant sound for Wright and his beleaguered Company A would have been whizzing bullets. While the 55th was spared the intensity of the attack carried out by Barskdale's Mississippi troops, Confederate snipers, frequently firing from civilians' homes, tormented the regiment throughout the day. Detachments would be sent out to clear an area of snipers, who seemed to almost immediately appear somewhere else.

Finally, two volunteers seemed to have some luck in suppressing the Confederate marksmen. Charles Stacey, renowned for his marksmanship, found a forward position and kept the Confederate snipers at bay for two hours with some sniping of his own. It was XI Corps commander O. O. Howard himself who asked for volunteers to stop another sniper in a brick building on Gettysburg's Washington Street. The 55th Ohio's Pvt. Benjamin Pease immediately rushed forward, only to glance around and discover that he was the only soldier who'd done so. Undeterred, he ran up to the building, pounded on the door with his rifle butt, and demanded that the sniper surrender. Five Confederates came out with their hands up, discovering, no doubt to their chagrin, that they'd been surrounded by Pvt. Benjamin Pease.[84]

Despite Sickles's blunder, the Confederates would fail to overpower the Union left on July 2, and the blame for this would fall on Lee's subordinate, James Longstreet, nicknamed "Old Pete," whom Lee himself referred to as "my warhorse." Longstreet was moody at Gettysburg. He strongly disagreed

---

[84] Harry F. Pfanz, *Gettysburg—Culp's Hill and Cemetery Hill.* University of North Carolina Press, 2011. pp 149-50.

with Lee's tactics, urging his superior to break off contact with the Union army to find another battlefield where the Army of Northern Virginia could build defensive works and let Meade do the attacking. It took the unhappy Longstreet–a proud man, he might have been sulky–all morning and most of the day to place his troops. Between about 4:30 and 5:30 p.m., they would attack in two great surges: first, against Sickles' misplaced corps, a near-success that would be checked by Meade's call-up of Union reinforcements, and second, against the extreme left of the federal line, on Little Round Top.

It was on this hill, in one of the most famous battlefield encounters of the war, that the second of Longstreet's surges failed when the 20th Maine's commander, Joshua Lawrence Chamberlain, launched a bayonet attack downhill against the tough Alabama soldiers who had themselves attacked the Maine regiment nine successive times. Chamberlain's charge was a desperate one: his men, after those nine assaults, were out of ammunition. The attack was also a stunning success. The Confederates either ran for their lives or surrendered. In a very real sense, the 20th Maine had saved the Union that afternoon. Had the Alabamians gotten around Chamberlain's men, they would have been in the rear of the entire Army of Potomac.

It was now nearly dusk on July 2, but the day's fighting wasn't done. At the other end of Meade's Union line, Richard Ewell began an artillery bombardment on the federal right once he'd heard the rolling cannon fire and musketry from Longstreet's assaults to the south, on the federal left. One of his objectives was to roll up the Union regiments positioned on the reverse slope of Cemetery Hill. Among the defenders there, behind a stone wall, were Erastus Fouch's friends from the 75th Ohio.

Ewell's assault was led by the irascible, profane, and aggressive General Jubal Early, and it hit the 75th Ohio at the worst possible moment. The regiment on their left, the 17th Connecticut, had been pulled out of line and sent to the right in anticipation of an attack from that direction, from nearby Culp's Hill. That meant that the 75th's commander, Col. Andrew Harris, had to account for the hole the 17th had left behind, in defending their section of the stone wall, by spreading his men across it. So it was on this thin line that a hard-fighting regiment, the Louisiana Tigers, fell.[85] They hit the weakened position hard,

Gen. Jubal Early. *Library of Congress.*

and the Ohio regiment collapsed. Some of them would join Fouch as prisoners of war. But the Union troops, bolstered by reserves, would hit back. A counterattack, one that included members of the 75th Ohio, met the Confederate surge. It was a man from Fouch's regiment who killed the Confederate major carrying the Tigers' colors.[86]

The next day, the final day of battle, would feature Lee's attack, after a monumental artillery barrage—140 field pieces from the Confederates' lines, answered by eighty from the Union center—that failed to dislodge the Union forces massed on Cemetery Ridge. This was Pickett's Charge. Over half the 12,500 Confederates who made up the assault were killed, wounded, or captured, and in their loss Robert E. Lee had finally and irrevocably lost his reputation for unerring

---

[85] "Reports of Colonel Andrew L. Harris, Seventy-fifth Ohio Infantry, commanding regiment and Second Brigade," July 5, 1863. http://www.civilwarhome.com/harrisgettysburgor.html

[86] Gary Adelman and Daniel Landsman, "East Cemetery Hill: Confederates on the Crest," The Civil War Trust. http://www.civilwar.org/battlefields/gettysburg/gettysburg-history-articles/east-cemetery-hill.html?referrer=https://www.google.com/ 2014.

battlefield leadership. This was the war's turning point: in Churchill's felicitous language, Gettysburg wasn't the beginning of the end, but it was the end of the beginning.

Erastus Fouch, one of 5,000 prisoners taken by Lee's Army of Northern Virginia, would be marched south under guard by soldiers from Pickett's division, men who, more than any others under Lee's command, were acutely aware of the magnitude of their commander's failure. On July 9, the prisoners were ferried across the Potomac and custody was turned over to a mounted infantry unit under Confederate John Imboden's command; one captive Pennsylvania cavalryman said that he "never saw anything but kindness shown to the prisoners" by Imboden's men, who marched their prisoners south for eleven days to Staunton, Virginia.

Fouch, then, was a lucky man. His luck would hold. After only fifty-one days, he was sent north in a prisoner exchange while others captured at Gettysburg would languish—or die—at the prisoner-of-war camp for enlisted men at Belle Isle, Virginia.[87] Later that year, the remnants of the 75th Ohio would be transferred to South Carolina and then to Florida, where Erastus Fouch would be mustered out of service, in Jacksonville, in January 1865. Eighteen months later, he married a Vinton County, Ohio, girl named Mary Emilie McClanahan, a marriage that would produce seven boys and two girls, and would take up farming in Minnesota. Like many of his comrades, Fouch wasn't done moving: census records show that by 1886, he and his family had moved to San Luis Obispo County; in 1900, Fouch was farming in the Huasna Valley and, by 1920, in the upper Arroyo Grande Valley.[88] Before he died in 1926, Fouch had made a successful life for himself, as suggested by Annie

---

[87] D. Scott Hartwig, "I can't tell you what we suffered" Prisoners, Part 2 – A Union Story," *From the Fields of Gettysburg: The Blog of Gettysburg National Military Park*. November 29, 2012. https://npsgnmp.wordpress.com/2012/11/29/i-cant-tell-you-what-we-suffered-prisoners-part-2-a-union-story/

[88] "Erastus Fouch," ancestry.com. http://person.ancestry.com/tree/983870/person/549903464/facts

Morrison's 1917 *A History of San Luis Obispo County and Environs:*

Attracted by the wonderful climate of California, he sold out and came West, coming almost immediately to San Luis Obispo County; and in the vicinity of Arroyo Grande he bought a home surrounded by thirty-three and a half acres. This land he has improved, devoting part of it to farming and part to the raising of fruit and alfalfa: and in addition he has rented considerable land and carried on general farming.

In practically every way Mr. Fouch has been successful as a farmer, and while enjoying domestic life to the full, he has never failed to give his support to civic affairs in which helpers are needed, but are often wanting. One instance of this is his relation to the local high school, for the establishing of which Mr. Fouch worked so hard.[89]

One of Gettysburg veteran Erastus Fouch's legacies is this graduating class from Arroyo Grande Union High School; this is believed to be the Class of 1898. *Photo courtesy of Randy Spoeneman.*

---

[89] Annie Morrison and John Haydon, "Erastus Fouch," *The History of San Luis Obispo County and Environs.* Historic Record Company, Los Angeles, CA: 1917, p. 573.

Gettysburg has one more connection to local high school education. Tim Culp was, for many years, a biology teacher at Mission Prep in San Luis Obispo, and it was his ancestors who gave one battlefield site, Culp's Hill, its name. Few Civil War stories are more poignant than one that involves a Culp who fought at Gettysburg.

Three Mission Prep teachers in the early 1990s in front of the high school on San Luis Obispo's Palm Street: the author, biology teacher Tim Culp, math teacher Phyllis Brudney. *Photo courtesy Evelyn Morgan.*

Henry Culp had bought the property that included the hill named for him a decade before Fort Sumter. Culp's nephew, Wesley, grew up in Gettysburg, learning the same trade, working with leather, that had sustained Ulysses Grant in Galena, Illinois, when his fortunes were at low ebb. Wesley's boss moved his business to Virginia in 1858, and Wesley moved with him, although the young man kept in touch with friends he'd grown up with, like Jack Skelly and Skelly's sweetheart, Virginia (Jennie) Wade. But he'd made new friends in Virginia, so when the war broke out, Wesley enlisted in the 2nd Virginia Infantry and fought for the Confederacy. Wesley's brother, William, fought for the Union in the 87th Pennsylvania, and the two regiments faced off during a firefight in Stonewall Jackson's Shenandoah campaign in 1862. Neither Culp was hurt.

Another Union soldier in the 87th wasn't so lucky. In one of the many coincidences that marks wartime, when great numbers of people are put into motion, Wesley Culp found his old friend Jack Skelly in late June 1863, badly wounded and in a Confederate field hospital. Skelly knew that he would never see Jennie Wade again, and he asked his Gettysburg friend to find a way to deliver a last letter to her. Wesley Culp promised that he would.

Culp and the 2nd Virginia came back to his old hometown as part of Richard Ewell's Confederate corps, and the regiment fought on his uncle's property on July 2 as part of the sequence of attacks that involved the 75th Ohio on nearby Cemetery Hill. Wesley Culp survived that intense fighting but died the next day, the only soldier in the 2nd Virginia's Company B killed at Gettysburg.

So Jack Skelly's letter never got to Jennie Wade.

But Jack never knew that Jennie had died at Gettysburg, as well. On the same day, July 3, that Wesley Culp was killed in action, Jennie was kneading dough in her sister's kitchen to make biscuits—her sister had just delivered a baby.

A bullet penetrated the heavy kitchen door. The bullet hole, widened by generations of tourists' index fingers, is still there. It struck her in the back and killed her instantly. She was the only civilian killed at Gettysburg.

Nine days later, Jack Skelly died from his wounds.

Jennie Wade was nineteen. Jack Skelly was twenty-one. Wesley Culp was twenty-four.

Wesley Culp (left); Jennie Wade, Jack Skelly.

One hundred thirty years later, Mission Prep biology teacher and basketball coach Tim Culp would return to his roots in Pennsylvania to earn a doctorate in microbiology and immunology from Penn State and now works as principal scientist for a pharmaceutical company headquartered in West Point, Pennsylvania. It takes about two hours today to drive from West Point to Gettysburg, but the residents of

West Point might have been close enough on July 3, 1863, to have heard the distant rumble of massed artillery fire on the last day of the battle. After the fighting was finally over, searchers on the Culp farm found a rifle stock with Wesley's name carved in it. Although his 2nd Virginia friends thought they'd buried Wesley on Culp's Hill, his body was never found.

Chapter 5.
"You Hung Him Yesterday."
War on the Sioux and Cheyenne, 1862–65

Although wrongs have been done me I live in hopes. I have not got two hearts.... I once thought that I was the only man that persevered to be the friend of the white man, but since they have come and cleaned out our lodges, horses, and everything else, it is hard for me to believe white men anymore.

–Black Kettle, Cheyenne Chief

The John Rice home, Arroyo Grande. *Author photo.*

The yellow stone quarried from Mt. Picacho, just south of Arroyo Grande, is unusually strong. A nail driven into it can't be removed.[90] This was the building material, the same rock used for the IOOF Hall on Bridge Street and the Brisco Hotel, now a coffee house on Branch Street, that John S. Rice would select for the two-story home he built on Myrtle Street in 1894. The strength of this structure is a mirror-reversal of the vulnerability of Minnesota settlers, from Rice's wartime home state, who fled for their lives during an 1862 war with their Sioux neighbors.

John Rice's Civil War, then, was one more familiar to American history; he would fight in yet another Indian war.

---

[90] Aileen Nygaard, City of Arroyo Grande. "Historical Resource Designation: 756 Myrtle St. (Rice House), December 13, 2013.

He enlisted in the 10th Minnesota Infantry intending to fight Confederates but began his war by fighting the Dakota, or Santee Sioux, woodland cousins to the Plains Indians who would, at their zenith of power in 1876, inflict a spectacular defeat on George Custer's 7th Cavalry.

By 1862, the Santee Sioux were hungry, a factor that was key to the outbreak of violence. The uprising began not as a principled stand, but as the spontaneous act of hungry young men. Four Santee Sioux were returning from a hunt in southern Minnesota where there'd been flare-ups before, when young men went hunting on settlers' farmland. This day, the four hunters helped themselves to a nest of eggs laid by a Meeker County farmer's hen, and, within minutes, a confrontation with the farmer had escalated into murder: the four young men shot and killed five people—the farmer, two other men, a woman, and a little girl who'd witnessed the killings. Within days, whites and Indians on the Minnesota frontier were at war.[91]

What would be called the Sioux Uprising came despite months of effort on the part of the Santee leader, Little Crow, to prevent violence. But by the summer of 1862, his people, confined to the corner of Minnesota assigned them under a treaty signed by Little Crow himself, were beginning to starve to death. The game on their small reservation, reduced in size by a second treaty in 1858, was gone, and the 1862 annuity payments due them were late. The payments, to make the situation worse, went not to the Sioux but to the same Indian agents who warehoused the bacon, flour, and beef Little Crow's people needed. When the Santee asked one agent to extend them credit for food, he refused and said, in a phrase that could have been taken from Marie Antoinette, that the Sioux could eat grass if they were hungry. When the fighting

---

91 "How it Started," *The Sioux Uprising of 1862.* *http://www.d.umn.edu/~bart0412/project.htm*

broke out, the agent's body was found with his mouth stuffed with grass.[92]

Little Crow. From *The Indian Dispossessed*, by Seth K. Humphrey, 1906.

Even if Little Crow hadn't wanted it, it was his own pride that became a factor in causing the war between the Santee and white settlers. When the young men who'd started the killing over the hen's eggs confessed what they'd done to the chief, Little Crow was furious. A debate followed. As Little Crow and a few other elders argued

---

[92] "1862 Dakota War: Minnesota's Other Civil War,"
http://www.exploringoffthebeatenpath.com/Battlefields/DakotaWar/index.html

against going to war, one young man called the chief a coward. Little Crow's anger got the better of him. The accusation, the diminishing of his people and of their land, and their hunger, all seemed to have a deep emotional impact on Little Crow. He changed his mind and called for war.[93] Meanwhile, John Rice had enlisted in the 10th Minnesota on August 16. The killings happened on August 17. The enlistees of the 10th, expecting to take a train east to fight, had their transport orders countermanded. Their war would be close to home.

Minnesota settlers fleeing their homes in August 1862. *Library of Congress.*

For the next five weeks, the Sioux Uprising would see raids on isolated settlers, military outposts, and even on frontier towns. Thirty-four whites were killed in an attack on

---

[93] Dee Brown, *Bury My Heart at Wounded Knee.* Holt, Rinehart and Winston: New York: 1970, pp. 42-45.

the town of New Ulm on August 23. John Rice and his inexperienced comrades in the newly-raised 10th Minnesota were sent immediately into the war. They served as scouts and, over the winter of 1862, as guards over the Winnebago reservation, their presence intended to prevent the spread to that people of the war that the Santee Sioux had started. The following July, however, the 10th would take part in two battles during a punitive campaign led by Gen. Henry Sibley. At Big Mound, in what is today North Dakota, a peace parley between a military surgeon and the Sioux dissolved when the surgeon was suddenly shot. Sibley's infantry and artillery opened fire and drove the warriors from the field. Four days later, Sibley's detachment was attacked, and in a running battle, near Stony Lake, North Dakota, his men managed to drive the Sioux off, but Sibley, short on supplies and with his animals and men exhausted, turned back to Minnesota.[94]

In was in Mankato, Minnesota, where the most memorable event of the uprising occurred on the day after Christmas, 1862. Once the uprising of the late summer of 1862 had been put down, 38 of Little Crow's warriors were executed in Mankato on a massive gallows especially erected for their hangings. Four thousand Minnesota settlers converged on Mankato on execution day. The 10th Minnesota, with Rice's F Company mounted that day, were among the troops gathered to prevent the onlookers from taking the law into their own hands. The settlers stood beyond the barrier of soldiers, waiting expectantly and craning their necks to catch a glimpse of the condemned men who would emerge under guard with their hands tied behind them.

An army commission, in a series of trials made efficient by the absence of defense counsel, had originally sentenced

---

[94] Jeff Williams, "This Week in the American Civil War," July 22, 2013.
http://mncivilwar150.com/this-week-in-the-american-civil-war-july-22-28-1863/

303 Santee to death. When the general in charge of the proceedings, John Pope, telegraphed the lengthy list of the condemned and the lengthier charges against them to the White House for the customary presidential review, the telegram cost $400; the New York *Times* howled in protest and suggested that the money be deducted from Pope's salary.[95] Lincoln customarily argued for leniency in cases of military justice and so commuted the executions of all but 38 of the men, those who could be tied most clearly to the most violent acts of the uprising. There would be no mercy for men judged guilty of rape.

The execution of 38 Sioux men, Mankato, Minnesota, 1862. *Library of Congress.*

One of the condemned men was to be released. Chaksa had seized a woman and her children in one raid, but the woman, Sarah Wakefield, demanded to speak on his behalf

[95] Daniel W. Homstad, "Abraham Lincoln: Deciding the Fate of 300 Indians Convicted of War Crimes in Minnesota's Great Sioux Uprising," *American History Magazine*, December 2001. http://www.historynet.com/abraham-lincoln-deciding-the-fate-of-300-indians-convicted-of-war-crimes-in-minnesotas-great-sioux-uprising.htm

and told the tribunal that he had taken them captive in order to protect them from other warriors who wanted to kill them. The Wakefields owed their lives to Chaksa.[96]

Since his company was on horseback the day of the hangings, John Rice may have been among the first that morning to see the condemned men. As they approached the scaffold, the Santee stunned the crowd. They rushed it, jostling for position in mounting the steps, as if they were eager to die. They would stand on a board that would collapse when a rope that held it in place was severed. The man charged with that duty, holding an axe as the Sioux shuffled into their places, was William J. Duley, whose wife and children had been murdered in the uprising. A correspondent for the New York *Times* recorded what happened on the scaffold:

As they came up and reached the platform, they filed right and left, and each one took his position as though they had rehearsed the programme. Standing round the platform, they formed a square, and each one was directly under the fatal noose. Their caps were now drawn over their eyes, and the halter placed about their necks. Several of them feeling uncomfortable, made severe efforts to loosen the rope, and some, after the most dreadful contortions, partially succeeded. The signal to cut the rope was three taps of the drum. All things being ready, the first tap was given, when the poor wretches made such frantic efforts to grasp each other's hands, that it was agony to behold them. Each one shouted out his name, that his comrades might know he was there. The second tap resounded on the air. The vast multitude were breathless with the awful surroundings of this solemn occasion. Again the doleful tap breaks on the stillness of the scene. Click! goes the sharp ax, and the descending platform leaves the bodies of thirty-eight human beings dangling in the air. The greater part died instantly; some few struggled violently, and one of the ropes broke, and sent its burden with a heavy, dull crash, to the platform beneath. A new rope was procured, and the body again swung up to its place. It was an awful sight to behold. Thirty-eight human beings suspended in the air, on the bank of the beautiful Minnesota; above, the smiling, clear, blue sky; beneath and around, the

---

[96] Douglas O. Linder. "The Dakota Conflict Trials,"
http://law2.umkc.edu/faculty/projects/ftrials/dakota/Dak_account.html

silent thousands, hushed to a deathly silence by the chilling scene before them, while the bayonets bristling in the sunlight added to the importance of the occasion.[97]

The hanged men were left up for a half-hour, and then a detail, some of John Rice's comrades from Company K, buried them in a sand bank on the Minnesota River at the edge of town. The bodies were laid out in two rows, feet to feet, covered in their blankets and then in sand. They saw little rest because they were soon dug up by macabre souvenir hunters. Several would be sold to be dissected by medical students. One skeleton, that of a Santee leader named Cut Nose, became the property of Dr. William Mayo, the father of the founders of the famed clinic.

The next day, a warder came to release the man who had saved Sarah Wakefield's life. When he called out Chaksa's name, a prisoner called back: "You hung him yesterday." Chaksa, Prisoner 3, had been confused with Chaskey-etay, Prisoner 121, condemned for murdering a pregnant woman.

On July 3, 1863, the Santee leader Little Crow was picking berries with his son, Wowinape, when a farmer shot him dead. Wowinape fled but returned to the scene to wrap his father's body in a blanket and put new moccasins on his feet for his next journey. Soldiers investigating the encounter found Little Crow's body the next day. They scalped the corpse then dumped it in the middle of the street of a nearby town, where little boys celebrated July 4th by stuffing firecrackers into Little Crow's nostrils and ears and setting them off. When they'd gotten tired of this, his body was dumped onto waste ground to become food for hogs.

John Rice would leave Minnesota and farm for a decade in Iowa before coming to Arroyo Grande. He and his brother, Daniel, would make their marks on the Valley:

---

[97] "The Indian Executions: An Interesting Account, from our Special Correspondent." New York *Times*, Dec. 26, 1862. http://www.startribune.com/dec-26-1862-38-dakota-men-executed-in-mankato/138273909/

Daniel transformed local cattle and Indian trails into serviceable roads. John's fruit orchards would typify the transition Arroyo Grande was making from the cattle-ranching of Francis Branch's day to the community of farmers who would cultivate the Arroyo Grande Valley after the war.

In Minnesota, the farmer who had shot Little Crow received $500 and the gratitude of the state legislature.[98]

A Pennsylvania cavalry unit attempts, with some success, to look nonchalant for a Civil War photographer. They've stacked cavalry lances, an anachronism in a war when cavalry battles would be decided by carbines and revolvers. *Library of Congress.*

---

[98] Duane Schultz, *Over the Earth I Come: The Great Sioux Uprising of 1862.* St. Martin's Press, New York, 1992. pp. 272-73.

Three Arroyo Grande area settlers—James Dowell, Thomas Keown and Harrison M. Bussell— served in cavalry units that fought both Confederates and Plains Indians. In both the frontier West and in the Civil War, cavalry soldiers were indispensable. In the East, they were the "eyes" of the larger army; their mission was to seek out and locate the enemy or to screen the larger army, protecting it from detection when it was on the march. These were jobs that the most celebrated Confederate cavalry commander, J.E.B. Stuart, failed to do for Lee during the 1863 Pennsylvania campaign. Stuart was on a daring cross-country raid, riding completely around the Army of the Potomac, but in the process, he had separated himself and his command from Lee and so the Army of Northern Virginia blindly blundered into Meade's forces at Gettysburg.

Infantry soldiers thought horse soldiers useless and were noted for the sardonic saying that there was no sight rarer on a battlefield than that of a dead cavalryman. Luckily for historians, if not for cavalrymen, there were such things and, in recent years and thanks to forensic science, horse soldiers have been given a voice that suggests their lives were no easier than those of the infantry.

In fact, for Civil War cavalrymen, the most poignant evidence for the difficulty of the lives they led comes from slightly younger contemporaries—the remains of the troopers who died with George Custer at the Little Bighorn in 1876. 20th-century forensic studies indicated that spinal problems— arthritis of the neck, degeneration of the disks of the mid- to lower spine, hyperflexibility of hip and ankle joints, and even muscle markings at their attachments to the jaw, suggesting a regular clenching of teeth while on the move—had given men in their mid-twenties the aches and pains of men in their seventies; in fact, the only part of their bodies that may have hurt worse than their backs would have been their teeth, which showed poor dental care and extensive tobacco use.[99] Arroyo Grande veteran James A. Dowell, 16th Kansas, was plagued by another ailment common to cavalrymen— hemorrhoids.[100]

George A. Custer, May 1865. *Library of Congress.*

Despite letting Lee down at Gettysburg, for most of the Civil War, it was Gen. J.E.B. Stuart and his Confederate contemporaries, Fitzhugh Lee, Joseph Wheeler and Nathan Bedford Forrest, who had the reputation for fielding cavalry that was far better, in both mounts and in troopers, than Union cavalry. This was a gap that would begin to close in

[99] Douglas D. Scott, *Uncovering History: The Legacy of Archaeological Investigations at the Little Bighorn Battlefield National Monument,* United States Department of the Interior; Lincoln, Nebraska: 2010, pp. 119-25

[100] "James A. Dowell," *Register, Sawtelle Home for Disabled Veterans,* Los Angeles, CA, http://interactive.ancestry.com/1200/MIUSA1866_113910-00655?pid=249017&backurl=http://person.ancestry.com/tree/9147826/person/-548408604/gallery&usePUB=true&_phsrc=uub9&usePUBJs=true

the war's last year. George Custer, for example, was noted for the kind of boldness that Stuart embodied, a trait that would get both men killed. A similar gap would never be overcome between cavalrymen like Dowell and a comrade of his, Thomas Keown of the 12th Missouri Cavalry, and the masterful Plains Indian horsemen they faced.

A fictional Confederate veteran, Charles Portis's Rooster Cogburn, unwittingly points out a disadvantage that would plague these men when, in the novel *True Grit*, he disparages the officious Texas Ranger LaBoeuf's Appaloosa by posing the question "How long have you boys been riding sheep down there?"[101] But it was in fact the compact mustang, like LaBoeuf's mount, descendants of Andalusian horses the Spanish had brought with them to the New World, that made tribes like the Cheyenne, the Sioux and the Comanche the finest light cavalry in the world. In their biography of Sioux leader Red Cloud, historians Bob Drury and Tom Clavin make an unfavorable comparison between the cavalryman's mount, descended from "the hulking, grain-fed steeds" of Northern Europe and the Indian mustang, "easy to break and able to travel great distances without water."[102]

So the mobility of Plains Indians made them elusive for aggressive Union officers like Gen. Patrick Connor, who led three columns of cavalry into the Powder River Country of Montana Territory in the summer of 1865 on an expedition that included James Dowell–his descendants would become prominent in farming, business and in the law in both Arroyo Grande and Nipomo, just to the south–and Thomas Keown. Connor, who issued a standing order to kill every Native American male over the age of twelve, wouldn't find all that many to kill. The Sioux and Cheyenne, on the other hand,

---

[101] Film Script, *True Grit*, Screen adaptation by Joel and Ethan Coen, based on the book by Charles Portis, p. 43, http://moviecultists.com/wp-content/uploads/screenplays/true-grit.pdf
[102] Bob Drury and Tom Clavin, *The Heart of Everything That Is: The Untold Story of Red Cloud, An American Legend*, Simon and Schuster, New York: 2014, p. 52.

would find Connor with ease, and if they'd only been armed as well as the soldiers, they would have killed the men in Connor's command, Dowell and Keown included.

The Powder River Country includes vast areas of the Dakotas, Wyoming, and Montana. The area had been among the traditional and most valuable hunting grounds, confirmed to tribes, including the Sioux, in an 1851 treaty. It was the discovery of gold in Montana in 1863 that suddenly made the area potentially valuable to whites. A trail to the gold fields established by John Bozeman and John Jacobs would lead to an alarming rise in the number of whites penetrating Indian territory. In 1864-65, attacks on miners increased. So the War Department ordered Gen. Patrick Connor, a County Kerry native and a veteran of Harry Love's California Rangers—the tough outfit credited with killing the legendary bandit Joaquin Murrieta in 1853—to secure the Bozeman Trail.

Brig. Gen. Patrick Connor. *Library of Congress.*

Connor's expedition moved out in July 1865, and the two future neighbors, Dowell and Keown, fought together in one of Connor's columns under the command of Col. Nelson Cole. One of the first things the commanders did, and they did it rapidly, was to get lost. Connor sent out scouts to find Cole's column. Cole did the same. They failed. Cole, meanwhile, had unknowingly marched his men into the

130

midpoint between two large encampments and between two of the most inspirational leaders the Sioux would ever produce: Sitting Bull and Red Cloud. Sitting Bull's men found Cole's command and they "jumped like angry badgers" on Dowell and Keown and their comrades.[103] At the moment of their attack, the weather—as capricious on the Great Plains as the English Channel's weather would be in the week before D-day—took a turn for the worse.

Cheyenne leader Roman Nose in old age. *New York Public Library.*

As the Sioux attacked on September 1, 1865, the temperature dropped seventy degrees and, although the Indians disappeared, a freak blizzard attacked Cole's detachment instead, killing many ill-fed and exhausted horses. Cole's men, some of them now and by necessity infantry, continued their march up the Powder River,

---

[103] Ibid, p. 214.

fighting the whole time and harassed the whole time by detachments of Sioux and Cheyenne who picked off isolated troopers and made off with even more Union Army horses. A week later, Cole's column found themselves, accidentally and uncomfortably, near a camp whose leader was yet another man famed to the Plains Indians: the Cheyenne, Roman Nose.

On September 8, Roman Nose organized an attack on Cole's men, who had formed their wagons into a protective square. It was then that Dowell and Keown saw what modern American historians of the West almost would willingly die to have seen, since there is no known photographic image of the man, and he was perhaps the most famous of all the Sioux. Dowell and Keown saw this warrior gallop across their front on a "dare ride"—both to prove his own courage, already well-established, and more to the point, to draw out the soldiers. He was nearly nude, this young upstart from a people allied with the Cheyenne, except for moccasins and breechclout. His light, slightly curly hair was tied back, with a small stone behind his ear fixed in place by a leather strap, his medicine against the troopers' bullets, which worked perfectly that day against a hail of gunfire from the soldiers. He defiantly rode up and down the little stockade of wagons, taunting Cole's men.

His name was Crazy Horse.

The soldiers refused to take the bait and come out—not even when Roman Nose, imitative and probably envious of Crazy Horse, but more finely equipped, with a magnificent eagle-feather war bonnet that trailed over his white horse's rump, rode up to them only to have the horse shot out from under him.[104] The troopers stayed behind their barricade and responded to three attacks with breech-loading carbines and artillery canister. The weather again intervened: this time, a

---

[104] Ibid, p. 216.

thunderstorm turned the area into a swamp, making more Sioux attacks impractical but still making the lives of soldiers like Dowell and Keown miserable. Once again, after burning extraneous equipment and the corpses of dead cavalrymen, Col. Cole continued his march. By now, many of his men were suffering from scurvy and were eating their own mounts to stay alive. They were at what must have seemed the limit of their endurance when they finally made contact with their commanding officer, Patrick Connor, and his column. They had been no more successful in killing any Indians, twelve years old or otherwise. Connor led his dispirited command back to Fort Laramie in October 1865. The grandiose-sounding "Powder River Expedition" was a disaster.

Had the history of Harrison Bussell's 1st Colorado Cavalry somehow ended in 1862, the battle they'd fought against Confederates and the reputation they'd earned would have been among the Civil War's greatest success stories. But the First's war would continue, this time against Plains Indians, and in 1864, they participated in the attack on a Cheyenne and Arapaho encampment at Sand Creek, Colorado. Rather than a battle, this incident constituted what twentieth-century history would call a war crime. Bussell was almost certainly present at the success, the Battle of Glorieta Pass in 1862, but not the disaster of the attack at Sand Creek in 1864, which remains firmly attached to the reputation of the 1st Colorado Cavalry, the unit memorialized on Bussell's Arroyo Grande tombstone.

In 1862, Bussell's regiment turned back a daring Confederate invasion of New Mexico Territory. Henry Hopkins Sibley, a distant cousin to Gen. Henry Hastings Sibley, who'd led the punitive expedition against the

Minnesota Sioux that included John S. Rice, had overall command of the Confederate forces that Bussell and his 1st Colorado Cavalry faced in battle in 1862. Sibley was a restless, complex man, plagued by alcoholism, and an inventor; his Sibley tent and camp stove became common features of Civil War army life. Sibley resigned his commission in the Union army to form a brigade, made up of three Texas cavalry regiments, in San Antonio in the fall of 1861.[105] The following spring, he led an invasion of New Mexico Territory whose ultimate goals were ambitious: control of the Santa Fe Trail and Confederate access to the gold fields of Colorado. After initial successes, including the seizure of Santa Fe, Sibley's expedition ran into trouble at Glorieta Pass.

Among the Union leaders defending New Mexico was Harrison Bussell's commanding officer, John Chivington, an erstwhile Methodist preacher who'd won a major's commission from the governor of Colorado; at Glorieta Pass, he would prove himself a capable soldier, a reputation he would himself destroy two years later while waging war on the Cheyenne. But on March 26, 1862, Chivington's men pounced on Sibley's–about three hundred Confederate cavalrymen led by Maj. Charles Pyron–and drove them into retreat. Pyron's men were later reinforced by the 4th Texas Cavalry; while Chivington withdrew to reorganize his men, the Confederates' numbers grew to over a thousand troopers, and their new commander on the scene, Lt. Col. William R. Scurry, decided to seek out and attack Chivington. But Chivington had been reinforced, as well, by forces commanded by Col. John P. Slough, and they went searching for the Confederates at the same time Scurry was

---

[105] "In Search of a Southern Manifest Destiny: Sibley's Brigade – The Confederate Army of New Mexico," *Thoughts, Essays, and Musings on the Civil War: A Civil War Historian's Views on Various Aspects of the American Civil War,* January 13, 2012, https://bobcivilwarhistory.wordpress.com/2012/01/13/in-search-of-a-southern-manifest-destiny-sibleys-brigade-the-confederate-army-of-new-mexico/

searching for the Union forces. The two found each other on the morning of March 28 and the battle that followed, which featured an artillery duel, cavalry charges, and close-in fighting, lasted for over six hours before the northern forces withdrew.[106]

John Chivington. *National Park Service.*

Scurry thought he'd won the battle for Sibley's command, only to discover that Chivington's men had separated from the main Union force, rappelled down the steep canyon walls where Scurry had left his supply train, and burned his wagons and killed his draft animals.[107] The Confederates were forced to withdraw to Texas, and Sibley's invasion of New Mexico was over. John Chivington would

[106] Don Alberts, "The Battle of Glorieta: Union Victory in the Far West," The Civil War Trust, http://www.civilwar.org/battlefields/glorietapass/glorieta-pass-history-articles/glorietaalberts.html

[107] Carol L. Higham, *The Civil War and the West: The Frontier Transformed*, Praeger Books: Santa Barbara, California: 2013, p. 105.

find another war to fight, but at Glorieta Pass, he'd learned a lesson in using stealth and surprise to win battlefield victories.

By 1863 that new war loomed. Increasing tension and deteriorating communication between Colorado military and civil authorities and the Cheyenne would ultimately contribute to tragedy at Sand Creek. Colorado Governor John Evans began to hear rumors of a meeting among several Plains tribes—Cheyenne, Arapaho, Sioux, and Kiowa—planning a coordinated war on white settlers and soldiers. It was doubtless the Minnesota Sioux uprising the year before (Troops, including John Rice's 10th Minnesota, were still in the field on their punitive expedition.) that would have given Evans reason to believe those rumors.

Isolated but violent attacks seemed to confirm the threat of war: a band of Arapaho raided Isaac van Wormer's ranch southwest of Denver and stole some of his cattle; a year later, another party of Indians, assumed to be Cheyenne, returned to the van Wormer ranch and killed a young couple and their two small children. The mutilated bodies of the Hungate family were disinterred and put on display in Denver. Raiding would continue on the part of many tribes, including Utes, Sioux, and a Cheyenne warrior society, the Dog Soldiers, whose power seemed to be growing during 1863 and 1864. Meanwhile, elders like the Cheyenne chief Black Kettle were counseling peace with the whites. The aggressive Dog Soldiers would get a counterpart on the other side in John Chivington, who'd been placed in command of Colorado's volunteer troops. Now, in the summer of 1864, Chivington was among the increasing chorus of Coloradans, led by newspaper editors and both military and civil leaders, calling for, as one Denver newspaper put it, "the extermination of the red devils."[108]

---

[108] "John Chivington," PBS *The West*, *http://www.pbs.org/weta/thewest/people/a_c/chivington.htm*

The Camp Weld Conference, 1864. Kneeling in front are Maj. Edward Wynkoop and Lt. Silas Soule. Directly behind Wynkoop's hat is Black Kettle; on Black Kettle's left is One Eye. *National Park Service.*

That prospect was complicated by Black Kettle and other Cheyenne leaders when they came into Camp Weld, near Denver, in September to ask for peace. They were accompanied by Maj. Edward Wynkoop, the commander of nearby Fort Lyon, whose opinion of the Indians that he was charged with policing had been evolving: as he got to know Cheyenne like Black Kettle and another leader, One-Eye, he wrote that "I felt myself in the presence of superior beings, and these were the representatives of a race I had

137

heretofore looked upon without exception as being cruel, treacherous, and bloodthirsty. . . ."[109]

Neither Governor Evans nor Col. Chivington was pleased with Wynkoop's peace efforts: Evans had just raised a regiment of 100-day volunteers, the 3rd Colorado Cavalry, whose sole purpose was to exterminate hostiles, and Wynkoop's diplomacy threatened to make the governor look foolish and the 3rd Colorado redundant. So the Camp Weld conference ended inconclusively, without a peace agreement. Black Kettle and his people were told to come in to Fort Lyon and surrender to Wynkoop when they were ready to make peace. "Peace" meant giving up their traditional lives to become farmers.

Col. Chivington's opinion of Wynkoop became apparent when the young officer was relieved of his command and replaced six weeks after the Camp Weld conference by Maj. Scott J. Anthony. On November 28, Governor Evans's volunteers, the 3rd Colorado Cavalry, arrived at Fort Lyon, commanded by Chivington, who was quick in shoving post commander Anthony aside and taking over. Once he'd established his authority, Chivington informed the officers of the 1st Cavalry stationed there that he intended to take both regiments out to Sand Creek and attack Black Kettle's encampment there.

Several of the 1st Colorado's officers who had served under Wynkoop immediately protested, insistent on the good intentions of leaders like Black Kettle and One-Eye. Chivington overrode the protest, but one of the officers he failed to convince was Lt. Silas Soule; after the meeting, Soule made his position clear to his brother officers: "[I] told them," he wrote in a later letter to Major Wynkoop, "that any man who would take part in the murders, knowing the

[109] Stan Hoig, *The Sand Creek Massacre*, University of Oklahoma Press, Norman: 1974, p. 99

circumstances as we did, was a low lived cowardly son of a bitch."[110]

Despite his protests, Soule would ride out with his Company D, 1st Colorado Cavalry, as part of the attack force. He believed, perhaps, as Chivington had implied, that the expedition was going after hostile Dog Soldiers and not peaceful Indians. There is no evidence that Harrison Marion Bussell accompanied his Company G—only part of the 1st Colorado's troopers went along with Chivington—but there is reason to believe, based on the attitude of the First's officers, like Lt. Soule, that he would have approved of the company's conduct in what followed.

James Beckwourth, one of Chivington's scouts at Sand Creek. *Smithsonian Institute.*

Company G had responsibility for two of the four small mountain howitzers that Chivington's command, now about 700 soldiers, would bring   along with   them. The detachment also would bring along, as a guide, James "Medicine Jim" Beckwourth, the aging African American trapper and scout. In 1848, Beckwourth, carrying the mail north after a stop at William Dana's Rancho Nipomo, had discovered the bodies of the Reed family, brutally murdered by drifters from the gold fields, at Mission San Miguel and had sounded the alarm. The   murderers were eventually found by a posse and a shootout ensued on the beach at Summerland. They were captured and later executed in Santa Barbara by a firing squad commanded by then–Lt. Edward O. C. Ord, who, as a general, would play an important role in the 1865 Appomattox Campaign.

To the northeast, Black Kettle's encampment of some 650 Cheyenne and Arapaho would be awakened by barking dogs. Women beginning to prepare breakfast could feel and hear the pounding of hooves, which they at first assumed, hopefully, was a nearby herd of buffalo, but the vibration was followed almost immediately, as dawn broke, by heavy small-arms fire and the terrifying shriek of artillery shells from the mountain howitzers. What happened next will never be known definitively; apologists for Chivington argue that a substantial number of warriors was present at the encampment and quickly returned fire. The historical record, which includes testimony from two Congressional investigations, indicates something much more sinister happened on November 29, 1864. Twenty-four of Chivington's men were killed in combat that lasted from early morning until nearly sunset—about 3 p.m., in winter— but perhaps as many as 200 Cheyenne and Arapaho died. Many of them, perhaps most of them, were women and children.

Company D's soldiers, commanded by Lt. Soule, refused to open fire. Later, Soule recorded, in his letter to Wynkoop, horrific scenes:

> I tell you Ned it was hard to see little children on their knees have their brains beat out by men professing to be civilized. One squaw was wounded and a fellow took a hatchet to finish her, she held her arms up to defend her, and he cut one arm off, and held the other with one hand and dashed the hatchet through her brain. One squaw with her two children, were on their knees begging for their lives of a dozen soldiers, within ten feet of them all, firing – when one succeeded in hitting the squaw in the thigh, when she took a knife and cut the throats of both children, and then killed herself. One old squaw hung herself in the lodge – there was not enough room for her to hang and she held up her knees and choked herself to death. Some tried to escape on the Prairie, but most of them were run down by horsemen. I saw two Indians hold one of another's hands, chased until they were exhausted, when they kneeled down, and clasped each other around the neck and were both shot together.[111]

While many soldiers, especially from among the hundred-day volunteers of the 3rd Cavalry, participated in the killing—and in the sexual mutilation of bodies afterward—a September 2013 acquisition by Colorado College's Special Collections, a typescript of an account by a Company G trooper, Pvt. Isaac Clarke, suggests that the Bussell's comrades in his company acted that day much as Silas Soule's men had. Clarke, like Major Wynkoop, had become acquainted with One-Eye and respected the Cheyenne leader immensely; according to him, One-Eye came walking toward Chivington's soldiers carrying a white flag. The soldiers began to shoot at this target obligingly coming toward them. When a G Company trooper rode out to try to save One-Eye, a bullet finally found its mark and the Cheyenne leader fell dead. Moments later, the soldier's comrades, now shooting freely, killed him, too, as he trotted back toward the firing line. Isaac Clarke blamed the slaughter, now being inflicted even on their fellow soldiers, on the green volunteers who made up the 3rd Cavalry. It would take every effort,

---

[111]Ibid

141

Clarke reported, of Company G's officers "to keep us from turning our artillery loose on every hundred day man in the bunch."[112]

Ironically, Company G's use of the artillery may be indicative of the soldiers' disgust with Chivington's orders to attack the camp. They obeyed the order to open fire on the Cheyenne and Arapahos with their howitzers, but it was at that point in the battle that Indian survivors recalled explosions in the sky overhead. This suggests, according to Sand Creek historian Jeff Campbell, that G Company's men had cut the fuses short on the shells they'd fired, causing them to explode in mid-air. Other shells exploded far beyond the camp. Since Isaac Clarke, Harrison Bussell, and their comrades in the company had experience with handling the field pieces, this suggests they'd elevated the muzzles to deliberately overshoot their ostensible targets.[113]

So it appears that few of the men who served with Bussell's 1st Cavalry appreciated the accolades Denver showered on Chivington and his men once their mission had been completed. The Rocky Mountain *News* proclaimed, without proof, that the murderers of the Hungate family had themselves been killed and so had Cheyenne Chief Black Kettle. He had not: Black Kettle had survived, dragging his wounded wife to safety, away from their lodge, over which the chief had flown a large American flag, hoping for its protection.

---

[112] Isaac Clarke, "Sand Creek Memoir—'All One-Sided,'" *Colorado College Special Collections*. https://sites.coloradocollege.edu/ccspecialcollections/2013/09/11/isaac-clarkes-memoir-of-the-sand-creek-massacre/
[113] Jeff Campbell, email communication to author, March 1, 2016.

Black Kettle would live only a few years more. In a remarkable duplication of history, George Custer's 7th Cavalry troopers would kill him, along with as many 150 others, in yet another surprise attack on a winter camp, this one along the Washita River in 1868, an event depicted graphically in the Arthur Penn film *Little Big Man*. The just-promoted Capt. Silas Soule, after testifying against Chivington in the investigations that followed, was shot dead on a Denver street five months after Sand Creek. Chivington loyalists were suspected, but no man ever stood trial for the murder. Soule had been walking alongside his wife of five weeks when he was gunned down. Harrison Marion Bussell would marry an Ohio girl, Mattie Imus, and move to Arroyo Grande, where Mattie died in 1896 and Harrison ten years later. Censured by Congress, John M. Chivington would resign from the service and move away from Colorado. He returned in 1887 to visit Chivington, Colorado, the town named in his honor.

The Seventh Cavalry's attack at the Washita, 1868. *Harper's Weekly.*

Soule earned a different kind of honor. Each fall, young Cheyenne athletes participate in a "spirit run," a three-day race dedicated to healing the memories of the massacre. On the last day of the run, the runners and the older people, walkers, both Native American and white, come to Denver's Riverside Cemetery and they gather at Silas Soule's graveside. Here, they pray for him. They have never forgotten the soldier who sought peace and who, in the aftermath of the violence that came instead, insisted that the truth about Sand Creek be told.

Sand Creek, along with the 7th Cavalry's extermination of a Sioux band at Wounded Knee in 1890, remains one of the most controversial and painful episodes in American history. It also contributed to the Sioux and Cheyenne resistance that would bring James Dowell and Thomas Keown to the Powder River country, two men who, unlike Black Kettle and so many of his people, would survive what would become known as "The Indian Wars."

Tribute stones left on Silas Soule's grave, Riverside Cemetery, Denver. *Photo courtesy Carol Singer.*

144

Chapter 6.
"I Want the *American* Flag!"
Sherman's Atlanta Campaign, 1864

No Civil War campaign involved more Arroyo Grande veterans than Sherman's Atlanta Campaign in the spring and summer of 1864, and later his March to the Sea in November and December. Obscured in part by the imagery of Sherman's soldiers denuding the countryside, like Amazon ants, and the mythology of David O. Selznick's production of *Gone with the Wind* (retreating Confederates did as much damage as Sherman would do later when they blew up ammunition trains the day before Atlanta's fall),[114] no Civil War fighting had more political significance than Sherman's Georgia campaigns.

William Tecumseh Sherman. *Library of Congress.*

The twin victories of Gettysburg, where Lee's second invasion of the North was repulsed, and Vicksburg, where the Union finally secured control of the Mississippi and cut the Confederacy in two, did not mean that the war was won. Not only did nearly two years of fighting remain after those July 1863 victories, but the fighting would be so costly and the issue of ultimate victory so much in doubt that Abraham

---

[114] Frank Reeves, "The Burning of Atlanta, Seared into America's Memory," Pittsburg *Post-Gazette,* August 31, 2014, http://www.post-gazette.com/local/city/2014/08/31/The-burning-of-Atlanta-seared-into-America-s-memory/stories/201408310090

Lincoln stood a real chance, in November 1864, of losing his bid for re-election. He faced the threat of Democratic rivals who were calling for negotiating a peace with the Confederacy and so end the nation's ordeal short of emancipation and reunion, the goals so many were fighting for.

By then, Lincoln had at least found a general capable of carrying out his military and political will, the defeat of the Confederate armies and so the defeat of secessionism, in Ulysses Grant. The new commander of the Union armies conceived of a unified plan of war: he would move against Lee's Army of Northern Virginia with Gen. George Gordon Meade's Army of the Potomac. The other major Union army was based in the west, in Tennessee. There, Grant's friend and commander of the Military Division of the Mississippi, William Tecumseh Sherman, was to invade Georgia and so take the war to the resource-rich state that fed the Confederate war effort.

In May 1864, Grant entered Virginia with the mission to follow and so destroy Lee, and not, as earlier generals had sought, to capture Richmond. In a series of ghastly battles, from The Wilderness to Spotsylvania Court House to Cold Harbor and finally to the trench warfare of Petersburg, Grant followed Lincoln's advice faithfully: "Hold on with a bulldog grip, and chew and choke as much as possible,"[115] the president wrote him. Grant did exactly that, but at an appalling cost. The casualty lists posted back home were longer than they'd ever been in three years of fighting. The war was now looking hopeless and inconclusive.

It was Sherman who would bring a campaign of victories, a war of movement and a flood of hope to Northern newspaper readers and so to Lincoln's re-election prospects, and so also to the survival of the Union.

---

[115] Timothy P. Townshend, "Lincoln, Grant and the 1864 Election," National Park Service, http://www.nps.gov/liho/learn/historyculture/lincolngrant.htm

A pontoon bridge outside Petersburg, Virginia, 1865. *Library of Congress.*

Among the soldiers who would march with Sherman were Morris Denham, Irwin Ross, Jefferson Wright, Henry Bakeman, Otis M. Keesey, Vitalis Runels, and John H. Alcott, all men who would settle in the Arroyo Grande area after the war. Alcott, a carpenter, had been born during his immigrant parents' voyage from England to America; in the 1900 census he, too, was living in Arroyo Grande with his wife, Christena, and two children, Lillie, 18 and Samuel, 15, and in 1863-64 his carpentry skills were put to work, first under Gen. Rosecrans and then under Sherman. Alcott was placed on detached service from his 16th Wisconsin and became part of a pioneer unit[116]—the precursors of World War II's combat engineers—and it was the pioneers, along with the freed slaves who provided so much labor, who

---

[116] "John Henry Alcott," Civil War service record, State Historical Society of Wisconsin, February 28, 1995.

148

made Sherman's war of movement possible: they put down corduroy roads (roads surfaced with logs), cut roads, repaired bridges or built pontoon bridges at river crossings. All of these were tasks that were frequently completed under enemy fire, and they were invaluable in clearing Sherman's way.

Sherman's opposite and Georgia's defender was Gen. Joseph E. Johnston, commander of the Confederate Army of Tennessee (Union armies took their names from nearby rivers, so Union soldiers fought, for example, in the Army of *the* Tennessee), the man who had once commanded what was now Lee's Army of Northern Virginia until his wounding in the Seven Days Battles of 1862.

Ironically, Johnston faced another enemy just as implacable as Sherman. Unfortunately, it was Jefferson Davis, Johnston's president and commander-in-chief. Davis seemed to cultivate a deep professional and personal antipathy for Johnston, suspecting his general of timidity. Sherman's invasion of Georgia and his inexorable push toward the manufacturing and rail center at Atlanta only seemed to confirm Davis's suspicions: Johnston maneuvered, entrenched and feinted. But he was handicapped by his inferior numbers, so he did not win victories and he did not seem to slow Sherman. Jefferson Davis replaced him in mid-July 1864 with the aggressive John Bell Hood, the general who would ultimately command, later in the year, at the twin Confederate disasters in Tennessee, at Franklin in November and then at Nashville in December.

When Sherman had put these events in motion by invading Georgia from his base in Chattanooga in May, his command consisted of three armies totaling over 100,000 men. Just as they were in the East, the Union forces were twice the size of the opposing Confederates. Sherman would keep virtually every one of those soldiers in constant motion. The Atlanta campaign resembled Douglas MacArthur's "island-hopping" strategy in the Southwest Pacific in World

War II: Sherman would continually bypass and move beyond the entrenched positions that Johnston had established, or he would hit them obliquely, on the flanks, refusing to give the Confederate the battle that he wanted. In one of the first battles of the campaign, at Resaca, Georgia, on May 14-15 1864, it would be an Arroyo Grande veteran who participated in one such sidestep. In the process, Pvt. Henry Bakeman of the 2nd Iowa got considerably wet for his adopted country. Bakeman, the German-born Fort Donelson and Shiloh veteran who those in his regiment who crossed the Oostanaula River in pontoon boats garnered by his divisional commander, a one-armed general named Thomas Sweeny, who saw and seized an opportunity to fall on the Confederates from an unexpected direction. It may not have resembled the dramatic depictions of Washington crossing the Delaware to fall on unsuspecting Hessians, but it had essentially the same impact. It was a brilliant maneuver.

Sweeny's personal behavior was less so. The general was, said one acquaintance, multilingual, in "English, Irish-American and profane."[117] He reacted instantly and decisively to any slight, perceived or otherwise, against his personal honor. Several weeks after Resaca, the hot-tempered officer, Cork-born and a member of the Fenian Brotherhood, Irish republicans, would brawl with two brother generals with whom he argued (and with whom, it's presumed, he'd been drinking) in a command tent. He called his superior, Grenville Dodge, a "cowardly son of a bitch" and emphasized his point by hitting Dodge with his only available arm. He followed that by wrestling Brig. Gen. John Fuller to the ground. This would ultimately cost Sweeny his command, and he did himself no favors in 1865 when he was finally dismissed from the service altogether for being absent

---

[117] Donald S. Bailey and the Editors of Time-Life Books, *Battles for Atlanta: Sherman Moves East*, Time-Life Books, Alexandria, Virginia: 1985, p. 43.

without leave. He was absorbed in planning a Fenian
invasion of British Canada.[118]

Gen. Thomas Sweeny, Henry Bakeman's
divisional commander. *Courtesy the National Parks
Service and the Wilson's Creek Battlefield*

But at this battle, Sweeny's river crossing was a
fundamental threat to Joseph Johnston's southern flank while
the Confederate commander and his command seemed to be
absorbed by action along their northern lines, where a
horrific fight broke out that would prove essentially
meaningless, in contrast to Sweeny's flanking movement.
The two armies were fighting over four Confederate
cannons. The commander of that section of Johnston's lines,

---

[118] "Fighting Tom Sweeny," http://www.aohdiv1.org/sweeny.html

John Bell Hood, said the battery that was the Northerners' objective was made up of "four old iron pieces, not worth the sacrifice of even one man." Yet the struggle over the four guns left them surrounded by dead men from both sides, isolated in a no-man's land between the two lines, so that neither side was able to retrieve them. At nightfall, Union troops finally and stealthily hauled them away with ropes. By then, Sweeny's unexpected appearance meant that Johnston's Confederates were already outmaneuvered, so they conceded Resaca, laying green cornstalks across wooden bridges to the south to muffle the sounds of their retreat.[119] The capture of the guns had meant nothing.

Johnston and Sherman continued their deadly minuet into June—advance, entrench, outflank, retreat—when, on June 27, at Kennesaw Mountain, Sherman seemed to tire of maneuvering. This battle, fought in front of Marietta, about twenty miles north of Atlanta, resembled the head-on bludgeoning Grant was inflicting on Lee's forces, yielding grievous Union losses, in Virginia.

Johnston's army had the high ground and was disposed much as Meade's army had been at Gettysburg, as if it were aligned along a giant fishhook. Henry Bakeman's 2nd Iowa would attack the hook while Otis Keesey's 98th Ohio aimed at an objective on the fishhook's spine, on the Confederate left, at the junction of two Confederate divisions led by Patrick Cleburne and Benjamin Cheatham. Keesey was a musician in the 98th's regimental band, and musicians, in combat, were often put to work as stretcher-bearers, which meant that their life expectancy was no better than that of a rifleman's, who at least had the comfort of a rifle.

If Johnston's position resembled the Union position along Cemetery Ridge at Gettysburg, then Sherman's Northerners would endure the same kind of punishment that Lee's

---

[119] Bailey, pp. 47-48.

Southerners had endured during their assaults in 1863. Henry Bakeman's Iowa regiment was to "demonstrate," to attack without expectation of carrying the enemy position, uphill through dense vegetation and rocks. To Bakeman's right, Ohio regiments had to slog through a stretch of swamp to approach their objective, Pigeon Hill. Both morning assaults were thrown back with relative ease. On Pigeon Hill, the best one commander could do for his Ohio soldiers was to send forward shovels. They burrowed into the slope and hung on until dark.[120]

But these were demonstrations. Sherman's hopes for a breakthrough were to be fulfilled farther south, in an assault spearheaded by two brigades, one led by Col. Daniel McCook and one led by Otis Keesey's brigade commander, Col. John Mitchell. Although the opposing lines were only 400 yards apart, it was on this part of the battlefield where Sherman's assault would cost him the most men. The Ohioans were slowed by swampy ground, and when they approached Gen. Cheatham's position, held by veteran soldiers, they met accurate and intense rifle fire. Some Confederates were firing so rapidly that when they re-loaded their rifles, the powder charge flashed as soon as it entered the heated barrel, before they had the chance to ram home the bullet.[121] Adding to the carnage were two hidden artillery pieces that opened fire with canister when the Union men were only 45 yards away. The impact was devastating; Col. McCook managed to mount a rebel parapet and waved his brigade forward with his saber, but he was shot in the chest almost immediately. He would die, at 29, a few days later and the brigade's assault on Cheatham's men seemed to die with his wounding. Otis Keesey's brigade would come nearly as close as McCook had, so close that the Confederates were

---

[120] Capt. Alvah Skilton, "Account of the Battle of Kennesaw Mountain," from the blog *The Battle of Kennesaw Mountain: June 27, 1864,* https://kennesawmountain.wordpress.com/accounts/union-accounts/57th-ohio-captain-alvah-skilton/
[121] Shelby Foote, p. 395

hurling rocks down at the Ohioans. But the attack ebbed here, too, and so did Sherman's chance to carry Johnston's position. The place where McCook's and Mitchell's brigades fought would be known as "Dead Angle." Three thousand Union soldiers were killed or wounded on June 27; nearly a third from them in the assault on as Cheatham's position.[122] Sherman's stunning march on Atlanta had suddenly become difficult and deadly.

Union Army zouaves. These units wore uniforms were modeled on those of Napoleon III's colonial troops. These men are conducting an ambulance drill. *Library of Congress.*

Sherman was in a hurry to move on after the costly fighting at Kennesaw Mountain and this had dire effects on the Union men who had been wounded. Their commander

---

[122] Stephen Davis, "Cheatham Hill," The Civil War Trust, http://www.civilwar.org/battlefields/kennesawmountain/kennesaw-mountain-history-articles/cheatham-hill.html?referrer=https://www.google.com/

wanted to follow Johnston at close quarters, so orders came down to evacuate the 2,000 wounded within 24 hours, starting many of them on the long and hazardous path back to the rear, to Union hospitals in Chattanooga. But the train depots were miles away and rains had rendered roads nearly impassable, so men already in agony had to endure muddy and excruciatingly slow transport in every available wagon. The wounded then faced a train ride along a line in constant danger of being severed by Confederate cavalry. Many of these men were already debilitated by an outbreak of scurvy in Sherman's army. When they finally reached Chattanooga, a nurse named Lauretta Cutter was waiting for them.

Lauretta H. Cutter Hoisington in her later years at a reunion for Civil War nurses. *Courtesy of the Temple of the People, Halcyon, California.*

Cutter, born in Ohio in 1826, was a matron, or a "practical nurse," who must have felt a powerful call to serve the sick and wounded young men that the war produced in such prodigious numbers. Before the war, she'd had other causes. She'd been an ardent abolitionist in Ashtabula County, Ohio, a hotbed for the anti-slavery movement, and evidently an area frequently visited by John Brown, the man who would attempt to raise a slave rebellion by seizing the federal arsenal at Harpers Ferry in 1859.

After the war, she would continue her nursing career in Cleveland; in 1880, she married a minister, William Henry Hoisington, and she became immersed in the teachings of Theosophy, an outgrowth of 19th century spiritualism. Spiritualism popularized the possibility of communicating with the dead, a belief that captivated Mary Lincoln, who mourned two sons and, eventually, her husband. Theosophy grew beyond the faddish popularity of spiritualism to encourage the exploration of a kind of divine unity, in some ways evocative of the Transcendentalism of Emerson, Thoreau, and the intellectuals that made up the utopian community of Brook Farm, and so a faith respectful of other faith traditions. Theosophy spread worldwide and one branch, the Temple of the People, was founded in New York in 1898 and moved west to Halcyon in 1903, a utopian community still thriving today. Lauretta Cutter Hoisington arrived two years later to become "a devoted and efficient member of the Temple Staff."[123]

Those are the precise qualities Sherman's wounded men needed as they made their painstaking way back to the army hospitals in Chattanooga. A family history includes a brief memoir when Lauretta looked back at her wartime service with her "soldier boys:"

To steel the heart to suffering, and endeavor to comfort those I could not cure, was my experience as an army nurse. It is not pleasant to recall the time when glory was bought with the mutilation and suffering of brave and patriotic men; and the labor I performed in hospitals Nos. 1 and 2, at Chattanooga, Tenn., during the years 1864 and 1865, oftimes comes to me as

---

[123] "Faces of Friends," *The Temple Artisan*, Vol X No. 3 August 1909 pp. 45-47

a horrid nightmare. Surgeon Salter was in charge of No. 1 hospital, and by him I was first assigned to duty (early in May, 1864), in preparing 'light diet' for the most critical cases, and was assisted by Miss Babcock, of Chicago,--since deceased. A little later I was assigned to duty in the wards of hospital No. 1, a position which I continued to fill during my service Hospital No. 1 consisted of twelve long wooden buildings--with some tents--and almost daily received accessions from Gen. Sherman's army at the front, making room for them by sending to the north convalescents as soon as they were able to endure the trip.

The hospitals were divided into sections, with a surgeon in charge, and each section into wards. The sections were known by numbers, but many of the wards were designated by the class of diseases treated in them, as--gangrene ward, measles ward, typhoid ward, etc. The typhoid ward was somewhat isolated from the others, and I was told that I need not go into it, but in passing it the groans, and calls for lemonade impelled me to enter and minister to their wants as best I could. The result was that I contracted the fever, and for many days was so sick that I have no recollection of what occurred. I was taken from my tent to rooms, and so kindly cared for. ...In the meanwhile Sherman was marching on, and another hospital was necessary, which was called No. 2, and as soon as able I was assigned to it. I was agreeably surprised by finding here Miss Tuttle and Miss Dean, of Ashtabula County, Ohio, who were to be my comrades, and it was a happy meeting to us all.....As time passed by Miss Tuttle, who had been a nurse since the battle of Antietam in 1862, was transferred to No. 1, and Miss Dean to the kitchen of No. 2. Many convalescents were furloughed and went home to vote for President Lincoln, and we made it a point to add to their comfort from the stores at our command. I remember one occasion when we gave each man a few grapes and a pocket handkerchief. The thanksgiving dinner came, and royally did Miss Dean superintend the feast. It was like an oasis in a desert; and the hearty response of the boys, 'long may she live,' was a worthy recompense, as it came from the hearts of suffering, but brave soldier boys.[124]

Typhoid nearly killed Lauretta Cutter. Elsewhere, another matron, Hannah Ropes, an acquaintance of the author Louisa May Alcott, may have literally worked herself to death in January 1863 after six months of unrelenting labor in attending wounded soldiers in Washington D.C. For both

---

[124] L.N. Parker, *History and Genealogy of the Ancestors and Descendants of Captain Israel Jones who removed from Enfield to Barkhamstead, Conn., in the year 1759.* Laning Co, Norwalk, Ohio: 1902, pp. 261-63. Ancestry.com.

Cutter, with soldiers arriving from places like Kennesaw Mountain, and Ropes, with her soldiers coming back from Virginia battlefields, the first priority was to wash the carloads of filthy, helpless men as they came off the trains and into their care. Nothing, Ropes noted, transformed a wounded man more than a bath and clean sheets; one soldier, shot through the hand, whispered "Oh, mother" to Ropes as his head finally rested on perhaps the first pillow he'd slept on since joining the army.[125]

Convalescents in a Union Army hospital near Washington D.C. *Library of Congress.*

---

[125] *Civil War Nurse: The Diary and Letters of Hannah Ropes,* Edited and with an introduction and commentary by John R. Brumgardt, The University of Tennessee Press, Knoxville: 1980, p. 53.

"Mother" was a word heard frequently in both hospitals and on battlefields during the Civil War. In the lulls in the fighting, the combatants were tormented by the discordant chorus of wounded men, their groans and calls for help. They included heart-rending cries of the word "mother" that came from men who were utterly alone, lying between the lines. It was this word that figured in one of Hannah Ropes's most moving memories, that of a soldier who fought death as hard as any regiment fought on the battlefield:

> The young man who was shot through the lungs, to our surprise and, as the surgeons might say, contrary to all 'science,' lived till last night, or rather this morning. We considered him the greatest sufferer in the house, as every breath was a pang. I laid down last night and got asleep, when I was roused by hearing him cry, very loud, 'Mother! Mother! Mother!' I was out of bed and into my dressing gown very quickly, and, by his side…as they all are, he was on the battlefield, struggling to get away from the enemy. I promised him that nobody should touch him, and that in a few moments he would be free from all pain. He believed me, and fixing his beautiful eyes upon my face, he never turned them away; resistance, the resistance of a strong natural will, yielded; his breathing grew more gentle, ending softly as an infant's.[126]

Lauretta Cutter refers in her correspondence to "mutilated" men, and many of the wounded she would encounter on their arrival were amputees whose surgeries had been performed close to the battlefield—sometimes so close that another nurse, Red Cross founder Clara Barton, was turning her attention to a wounded soldier in a medical tent at Antietam when a bullet nicked her sleeve and killed him. Amputation, of course, would produce thousands of veterans who would be the most visible reminders of the war that postwar America wanted to forget, but the procedure was seen as a medical necessity to save lives.

Soldiers who'd been shot in the body or head often never lived long enough to make it to the surgical tents. Abdominal wounds, because of sepsis, were particularly deadly. Soldiers

---

[126] Ibid, pp. 67-68.

with these types of wounds were set aside, in a kind of triage, given morphine and water, if the former was available, and left to die. A surgeon could save the life of a soldier wounded in the arm. He couldn't always save the arm itself. When a heavy lead .58-caliber bullet, with a low muzzle velocity compared to that of modern weapons, hit a soldier in the arm or leg, the bone was shattered beyond repair, and the kind of fracture generated by a bullet wound invariably led to infection of the bone and eventually to the infection's spread. It was the infection that would do the killing.

A surgical tent at Gettysburg, July 1863. *National Archives.*

So amputation was a sad necessity and not a procedure that surgeons, despite their reputation as "sawbones," chose automatically. They saw it as a last resort, but an estimated 30,000 amputations were performed on Union Army soldiers during the war.[127] Once a surgeon had decided to amputate, soldiers were anesthetized, which generated another misconception that persists, one that physician and author Alfred J. Bollet corrected in a 2004 article:

At the time of the Civil War, ether or chloroform or a mixture of the two was administered by an assistant, who placed a loose cloth over the patient's face and dripped some anesthetic onto it while the patient breathed deeply. When given this way, the initial effects are a loss of consciousness accompanied by a stage of excitement. For safety reasons, the application was usually stopped quickly, which is why surprisingly few deaths occurred. The Civil War surgeon went to work immediately, hoping to finish before the drug wore off. Although the excited patient was unaware of what was happening and felt no pain, he would be agitated, moaning or crying out, and thrashing about during the operation. He had to be held still by assistants so the surgeon could continue. Surgery was performed in open air whenever possible, to take advantage of daylight, which was brighter than candles or kerosene lamps available in the field. So, while surgeons performed operations, healthy soldiers and other passers-by often had a view of the proceedings (as some newspaper illustrations of the time verify). These witnesses saw the clamor and heard the moaning and thought the patients were conscious, feeling the pain. These observations found their way into letters and other writings, and the false impression arose that Civil War surgeons did not typically use anaesthesia. That myth has persevered, but the evidence says otherwise.[128]

***

As the 1864 election approached, convalescing soldiers who had been in Lauretta Cutter's care and who were well enough to travel, as she reported, were furloughed so that they could go home and vote in the election that Abraham Lincoln might well lose. It was Lincoln's Secretary of War, Edwin Stanton, who ordered generous furloughs so that soldiers could vote—absentee ballots were still a rarity—and that policy may have been decisive, because by the fall of

---

[127] Alfred J. Bollet, "The Truth about Civil War Surgery," *Civil War Times Magazine*, October 2004, http://www.historynet.com/the-truth-about-civil-war-surgery-2.htm
[128] Ibid

1864, the Northern soldiers who fought the Civil War wanted a decisive victory, and in Lincoln they saw the man with the will to end the war without compromising the battlefield sacrifices they and their comrades had made.

The Democrats nominated a man some of them had once idolized: George B. McClellan, former commander of the Army of the Potomac, who transformed the defeated rabble of First Bull Run into a well-oiled and self-confident modern army. But McClellan continued to throw chances away, time after time, including at Antietam, to win victories with the wondrous organization he'd created. Now, in 1864, he was running as a "War Democrat." If elected, he would seek victory and reunion but was willing to leave slavery in place in the South as the price for peace. The former general, however, faced pressure from an extreme faction, "Peace Democrats," in his party who demanded an immediate end to the fighting and a negotiated peace, one that could result in an independent Confederate States of America.[129]

Meanwhile, at the Republican convention in Baltimore, Lincoln had to endure the minor humiliation of a rival candidate, and yet another general, John C. Fremont, Erastus Fouch's onetime commanding officer, whom he'd had to fire. As the Union commander in Missouri early in the war, Fremont had unilaterally begun emancipating Missouri slaves, a gesture that could have lost the state to the Confederacy. In 1856, Fremont had been the first Republican nominee for president and the boomlet for his 1864 candidacy subsided quickly, but it was emblematic of the depth of Lincoln's, and the war's, unpopularity.

Even the other side understood this. If the Confederacy could hang on for ten weeks, their diminutive vice president, Alexander Stephens, declared in the summer of 1864, until

---

[129] Doris Kearns Goodwin, *Team of Rivals: The Political Genius of Abraham Lincoln.* Simon and Schuster, New York: 2005, p. 654.

the election, Lincoln's defeat at the ballot box would pave the way to the South's victory. Lincoln himself seemed to be preparing for the possibility. "I am going to be beaten," he told a soldier, "and unless some great change takes place, *badly* beaten."[130]

The "great change" arrived in September. Sherman's army took Atlanta.

Atlanta was vital to the Confederate war effort. It was at the hub of several railways; its factories produced artillery, pistols, swords, uniform buttons, processed flour, and tanned leather for cavalry saddles and infantry belts, ammunition pouches and shoes. It had been Sherman's ultimate target in his May 1864 invasion, although his steady progress south, sparring with Joseph Johnston's army, had been blunted at Marietta at the Battle of Kennesaw Mountain. In July, Sherman faced a new Confederate commander, John Bell Hood, known for his aggressiveness. At just thirty-three, Hood was now the Confederacy's youngest full general thanks to his patron, President Jefferson Davis, and he wasted no time in exercising his new authority. Within three days of his promotion and appointment to the command of the army defending Atlanta, Hood did his "defending" by attacking Sherman on July 20 at Peachtree Creek.

Among Sherman's men was Jefferson Wright and his 55th Ohio, the regiment that had endured Stonewall Jackson's attack at Chancellorsville and intense sniper fire at Gettysburg; he and his comrades must have felt a sense of deliverance once they'd been transferred out of O. O. Howard's "Dutch" XI Corps to Tennessee and now Georgia.

---

[130] Anne J. Bailey, *The Chessboard of War: Sherman and Hood in the Fall Campaign of 1864*, University of Nebraska Press, Lincoln: 2000, p. 5.

Their feeling might have been tempered by the fact that their new corps commander would be the demoted "Fighting Joe" Hooker, who'd been in overall command of the Chancellorsville disaster. But Hooker was an excellent corps commander who, like the less gifted Howard, seemed to have a habit of attracting Southern attacks. Then, perhaps generating renewed unease among the men of the 55th, Howard was transferred to Georgia, as well, and now commanded IV Corps, fighting alongside Hooker.

Gen. John Bell Hood. *National Archives.*

Hood's plan was to catch Hooker's and Howard's corps as they crossed Peachtree Creek, perhaps with some of them midstream, but he would endure the same fate Lee had endured on the second day of Gettysburg because it took his subordinate commanders most of the day to get their attack formations into position. When the attack finally came, it was three hours late. Part of Hood's assault came tantalizingly close to success: it hit a gap between Hooker and Howard, but then three brigades–one of them included Wright's 55th Ohio–came up quickly, and this time Wright and his

164

regiment had the satisfaction of returning the compliment Jackson had paid them back in Virginia. The 55th stunned advancing Confederates with concentrated rifle fire as they reached the crest of a hill, inflicting heavy casualties. In the fighting that day, Hood was beginning to demonstrate a quality that would mark generals and so condemn private soldiers on the Western Front in 1914-1918: his real skill lay in getting his own men killed without appreciable result.

Like those generals, who seemed to lack any sense of empathy, John Bell Hood would persist. Two days after Peachtree Creek, on July 22, he launched another massive assault on Sherman's army. Among the regiments who would feel the force of the Confederate attack was Morris Denham's 12th Wisconsin. Denham was, like John Alcott, a gifted carpenter; he would settle in Arroyo Grande in 1894 and build his family a beautiful gabled cottage that still stands on Ide Street.

On July 22, of course, Wisconsin men like Denham who were facing Hood's attack couldn't have been thinking much about their futures. Near the center-left of Sherman's line and fighting under an extraordinary brigade commander, Manning Ferguson Force, they would have been far too preoccupied with the brigades on both their immediate left and immediate right, which were collapsing. The Wisconsin regiments—John Alcott's 16th Wisconsin was brigaded with Denham's 12th Wisconsin—struggled to hold their position, a salient on Bald Hill that they'd seized the day before; they were in imminent danger of being overrun. They may not have known it, and it would have been just as well, but Sherman's subordinate and their army commander, thirty-five year-old James McPherson, was also just to their left when he inadvertently rode into the middle of rapidly advancing Confederate skirmishers; the general had just realized the danger and turned his horse's head when a bullet killed him. McPherson had been a favorite of Sherman's and, before that, he'd been John Bell Hood's West Point roommate and math tutor (Hood finished near the bottom of his Class of 1853) and Hood would be genuinely touched once he'd learned of McPherson's death. He had never stopped thinking of McPherson as a friend.[131]

It took time for the Wisconsin men to understand that their brigade commander, Col. Force, was also their friend. When he'd been a regimental commander of the 20th Ohio, one of his soldiers, Henry Otis Dwight, described him:

A spare grave man with an eye that penetrated to the spine of a culprit, was in the habit of appearing on the drill ground and caused no small discomfort to both drill-master and men by so doing, for he was always critical, and when he spoke he made every one feel that his day of reckoning had come. He took the deepest interest in our welfare, and so was very strict with our follies. We all respected him for his justice and manliness, and before long we had learned to love him like a father.[132]

This stern father figure had trained his young men well. As the units on their flanks collapsed during the morning of July 22, Force's brigade held. The gunsmoke billowed around them so thickly that Col. Force called for a flag to mark his brigade's position. When a helpful lieutenant produced a white flag, Force was incensed. "Damn you, sir!" he bellowed. "I don't want a flag of truce; I want the *American* flag!"[133] Force got the proper flag, and he and his men hung on through repeated assaults by determined Texans. At 3 p.m., as he knelt to attend to a wounded officer, Force was hit squarely in the face; the bullet struck below one eye,

---

[131] Wayne Bengston, "Sherman Loses his 'Right Bower,'" *About North Georgia*, http://www.aboutnorthgeorgia.com/ang/James_Birdseye_McPherson

[132] David Mowery, "Manning Ferguson Force: A Tribute," Delivered at Spring Grove Cemetery, Cincinnati, Ohio, June 23, 2001

[133] Ibid

shattered his palate, and exited from the back of his skull. The brigade commander somehow remained conscious and active, but unable to speak; he used arm motions and pointed his sword to pantomime his orders. His men, including his Wisconsin regiments, threw the Confederates back. What would become known as the Battle of Atlanta resulted in another bloody repulse for Hood's army.

It would take another month of maneuver and siege, but finally, at the end of August, when Sherman threatened to cut Hood's supply line, the Confederate general evacuated Atlanta. Sherman's telegram to Washington followed on September 3: "Atlanta is ours, and fairly won," and Lincoln would win re- election eight weeks later in the same way.

Morris Denham's brigade commander, Manning Force, as a brigadier general. A small bandage under Force's eye is evidence of his terrible wound. *National Archives.*

Col. Manning Force heard the news of Atlanta's fall on as he was recovering from his bullet wound. He was promoted to general and would become a superior court judge after the war, but resigned the bench when the pain from his war wound finally overwhelmed him. For the two Arroyo Grande settlers in his brigade, Morris Denham and John Henry Alcott, there would be more fighting on a long road that would take them beyond Atlanta, to the sea and into the Carolinas. The South's ordeal, like Manning Force's, had only begun with Atlanta's fall.

Chapter 7.
The Woods that Grew Skulls
Grant and Lee, 1864

On May 4, 1864, Adam Bair began a forty-mile march into the darkest part of the Civil War with his 60th Ohio Volunteer Infantry Regiment. He would survive this journey to make another, by covered wagon, to California in the 1870s, where he would establish deep family roots in the Arroyo Grande and Huasna Valleys.

ARNOLD   SAN LUIS OBISPO, CAL.

A studio portrait of Adam Bair from the
1880s. *Courtesy the Robinson Family,*

That was far in the future. In the spring and summer of
1864, Bair and the boys and men of the 60th Ohio were
meant to be finishers. The regiment had begun training in
Columbus in February 1864 and was sent east to Washington
to prepare for what was to be the last great Virginia offensive,
the push to end the war. In April their training had
intensified at their camp near Alexandria. They were assigned
to IX Corps, commanded by Ambrose Burnside, the short-
lived commander of the Army of the Potomac who'd wasted
his men in frontal attacks on Lee's entrenched army on

170

heights above Fredericksburg in the winter of 1862. He had, after that disaster, gratefully accepted demotion to the lesser demands of corps command.

So under Burnside, the 60th Ohio, on the afternoon of May 5, crossed the Rapidan River at the Germanna Ford. From a rise, they could see dust clouds raised by Lee's army on the move[134] and began to march into The Wilderness, a vast tangle of forest and scrub so dense that it shut out the sun. Adam Bair was a corporal and therefore, like Richard Merrill had been at Antietam, a file closer. Bair must have been tired after the river crossing. His role was like that of a border collie, striving constantly to keep his company together and moving forward, cajoling potential stragglers, barking, like a collie, at men who'd packed too heavily when they had been warned to travel light.

The wake of the 60th would have been a Civil War treasure-collector's dream, strewn as it would have been with all manner of equipment: rubber blankets, coffeepots, needless overcoats and extra clothing, books that would never be read. Eventually, as the sounds of battle began to become more distinct, the 60th would leave behind what many Civil War soldiers left: playing cards, dice, flasks of brandy or whiskey, packets of what were euphemistically called "French postcards" with their leering plump models. These are not the items a man would want on his person if he "fell," to use another euphemism common to describing the indescribable violence of a Civil War soldier's death in combat.

Union soldiers would begin to see, as they crunched through the carpet of leaves in the closeness of the woods, dead soldiers grinning at them in their passage. These were

---

[134] James Lyman van Buren, "Diary of a General from the Battle of the Wilderness and Fortifications at Petersburg," http://ww.raabcollection.com/james-lyman-van-buren-autograph/general-jl-van-burens-battle-journal-person-effects#sthash.6PzmoQMt.dpuf

the skulls of the men who'd fought the year before at Hooker's debacle, Chancellorsville, either disinterred from their shallow graves by hungry animals, perhaps by a hardscrabble Virginia farmer's hogs, or simply lost and left where they'd fallen in the days when Lee and Jackson had played hammer and anvil with the Army of the Potomac.

Alfred Waud's sketch of Union soldiers, in The Wilderness, attempting to save their wounded comrades as fires spread. *Library of Congress.*

The woods themselves would become the enemy in this new battle, in 1864, because the dark wasteland made a mockery of combat drill; its density cut up infantry formations into little knots of soldiers who became separated from one another as they struggled forward, whipped by branches, tripping over roots, cursing in the close humidity and heat already descending on northern Virginia. For many Union soldiers, the dark was suddenly illuminated by the muzzle flashes of Confederate infantry with their bullets amputating tree branches, vaporizing leaves, buzzing like hornets past men's ears. Some of them, with a dull thud, a sound familiar to Civil War soldiers but now as lost as the sound of the rebel yell, found their targets in the bodies of young men. The flash of powder did something else: firefights sparked fires that would rage in the tangle of trees and scrub and the fires burned wounded men alive as they shrieked for help. No battle in the Civil War was more grotesque than the one fought in this forbidding place.

Adam Bair's comrades could hear the fighting that had already been going on all day; in Grant's army, IX Corps had come up last, and the 60th Ohio would go into camp on the edge of the battlefield during the late afternoon of May 5. Grant ordered them to attack early the next day through the woods between the Orange Turnpike and the Orange Plank Road. They were to find a seam in Lee's army that he believed to be there, then attack the rear of Confederate Gen. A.P. Hill's corps. Hill was a sickly man yet he was one of Lee's most formidable leaders in battle. It was his hard-marching light division that had very nearly won Antietam for Lee back in 1862. He, like the Italian nationalists who fought under the great Victorian hero Giuseppe Garibaldi, liked to wear a red shirt when he was fighting. To prepare to fight Hill, the tired Union soldiers would have been wakened at midnight to move out for the attack, scheduled for 4:30 a.m. It didn't get off until much later, a failing one diarist laid completely on Orlando Willcox, the 60th Ohio's divisional commander.[135] When Willcox's men finally moved up a country road through the woods, they would emerge in a clearing, in sunlight, where they discovered enemy artillery instead of the gap in Confederate lines they'd hoped for.

They'd run into James Longstreet's men, aching for their turn to fight behind screening fire from the artillery batteries. Longstreet's men were proud veterans and they hit hard. Burnside's IX Corps, including Willcox's division, quickly became so bloodied that they were forced to withdraw. Adam

---

[135] Ibid.

Bair and the 60th were brought up last and put in a blocking position to cover the retreat. By the end of the day on May 6, the battle was over, and Lee had mauled Grant's army: over 17,000 Union soldiers had been killed, wounded, or were missing in two days of fighting. Grant, in a technical sense, had lost the battle. But what mattered more than May 6 was what happened on May 7.

When McClellan, Burnside, or Hooker had been dealt the kind of punishment Lee inflicted on Grant in The Wilderness, they'd crept across the river fords and back to their encampments near Washington. But when Lee's men awoke on May 7, Grant's men were still there. In fact, they began marching south, moving around Lee's army. They were headed for Richmond, and Lee would be forced to follow them. It was a deadly strategic dance that resembled the campaign Sherman was waging at the same time against Joseph Johnston in Georgia. It would take eleven months for Grant to worry Lee's Army of Northern Virginia down to surrender but, like the bulldog Lincoln wanted his general-in-chief to emulate, Grant had a grip on Lee and he would not let go. Now, after The Wilderness, the two armies, a combined 150,000 men, ran a footrace to seize a crossroads at the tiny town of Spotsylvania Court House. If Grant could get there first, get in between Lee and Richmond, he could force a battle—with Lee the attacker this time–that might be decisive.

But Grant didn't move fast enough. Part of the problem was clogged roadways leading out of The Wilderness. Monumental traffic jams developed that were exacerbated, at one point, by a veteran regiment of Union cavalry who came upon a regiment of new recruits, their brass buttons still shiny and their uniforms, even under their layer of road dust, a more vivid blue. The veterans speculatively eyed the fresh and well-fed mounts of the rookies, eyed each other, and smiled. A battle within a battle soon broke out, knots of fistfights and wrestling matches in an hour-long riot that ended with one regiment riding off with the other's horses.[136] The melee was one of many factors that slowed the Union advance down. Another was sheer exhaustion; some infantrymen were nodding off on the march to Spotsylvania, and as they stumbled toward Laurel Hill, not far from their objective, they found, to their chagrin, Confederates behind the entrenchments that they'd just thrown up. Lee had won the race, and the fight that followed involved soldiers on both sides who were so tired that their hand-to-hand combat, as they began to claw at each other, was nearly in slow motion.

Adam Bair and the 60th Ohio came up to Spotsylvania on May 9, in the van of Gen. Willcox's Third Division, and it was Willcox himself who ordered them to form a line of battle. A veteran of the 60th described what happened next in a speech he delivered at a regimental reunion many years later:

> ...the enemy came out of the woods in front and on each flank, and opened on us, and then how the dust flew. After they had been engaged for some time, General Wilcox [sic] said: "The fools (meaning the 60th) did not know when they were whipped." Then he ordered one of his staff officers to go at once and order up other regiments to our relief. During that fight, which did not last long, we lost in killed or wounded, more than one-half of those actually engaged.[137]

It was in this engagement that Bair lost his first sergeant, a popular 23-year-old and "one of the finest-looking young men" of Wayne County named Michael Silver. What made Silver's death especially tragic was the fact that he didn't have to be in the fight that day:

> On a 40-mile hike from Alexandria, Michael Silver succumbed to sun stroke and was laid up at a field hospital for several days. After hearing of an upcoming battle at Spotsylvania, Silver and several of his

---

[136] Bruce Catton, *The Army of the Potomac: A Stillness at Appomattox*, Doubleday, New York: 1953, p. 95-96.
[137] John H. Ellis, "History of the 60th O.V.I. of 1864," Sept. 1890, http://freepages.genealogy.rootsweb.ancestry.com/~volker/history/civilwar/memoirs/60thmemellis.html

sick comrades left the field hospital to rejoin their regiment. On May 9th, at the Battle of Mary's Bridge, Michael Silver lost his life when he took up the flag after several color bearers before him had been wounded. "But as he waved the colors making himself a target of attack, he quickly became the victim of a bullet, being shot by a Confederate sharp-shooter. He was mortally wounded and died on the field of battle. His comrades later buried him on the battlefield, marking the grave the best they could before having to move on.[138]

It was a measure of the 60th's devotion to Silver and to each other that a year later Company B men located Silver's battlefield grave and brought his remains home to Wayne County, Ohio.

It was also a measure of the determination of the regiment, and of men like Adam Bair, that on May 12, the 60th Ohio locked itself into a firefight that lasted, all told, seventeen hours; bullets from the two sides pulverized a tree twenty-two inches in diameter. At the war's end, Sherman's "little devils," on their way to Washington City for the Grand Review, were awestruck at this remnant of the kind of battlefield savagery they'd rarely seen since they'd left Atlanta the previous fall. The Westerners stopped to whittle away fragments of the shattered tree stump as souvenirs until nothing was left.[139]

After nearly three weeks, Grant disengaged and again moved south toward Richmond with Lee and the Army of Northern Virginia following on parallel roads. The two armies had lost 32,000 in killed, wounded or missing men, but the losses had a grim calculus: Grant could absorb casualties like these, given the North's superior population, and Lee couldn't. Now, in the late spring of 1864, it appeared that Civil War was beginning to evolve into a war of

---

[138] S. Zimmermann, "Michael Silver Killed in Action during Civil War," Wayne County Historical Society, October 11, 2012,
http://waynehistoricalohio.org/2012/10/11/michael-silver-killed-in-action-during-civil-war/
[139] Ellis.

attrition, whose only objective was killing. In the next battle at Cold Harbor, Grant's tactics seemed to confirm that.

❧

If the South couldn't sustain the level of casualties that Grant was inflicting, neither could it match the machinery of a war that was now being fought by factory workers as well as by soldiers, a point perfectly made by Margaret Mitchell and the 1939 film adaptation of her novel, *Gone with the Wind:*

> Charles Hamilton: Are you hinting, Mr. Butler, that the Yankees can lick us?
>
> Rhett Butler: No, I'm not hinting. I'm saying very plainly that the Yankees are better equipped than we. They've got factories, shipyards, coal-mines . . . and a fleet to bottle up our harbors and starve us to death. All we've got is cotton, and slaves and . . . arrogance.[140]

Had the gentlemen gathered in the parlor at 1861 Twelve Oaks been able to see City Point, Virginia, in 1864 and 1865, the reality of Butler's prophetic words would have shocked them. City Point, along the junction of the James and Appomattox Rivers, was Grant's headquarters and base of supply for the campaign against Lee, and a future Arroyo Grande resident, George Monroe, 148th Ohio, was stationed there when Confederate agents tried to blow it up.

City Point was a valuable target and would have astounded the men attending *Gone with the Wind's* barbecue because of its acres of artillery parks, stacked cannonballs, warehouses full of shoes, Springfield rifles, boxes of hardtack—the army cracker almost durable enough to build a house, and just as indigestible—row after row of tents in a

---

[140] Sidney Howard, final script, *Gone with the Wind*, p. 31.
http://www.dailyscript.com/scripts/Gone_With_the_Wind.pdf

city of soldiers, even its bakery, capable of turning out 100,000 loaves of bread a day. Quartermaster wagons offloaded cargo along a river controlled by navy ironclad gunboats; the wagons and military trains traveled in never-ending streams so busy that the scene might have reminded the gentlemen from Margaret Mitchell's Georgia of worker ants, charged with energy and purposeful.

The reach of the North's industrial base is suggested in this photo of Napoleon 12-pounder cannon under guard at City Point. *Library of Congress.*

By 1865, even Lincoln's presidential yacht, the *River Queen,* was anchored in the river when he visited with Grant and Sherman to sketch out the final acts of the war. Lincoln treasured these trips to see his soldiers, away from the constant assault of favor-seekers who paraded through his office. On another visit earlier in the war to McClellan's headquarters, Lincoln had idly picked up an ax on the deck of the Treasury Department yacht *Miami,* smiled, and lifted it, holding it straight out at arm's length for several moments. None of *Miami's* sailors, when they attempted it, could do the same.[141] On April 14, 1865, John Wilkes Booth's bullet would traverse Lincoln's brain; logically, it should have killed him instantly, so it was only Lincoln's will and physicality that allowed him to live for nine hours after the shot had been fired. George Monroe would have felt the president's loss in a very personal way: the 148th Ohio Infantry and Pvt. Monroe had been the recipients of a thank-you, a short Lincoln speech, in August 1864.

Monroe and his comrades were short-termers, hundred-day men, usually relegated to guard duty on railroads, at strategic bases like City Point, or as support troops, and so out of harm's way. But the 148th came close, thanks to the spectacular attempt at sabotage, to never seeing Lincoln at all. On August 9, 1864, two Confederate secret agents penetrated the picket line that surrounded the wharves simply by crawling through it on their hands and knees. The letdown in security might at in part be traced to the heat that day. City Point's pickets may have found themselves dulled by the kind of torpor ninety-eight-degree temperatures and Virginia humidity can induce. Even the stoic Grant found it hard to deal with the heat; he emerged from his tent and was doing his paperwork in his shirtsleeves. While Grant was at his labors, the lead Confederate agent, John Maxwell, left his companion behind and approached a barge, the *J.E. Kendrick.* From Maxwell's report:

> I approached cautiously the wharf, with my machine and powder covered by a small box. Finding the captain had come ashore from a barge then at the wharf, I seized the occasion to hurry forward with

---

[141] Doris Kearns Goodwin, *Team of Rivals: The Political Genius of Abraham Lincoln,* Simon and Schuster, New York: 2005, p. 436

my box. Being halted by one of the wharf sentinels I succeeded in passing him by representing that the captain had ordered me to convey the box on board. Hailing a man from the barge I put the machine in motion and gave it in his charge. He carried it aboard.[142]

Railroad sheds at City Point. *National Archives.*

The hapless man from the barge had no idea he'd been handed a twelve-pound bomb. Maxwell and his accomplice had no idea, even as they were attempting both nonchalance and rapid flight at the same time, that the box they'd delivered was now aboard an ammunition barge.

What a Union soldier heard ten miles away, in the trenches outside Petersburg, Virginia, was like a thunderclap. What a group of officers near Grant's headquarters heard in the middle of their poker game was the angry buzz of a cannonball, propelled by the explosion, as it ripped through

---

[142] "Report of John Maxwell, Secret Service, Confederate States, of explosion at City Point, December 16, 1864," The Siege of Petersburg Online, http://www.beyondthecrater.com/resources/ors/vol-xlii/part-1-sn-87/number-375-petersburg-campaign-report-of-john-maxwell-secret-states-of-explosion-at-city-point/

the canvas of their tent from one side to the other. What one soldier felt was immense sorrow at the sight of a white horse, on which a woman had been seated at the moment when the time bomb detonated. The woman was gone, and a Whitworth bolt—a shell from an artillery rifle—had gone through her horse, now shivering in shock. The soldier held the muzzle of his rifle next to the animal's head and fired. What a woman on a riverboat nearby felt was a dull thud on the deck beside her. She noticed it was a human head. She picked it up by its hair and placed it carefully in a fire bucket. The only other person as nonplussed as she was Grant, who looked with concern after some slightly wounded staff officers, gave a few orders, and returned to his paperwork.[143]

The barge *Kendrick* was gone, as was much of the City Point wharf. So were unknown numbers of contrabands, former slaves who were working for pay as stevedores. Three members of Monroe's 148th Ohio were killed, along with forty other soldiers, clerks and civilians, and over a hundred were wounded. The disaster was deemed an accident—not until after the war would it be revealed that it had been the act of John Maxwell, who had escaped.

Nine days later the wharf at City Point had been rebuilt and was as busy as it had been in the moments before Maxwell's bomb detonated. What happened at City Point was a tragedy, but it did nothing to stop the industrial machine that would continue to grind the Confederacy down. George Monroe and the 148th Ohio would soon be headed home; Adam Bair and the 60th Ohio were three-year men, not 100-day men, and so they were headed for wherever Ulysses Grant was headed, and Grant was headed for wherever Robert E. Lee was headed.

---

[143] Brager.

Grant and his staff using pews from a rural Virginia church for a council of war, 1864. Grant is seated between the twin trees. To his left is Assistant War Secretary Charles A. Dana, a member of the New England family that included Nipomo rancher William Dana and *Three Years Before the Mast* author Richard Henry Dana. Gen. Meade, with the downward-sloping hat brim, studies a map at the left edge of the photograph. *Library of Congress.*

Bruce Catton has brilliantly described Grant's movements in Northern Virginia, cut from west to east by river after river, to that of a sailing ship tacking against the wind. Grant would move toward Richmond to draw Lee south. Lee would head Grant off and throw up his entrenchments. Grant would probe Lee's position and then slip around it, usually to the east, or Lee's right, by several miles, ford the inevitable river in his path, and then jog to the left, to the west, and slightly south, incrementally closer to Richmond, which interested Grant not at all. What Grant wanted was to interpose himself between Lee and Richmond, and then let the great man throw his forces on the northerners' entrenchments in exactly the same way Hood would throw his against Schofield's at Franklin, Tennessee, later in the year.

It wasn't military genius that made Grant a battlefield master so much as it was an acute understanding of strategic and spatial reality. This business of tacking right and then reversing course left was interrupted only by battles that were enormously costly to both sides but, because of his inferior numbers, those battles were always more costly to Lee. It was an inelegant strategy but it was necessary.

But by the late summer, Grant was running into Virginia delta—marshy and impassable—so there was no more room for tacking to Lee's right because there was no more right on which to move 100,000 men and their baggage. He would have to confront Lee more directly, and that confrontation came at Cold Harbor in late May.

Cold Harbor was another tiny Virginia hamlet; it was neither near a body of water nor was it cold. It was instead oppressively hot, the kind of heat that makes it nearly impossible, for those not accustomed to it, to move or even to breathe. Neither was it especially attractive; Catton notes that many Union soldiers talked of someday returning to the verdant Virginia farm fields where they'd fought Lee. Nobody ever talked about coming back to visit Cold Harbor. The battle that began there at the end of May was another marathon, like Spotsylvania, which had lasted thirteen days. So would the Battle of Cold Harbor. By the time it was over, Grant would have lost, from the beginning of May to mid-June, nearly 48,000 soldiers, killed, wounded and missing.

What Grant did at this battle was such an error in judgment that it is certain that even a young corporal like Adam Bair would have seen it; it would have produced an inward wince like one a perceptive student might feel when a favorite professor misattributes a quote in an otherwise brilliant college lecture. Misattributed quotes don't kill young men. Grant did. But Grant was not a cold-blooded man. For a killer, which is after all the business of all generals, Grant, perhaps the best horseman of all Civil War generals, could not bear cruelty to animals. When he once saw an army teamster beating a team of horses, he leaped from his mount, grabbed the teamster by the throat, took the man's whip away, and then ordered him tied to a tree for six hours. It was not a lesson the teamster was likely to forget; Grant was no more likely to forget Cold Harbor.

It was a case of overconfidence. Grant believed that Lee was nearly finished. Again, if Union losses had been heavy, Lee's were nearly as heavy and he couldn't replace the men he'd left dead on the May battlefields. After Grant's cavalry commander, Philip Sheridan, found a mixture of Confederate cavalry and infantry at Cold Harbor, Grant and his subordinate commander, George Meade, began feeding division after division into the battlefield to support the fight the combative Sheridan had started. It was yet another battle, like Gettysburg, that seemed to take on a life of its own. After four days of combat, it was Adam Bair and the 60th Ohio's turn. On the morning of June 3, the Union army, shrouded in mist, moved across the open ground that led toward the Confederate entrenchments.

The 60th was to assault Lee's left. Unlike the general staff—coordination and communication throughout June 3 would be chaotic, and staff had not adequately scouted the ground to Lee's front—private soldiers were fully aware of what they were up against; many wrote their names on pieces of paper and pinned them to their uniforms. The

Confederates, as they'd done under John B. Gordon at Bloody Lane at Antietam, held their fire until the last possible moment, and what Bair would have seen resembled nothing so much as the terrible punishment Gordon's men had inflicted that day before they finally had to give way. Under withering rifle and artillery fire, soldiers fell, not singly or in pairs, but in large groups. To observers raised in a more agrarian America, that day looked as if young men were being harvested like wheat. To Bair's left, a small group from Winfield Scott Hancock's corps stood for the briefest of moments above the enemy's entrenchments before it was swept away.[144] The entire federal line—five army corps—shivered and buckled under the intensity of the fire; Grant called off the attack hours later. He'd lost perhaps as many as 7,000 men in the first forty minutes of the Battle of Cold Harbor alone, an attrition rate that wouldn't be equaled until the British assault on German machine-gun teams at the Somme in 1916.

Grant had not properly surveyed the ground before Cold Harbor, he had tragically underestimated Lee and the strength of Lee's troops, he had ordered a frontal attack on positions that were expertly built and so virtually impenetrable, and he had persisted in that attack until noon because he and his junior officers had failed to communicate clearly once it became apparent that the assault was fruitless. That night, Grant told his subordinates that he had never regretted an assault so much as the attack on June 3, 1864. After that, he rarely—if ever—spoke of Cold Harbor again.[145]

Two weeks later, on June 17, Adam Bair was wounded—evidently, a minor wound in the arm[146]—during another assault on Confederate trenches that described a south-facing

144 Robert N. Thompson, "Battle of Cold Harbor: The Folly and Horror," *Civil War Times Magazine.*

145 Ibid

146 Adam Bair obituary, posted May 2, 2013, Ancestry.com, http://mv.ancestry.com/viewer/60b4d97b-28c8-4d1a-bdc1-85c0fc9069dd/51511777/13212990675

arc around Petersburg, Virginia, a rail and industrial center below Richmond.

One of the ghastliest images of the Civil War is of this burial party on the Cold Harbor battlefield. *National Archives.*

If Lee, now committed to the defense of Richmond, was to hold the Confederate capital, he had to have Petersburg as a supply base—and supplies were already problematic for his Army of Northern Virginia. While Union soldiers wrote of fresh vegetables brought down from Grant's base at City Point, Confederates complained of eating nothing but corn dodgers for days on end. Meanwhile, Grant had ordered his men to dig their own trenches. So what followed for Bair and his comrades was nine months of trench warfare, of the scuttling of rats, of infestations of lice called "graybacks," of mud, which permeated even what soldiers ate, of disease caused by vermin and foul water, of intermittent and lethal

186

sniper fire that claimed any tired solider who lapsed into even a moment of inattention, of intense discomfort felt by soldiers who could never get completely dry in the winter and who baked in the heat and choked in the dust of summer, and all of this amid the treeless moonscape they'd created from constant digging and constant heavy artillery bombardment—all a foretelling of the horrors of the First World War.

Gen. Ambrose Burnside, the advocate for the assault on The Crater. *Library of Congress.*

That war's catastrophic 1916 Battle of the Somme would begin with the detonation of a massive mine under German lines—the crater it created remains today, looking like a massive sinkhole amid a patchwork of farm fields. A mine explosion also would mark a surrealistic and shocking moment in the trenches of Petersburg. The crater that explosion left behind was, of course, *The* Crater, and Adam Bair and the 60th Ohio were eyewitnesses to the tragedy that followed.

Unlike the debacle at Cold Harbor, the assault on Confederate lines in the Battle of the Crater had logic, foresight, and planning. It was the execution of the plan that verged on criminality, and it would finally cost the genial, consistently incompetent Ambrose Burnside, Bair's IX Corps commander, his job.

In July, Union soldiers who had been peacetime coal miners began digging a tunnel over 500 feet long to a point underneath trenchworks held by soldiers from South Carolina. Meanwhile, Burnside decided to use inexperienced troops, but troops that were highly motivated and would be specially trained to move through the tunnel and into the Confederate trenches, once four tons of powder were detonated beneath the South Carolinians. The troops that began training for the assault were African Americans—the nine regiments of U.S. Colored Troops that made up Burnside's Fourth Division. These were men who understood completely what would happen to them in battle—there would be no quarter for black troops, a precedent that had already been set at Fort Pillow in April, when Nathan Bedford Forrest's cavalry had attacked and overwhelmed a detachment of black troops in Tennessee and murdered soldiers trying to surrender. The Fourth Division chose "Fort Pillow!" as its battle cry for the day they would go into the coal miners' tunnel and emerge on the other side.[147] In a letter to his mother two days after the Battle of the Crater, a Union soldier wrote admiringly of the black troops: "they would charge into the city [Petersburg] if the order had been given...They don't know when to stop."[148]

The orders seemed clear-cut:

---

[147] Richard Slotkin, "The Battle of the Crater," New York *Times*, July 29, 2014, http://opinionator.blogs.nytimes.com/2014/07/29/the-battle-of-the-crater/?_r=0
[148] "Sgt. Thomas Brown Provides His Mother with an Eyewitness Account of the Disastrous Battle of the Crater," Aug. 1, 1864, http://www.rhinelander.k12.wi.us/faculty/rhslibrary/globalstudies/Letter%202%20-%20Civil%20War.pdf

At 3.30 in the morning of the 30th Major-General Burnside will spring his mine and his assaulting columns will immediately move rapidly upon the breach, seize the crest in the rear, and effect a lodgment there. He will be followed by Major-General Ord, who will support him on the right, directing his movement to the crest indicated, and by Major-General Warren, who will support him on the left. Upon the explosion of the mine the artillery of all kinds in battery will open upon those points of the enemy's works whose fire covers the ground over which our columns must move, care being taken to avoid impeding the progress of our troops. Special instructions respecting the direction of fire will be issued through the chief of artillery.[149]

Union troops stream into the tunnel entrance as the Battle of the Crater rages in the distance. *Library of Congress.*

The detonation of the mine was spectacular. Adam Bair and the 60th Ohio, held in reserve to the left of the planned assault, would have watched in awe when the explosion went off at 5 a.m. on July 30, 1864, and scores of unfortunate South

---

[149] General Order No. 8, Army of the Potomac, July 29, 1864, *Record of the Court of Inquiry on the Mine Explosion during The Battle of the Crater, July 30, 1864,* http://www.beyondthecrater.com/resources/ors/vol-xl/part-1-sn-80/or-xl-p1-004-coi-mine-explosion-battle-of-the-crater-july-30-1864/

Carolinians were vaporized or blown high into the sky. Eighty-five Union artillery pieces then opened fire on the Confederate lines. It was at that moment that the Union troops charged into the tunnel to follow the shock of the explosion with the shock of a concentrated infantry assault.

The problem for Grant is that they were the wrong troops. George Gordon Meade, Grant's subordinate and commander of the Army of the Potomac—a command he held uneasily, sharing his ill-defined role with the general-in-chief—at the last moment changed Burnside's plans. Meade didn't trust black troops—unlike the soldier who'd written his mother, Gen. Meade didn't understand, or didn't care to understand, their motivation and discipline, and he ordered Burnside to replace them. The assault would be led by white troops.

African American infantrymen, June 1865. *Library of Congress.*

Burnside became petulant and had his divisional commanders draw straws for the dubious privilege of leading the attack. The winner was Brig. Gen. James H. Ledlie, who was both safe and drunk in his bombproof shelter when his men entered the tunnel. Once they emerged in the crater, they stayed. The black troops had been trained to skirt around the edges of the crater and not to go into it, where they would be trapped, as Ledlie's men were now. Subsequent attackers, including the black soldiers, ran into what essentially was a human traffic jam inside the tunnel and in the crater on the other side. The Confederates brought up reinforcements and began firing into the masses of soldiers below. When they closed with the U.S. Colored regiments, they showed no mercy: wounded soldiers were bayoneted, and soldiers trying to surrender—or soldiers who had surrendered, and were being led to the rear—were shot. A Virginia officer watched, sickened, as two soldiers tormented their black prisoner, whipping him with a ramrod, shooting him in the hip, and finally killing him with a second shot to the stomach.[150]

Over 400 African American soldiers would be killed and 750 wounded in the four hours of fighting after the mine's detonation. Generals Burnside and Ledlie were relieved of command and sent home. Other soldiers, like Adam Bair, were condemned to seven more months in the trenches around Petersburg.

---

[150] Bryce A. Suderow, ""The Battle of the Crater: The Civil War's Worst Massacre," http://www.goordnance.army.mil/history/Staff%20Ride/ADDITIONAL

Chapter 8.
The Burning
The Shenandoah Valley, Sherman's
March
1864-65

When Timothy Munger died in Arroyo Grande in 1911, he was a well-liked man whose funeral, according to a San Luis Obispo newspaper account, was heavily attended and observed with full military honors. Munger was 73, a former justice of the peace, and had just been elected city clerk when his health began to decline. [151] This veteran had survived the Confederate prisoner of war system—in his case, Libby Prison in Virginia, a former tobacco warehouse. So had Erastus Fouch, who had the good luck to be exchanged out of the Belle Isle camp fifty-one days after his capture at Gettysburg. At least five of Fouch's Company I, 75th Ohio comrades weren't so lucky: they died as Confederate prisoners of war.[152]

Libby Prison, Richmond, after its liberation. *Library of Congress.*

If there was luck in being captured, it was only in the timing. Munger was captured near the end of the war and at the end of Gen. Philip Sheridan's campaign against Confederate Gen. Jubal Early in the Shenandoah Valley;

[151] San Luis Obispo *Breeze*, October 7, 1911, p. 1.
[152] *Roster of the 75th Ohio Volunteer Infantry Regiment*, http://www.civilwarindex.com/armyoh/rosters/75th_oh_infantry_roster.pdf

Munger's 8th Ohio Cavalry was surprised by Early's troops in January 1865, and 500 of them were taken prisoner. Munger and his comrades wouldn't have felt lucky. They were, according to one source, "marched through snow, barefooted, and with scarcely any food, to Staunton, where they were loaded on stock cars and sent to Libby Prison. The sufferings of the men were dreadful at the hands of a cruel and relentless foe."[153] Their suffering did not last long: they were paroled in February. By then, according to the journal of a less-fortunate Union officer imprisoned at Libby (the parole and prisoner exchange sytem was arbitrary and capricious in the war's last two years), the menu consisted of bread, turnips, rice, and, very rarely, meat—a diet so meager that a visiting Catholic priest, a Southerner, complained to the Libby commandant.[154] Records are incomplete, but an estimated 30,000 Union prisoners died in Confederate custody during the Civil War—the most notorious camp, whose commandant, Henry Wirz, would be executed after the war, Georgia's Andersonville, accounted for 13,000 deaths—but ironically, part of the blame for the subsistence rations at Libby and elsewhere lay in the battlefield success of Union generals like Philip Sheridan. Sheridan was pursuing, as Sherman soon would be in Georgia, a policy of total war, including the destruction of crops, and Timothy Munger had been captured in one of the most important food-producing regions in the Confederacy.

The Shenandoah Valley was a constant torment to Lincoln and the Union. Not only was it supplying food, including wheat, corn, and pork, to Southern armies, but it was a natural invasion route, analogous to the Ho Chi Minh trail used by North Vietnam to feed troops and supplies into the Mekong Delta during America's war in Vietnam. Early in the war, Stonewall Jackson's troops had played hide-and-seek

---

[153] "8th Ohio Cavalry," http://www.ohiocivilwar.com/cwc8.html
[154] Bartleson, Frederick A., *Letters from Libby Prison,*

in the Valley—killing, in the process, Erastus Fouch's brother, Leonidas, at the Battle of McDowell—and tying down 60,000 Union troops. The Blue Ridge Mountains on the valley's eastern flank had effectively shielded Lee's army from sight during his invasions in the Antietam Campaign in 1862 and the Gettysburg Campaign in 1863. In 1864, Confederate Gen. Jubal Early had threatened Washington D.C. with invasion, an event that featured a future Supreme Court justice, Oliver Wendell Holmes Jr., then a young Union officer, bellowing "Get down, you damn fool!" at a civilian in a stovepipe hat watching the combat, enraptured, at Washington's Fort Stevens. The civilian was President Lincoln.[155]

So, in August 1864, Ulysses Grant dispatched the small, aggressive, and brilliant general, Philip Sheridan, to the Shenandoah Valley to deal with Jubal Early and to deprive the Confederacy of the food the Valley provided, once and for all. At least six Arroyo Grande settlers, including Timothy Munger, served under Sheridan in the Valley, but they and Sheridan had more than a match in Early, arguably one of the South's most able generals. And Early had inherited elite troops: among the men under his command were those who had fought with Stonewall Jackson in the Valley campaign of 1862 and in two decisive victories that Jackson had delivered beyond the Valley—at Second Bull Run in 1862 and in the brilliant flanking maneuver at Chancellorsville in 1863.

Early, even in losses like Gettysburg, had a reputation for hitting Union troops hard, and he had been effective in consistently outwitting and outfighting Union forces earlier in 1864, when Lee had first dispatched him to the Shenandoah Valley. Early must have seemed a reincarnation of Stonewall Jackson: not only did he threaten Washington, but on July 30, he ordered his cavalry to burn Chambersburg,

---

[155] "Civil War Defenses of Washington," National Park Service, http://www.nps.gov/cwdw/learn/historyculture/president-lincoln-under-direct-fire-at-fort-stevens.htm

Pennsylvania, during a raid; 200 homes and buildings were destroyed. Early was so successful in raiding, fighting, and disappearing that he went through two Union generals—Franz Sigel and David Hunter—before Sheridan was summoned by Grant to take command. Lincoln had pressured Grant, now bogged down in trenches outside Petersburg, Virginia, for a change in command because the election was approaching and Early was as much a political as a military threat. His victories were sapping civilian morale and that meant Lincoln was losing potential votes. Losing the election (Sherman had not yet captured Atlanta) could mean losing the war.

But, given how roughly Early had handled the two earlier Union commanders, Grant's orders carried an explicit footnote for Sheridan: Don't lose. And Sheridan, who took over August 7, avoided risk at first. This was in part because he overestimated the size of Early's forces. Sheridan didn't realize he had 50,000 men to Early's 14,000, but the Confederate army seemed much larger, which was a credit to how well and how quickly Early moved his men up and down the Valley between his victories. Meanwhile, Early's commander, Lee, underestimated the size of Sheridan's army, failing to convince Early that it was as small as Lee insisted it was. The result was three weeks of the two armies sparring at a distance and an evolution in Early's opinion of the other side: they might outnumber him, but their commander, Sheridan, was timid.

Early, of course, was wrong. He wouldn't find this out after Sheridan launched his first real offensive in the Valley, which came only after Sherman took Atlanta early in September. This was enough of a turning point—it lifted the cloud that was hanging over Lincoln's chances for re-election—so Grant ordered Sheridan to go deep into the valley, to destroy Early, and to leave the Shenandoah "a barren waste."[156] The gloves were off.

Shenandoah Valley veteran Timothy Munger married Charlotte Brenner shortly after he'd mustered out of the 8th Ohio Cavalry; the marriage would produce seven children. *Photo courtesy Mark Dias.*

---

[156] Lt. Col. Joseph W.A. Whitehorne, "The Battle of Cedar Creek: A Self-Guided Tour," Center of Military History, United States Army, April 1991.

It was Sheridan's cavalry, including Timothy Munger's 8th Ohio, who would be behind the force of the first blow that the Union general landed on September 19, 1864. Early's army was again on the move, but it was divided. A division under Confederate Gen. Stephen Ramseur was discovered dangerously isolated near Winchester, along Opequon Creek. When Sheridan then went after Ramseur, he was late—his infantry was slowed because it had to advance through a narrow canyon that the cavalry had cleared of Confederates—but he hit hard, driving the Confederates back. Then Sheridan himself was stopped as the rest of Early's command arrived to rescue Ramseur's division.

What had been intended to be a lightning attack was now a slugging match that included Isaac Dennis Miller's 24th Iowa regiment; Miller would, after the war, farm in Morro Bay and Cayucos. He later came to Arroyo Grande to farm the Upper Valley and run a butcher shop on the side. This battle was a turning point in Miller's life; as the 24th Iowa emerged from a woods, they were flanked by a hidden Confederate unit that opened fire with devastating results. Among those cut down was Miller, with three bullet wounds to his right leg and a piece of shrapnel in his ankle. Evacuated to a field hospital, Miller refused amputation; the leg was saved, but he would have difficulty walking the rest of his life.[157] Meanwhile, the Union assault had been stopped cold.

Sheridan improvised. He sent two divisions of cavalry, including Munger's regiment, to the far left of the Confederate line along with two divisions of George Crook's VIII Corps, which included two more men who would settle in Arroyo Grande—Samuel McBane, 123rd Ohio, and George Purdy, 11th West Virginia. The cavalry and infantry were moving out together when Sheridan appeared and rode among them, shouting at them to "kill every son of a

---

[157] Troy B. Goss, "Pvt. Isaac Dennis Miller," *Troy's Genealogue,* http://genealogue.net/millcivwar.html

bitch!"[158] The infantry hit Early's left while the cavalry looped around to his left flank. Somewhere in between, Confederate Col. George Patton, the grandfather of the World War II tank commander, was killed, and Early's men collapsed. The use of massed cavalry had been especially telling, and Sheridan was using units like the 8th Ohio in a way that would presage the armored tactics of generals like Patton in the Second World War; at this point in the Civil War, superior Union mounts and better-trained troopers would prove decisive in the Valley. But Early, defeated at what would be called the Third Battle of Winchester, wasn't finished yet.

Confederate prisoners taken during Sheridan's Valley Campaign under guard, September 1864. *Library of Congress.*

---

[158] Jeffrey D. Wert, "Closing the Back Door: The Shenandoah Campaign of 1864," *Hallowed Ground Magazine*, Winter 2004,
http://www.civilwar.org/battlefields/cedarcreek/cedar-creek-history-articles/shenandoah1864wert.html

Neither was Sheridan. After Winchester, he turned to the second of Grant's goals, to deprive Early and Lee of the Shenandoah's food and forage: for the next two weeks, a campaign was waged on crops in the field. Valley farmers called it "The Burning;" on a smaller scale, it was the same kind of war, on civilian property, that Sherman would soon wage far to the south in Georgia. Like the soldiers Sherman referred to fondly as his "little devils," Sheridan's men burned enthusiastically.

"I shall never forget that day," one Valley woman wrote of the arrival of Sheridan's men, "it looked to me like the day of judgement [sic], our Father's old mill & barn and [cloth] mill and all the Mills and barns ten miles up the creek were burning at once and the flames seemed to reach the skies it was awful to watch."[159] One elderly farmer was spared; when a detail of Sheridan's men arrived at his farm, he was waiting for them with a hearty dinner, which he and his wife cheerfully offered them. They ate the way hungry young men will, and afterward, they hesitated as to what to do next. Their lieutenant eyed the farmer's barn and reminded his men that they were not obligated to burn an empty barn. Both the officer and his detail agreed that the barn looked empty to them. They rode away and left it untouched. Two thousand other barns, Sheridan estimated, were burned to the ground.[160]

The Burning had a practical short-term military effect: running short on food for his Army of the Valley, Early's hand was forced: he would have to attack Sheridan while his army was still capable of it.

---

[159] Linda Wheeler, "Flames consume Shenandoah Valley in Union campaign," Washington *Post*, September 11, 2014, https://www.washingtonpost.com/lifestyle/style/flames-consume-shenandoah-valley-in-union-campaign/2014/09/11/cc7cc46c-349b-11e4-9e92-0899b306bbea_story.html
[160] Ibid.

George Henry Purdy must have been an exceptional soldier; he enlisted as a private in the 11th West Virginia Infantry and emerged from the war as a captain. By the turn of the century, he was living in Arroyo Grande, when exploration for oil was ongoing in both Arroyo Grande and the Huasna Valley[161] and, later, in northern Santa Barbara County, where he's listed as an "oil refiner" and an "oil pumper."[162] Samuel McBane of the 123rd Ohio lived in Nipomo; on his death in 1901, the San Luis Obispo *Breeze* lauded him as a man with "an open heart and an open hand...His fireside was a place of welcome and good cheer to all who happened there." [163] Both men were part of Sheridan's VIII Corps, commanded by George Crook, who had given Early's men such a hard time at Winchester. Now, as they were waking on the morning of October 19, 1864, in their encampment near Cedar Creek, Early's men would return the favor.

VIII Corps, and much of Sheridan's command, were lulled by what many remembered as one of the most beautiful autumn days they'd ever experienced in lives at their bivouac in the Shenandoah Valley, one of the most beautiful places in America. A cavalryman nearby described it this way:

> The 18th of October in the Shenandoah Valley was such a day as few have seen who have not spent an autumn in Virginia; crisp and bright and still in the morning; mellow and golden and still at noon; crimson and glorious and still at the sun setting; just blue enough in the distance to soften without obscuring the outline of the mountains, just hazy enough to render the atmosphere visible without limiting the range of sight. As evening closed above the Valley, the soft pleadings of some homesick soldier's flute floated out through the quiet camp, while around a blazing campfire an impromptu glee club of Ohio boys

---

161 Ralph Arnold and Robert Anderson, *Geology and Oil Resources of the Santa Maria Oil District, Santa Barbara County, California,* United States Geological Survey, Government Printing Service, Washington D.C., 1907, pp. 107-109.
162 "George Henry Purdy," ancestry.com
163 San Luis Obispo *Breeze,* October 28, 1901, p. 1.

lightened the hour and their own hearts by singing the songs of home[164]

The next morning nearly replicated the Confederate attack at Chancellorsville in 1863. This time, the surprise was the brainchild of one of Early's subordinates, John B. Gordon, the survivor of Bloody Lane at Antietam in 1862, who found a path through the mountains that led directly to the exposed flank of VIII Corps, camped on the eastern side of the Valley Pike, and from a place, like the woods that had flanked Gen. O. O. Howard's XI Corps at Chancellorsville, that was felt to be so rugged that it would preclude any Confederate attack. But Gordon had found a way. At 5 a.m., the Confederates were so close to VIII Corps that they could hear the early risers among the Union soldiers as they chatted inside their tents.[165] Crook, who would win fame fighting Apaches after the war, had blundered by not throwing out pickets around his camp, so when the Confederates rose and opened fire, among the first victims were the soldiers of McBane's and Purdy's regiments. The panic that followed the attack was so intense that, within twenty minutes, VIII Corps had disintegrated and was, for the most part, now out of the fight.

But while VIII Corps broke just as Howard's XI Corps had back in 1863, some of them made a stand while their commander, quite literally, rode to their rescue. Sheridan was twenty miles away, just back from Washington and that morning in Winchester, at breakfast, when he heard the sound of cannon fire in mid-bite. Sheridan swung into the saddle of his mount, Rienzi, and started to ride toward the sound. And then he began to gallop, with frantic staff officers, including young William McKinley, trying to keep up. As Rienzi and Sheridan closed on the battlefield, the little general began to holler "Goddamn it, boys, we'll be making coffee out of Cedar Creek tonight!" and to wave his porkpie

---

[164] Whitehorne, "The Battle of Cedar Creek."
[165] Ibid.

hat. His men, including those of VIII corps, lining the road in retreat, watched open-mouthed as Sheridan galloped past them.

It worked. Sheridan left in his wake men who had been whipped, but their full-throated cheers followed Rienzi and then they turned around and began following, too.

Sheridan's Ride, by Thure de Thulstrup. *Library of Congress.*

Meanwhile, Early and his Confederates made the mistake of pausing to rest. The rations in the Union camp, as they had been at Shiloh, were too much for the perpetually hungry rebels to resist. The pause gave Sheridan time to get Horatio Wright's VI Corps, which had been putting up a stubborn defense, and William Emory's XIX Corps re-formed for a counterattack. Among Emory's command was the 24th Iowa's 1st Lt. William Lane, a veteran of Champion

Hill in the Vicksburg Campaign. In his report afterward, the 24th's commanding officer, Lt. Col. Edward White, summarized what Lane and his comrades did that afternoon as they made good on Sheridan's promise about Cedar Creek:

> About 12 o'clock I was ordered to move the Twenty-fourth Iowa to the extreme right of the Nineteenth Corps and protect the flank. I immediately moved to the place indicated, took position, and threw out a skirmish line. In this position I remained until 3 p. m., when I received orders to call in my skirmishers and take my place in the line as it was going to advance. My skirmishers had just reported when the advance was sounded. In order to get my position in the line I had to double- quick about one mile, and during the greater part of this distance we had to pass through the fire of the enemy's guns, which overshot our advancing columns, the shells exploding in the rear. About 3.30 o'clock I got my place in the line, which steadily advanced, driving the enemy from every position taken until we reached the camp we left in the morning. Here we halted and made some coffee (those of us who were fortunate enough to have any), the first we had tasted since the evening of the 18th.[166]

Sheridan's cavalry completed the success of the counterattack: it was George Custer's division this time that got into the rear of Early's troops, generating a panic equal to that the Union soldiers had felt that morning; it only intensified when a bridge collapsed in the path of the Confederates' retreat. What was left of Early's army would no longer pose a serious threat in the Shenandoah Valley, and what happened that day on the battlefield resonated three weeks later in the re-election of Abraham Lincoln.

✖

To my smoke-house, my dairy, pantry, kitchen, and cellar, like famished wolves they come, breaking locks and whatever is in their way. The thousand pounds of meat in my smoke-house, is gone in a twinkling, my flour, my meat, my lard, butter, eggs, pickles of various

---

[166] Lt. Col. Edward White, "Cedar Creek Report, Commander, 24th Iowa, 4th Brigade, 2d Division, 19th Corps," http://www.history.army.mil/books/Staff-Rides/CedarCreek/24IA.htm

kinds - both in vinegar and brine - wine, jars, and jugs are all gone. My eighteen fat turkeys, my hens, chickens, and fowls, my young pigs, are shot down in my yard and hunted as if they were rebels themselves. Utterly powerless I ran out and appealed to the guard.

'I cannot help you, Madam; it is orders.'[167]

This was Dolly Summer Lunt's lament in 1864 Covington, Georgia, and protests like this would be broadcast throughout Georgia and the Carolinas and then handed down through the generations for the next 150 years. She estimated that the plantation she, a widow, had inherited had been left $30,000 poorer by the passage of Sherman's army. In agonizing over her loss, Lunt, like most wealthy Southern landowners, failed to appreciate the irony of the generations of theft she and her husband's ancestors had committed in extracting the labor of enslaved men, women, and children.

Ruins of the Millwood plantation house near Columbia, South Carolina, destroyed by Sherman's army. *National Park Service.*

167 "Sherman's March to the Sea, 1864: A Southerner's Perspective," http://www.eyewitnesstohistory.com/sherman.htm

It would be equally short-sighted to suppose that Sherman intended to bring the fires of abolitionism with him as his men set alight tobacco sheds, cotton mills, barns, and manor houses during what would become known as the March to the Sea, five weeks of destruction lasting from mid-November until December 21, 1864. Sherman was a product of his times: he

was a racist who had written his wife on the eve of the war, when he was headmaster of a Louisiana military school, that for America, slavery was a necessity for whites and blacks: "Two such races cannot live in harmony save as master and slave."[168] Ironically, few men did more and in a more practical way to destroy slavery than Sherman, especially as his target was the slave-based economy of the wealthiest state in the Confederacy. And, for a man who constantly cited the cruelty of war, and sometimes exulted in it—"I will make Georgia *howl!*" he crowed in a telegram to Grant—he just as constantly asserted that his objective was to inflict his cruelty in the name of humanity, in a way that would bring the war to a more rapid and decisive end and so save tens, and perhaps hundreds, of thousands of lives.

The 62,000 men he took with him, his "little devils," were a mixture of very young soldiers, and among them were young men who would later settle in Arroyo Grande. Vitalis Runels was nineteen, John D. Brown (like Otis Keesey, Pvt. Brown was a musician, in the 34th Illinois Infantry) was 22. There were also older men with much battle experience: Jefferson Wright was 28, Morris Denham 31, and English immigrant John Alcott was 35. What Sherman intended to do was to march them from Atlanta to Savannah, Georgia on four days' rations. When those were gone, the army would live off the land, destroy what it couldn't eat or carry, and

---

[168] Thom Basset, "Sherman's Southern Sympathies," New York *Times*, January 17, 2012, http://opinionator.blogs.nytimes.com/2012/01/17/shermans-southern-sympathies/?_r=0

cripple Georgia's ability to supply armies like those of John Bell Hood, now moving north and so safely out of Sherman's way, in Tennessee, and Lee's Army of Northern Virginia, now locked in its trenches with Grant's forces south of Richmond. What Sherman would do in Georgia and later, in the Carolinas, was not necessarily a new way of making war. Imperial Hapsburg troops had devastated Protestant Germany with great zeal during the 17th-Century Thirty Years War and it had taken the North German states decades to recover; one of them, Prussia, in response to the destruction, would begin to build a military tradition that would haunt the twentieth century.

Sherman's men destroying railroad track in Atlanta. *Library of Congress.*

Grant and Sherman, in deliberately pursuing a scorched-earth policy begun in Atlanta as a strategic end in itself, made a much-condemned decision, but Atlanta was no Guernica or Dresden or Tokyo. A third of the city had already been destroyed by John Bell Hood's retreating Confederates in September; by November 15, the eve of Sherman's jump-off date, most of Atlanta's citizens had been evacuated. The Union commander then ordered structures that might have any potential military use to be razed. But arson fires had already begun as early as November 11, evidently the work of the "little devils" ostensibly under Sherman's command, and this destruction was a product of the loose rein Sherman would continue to exert over his men throughout the March to the Sea. So the fires set at Sherman's orders on November 15 were augmented by Union freelancers and the destruction was more than Sherman intended, a fact tacitly admitted by the brevity in his own memoirs about the burning and the condemnation of it by many of Sherman's own soldiers as they set out on the roads beyond Atlanta, headed for the sea.[169]

Meanwhile, for younger soldiers like Runels and Brown, this new campaign that Sherman was launching was an adventure, and, as young men will do, many brought their pets with them as they set out on November 15. Historian Burke Davis catalogued the menagerie that accompanied Sherman's 62,000 troops on the march. The most famous was Old Abe, the "battle eagle," a bald eagle kept by the 8th Wisconsin; Morris Denham's 12th Wisconsin had started the war with a bear, reluctantly sold in Kansas, but brought a raccoon with them to Georgia. One soldier kept a squirrel named Bun, contentedly munching hardtack on his master's shoulder. Minerva the owl accompanied another regiment and, of course, there were hundreds of dogs, some trotting

---

[169] Phil Leigh, "Who Burned Atlanta?" *New York Times*, November 13, 2014, http://opinionator.blogs.nytimes.com/2014/11/13/who-burned-atlanta/

alongside their adoptive companies, some perched on saddles with their cavalrymen.[170] (Sallie, a pit bull beloved by the 11th Pennsylvania—Lincoln had delightedly tipped his hat to her as she marched with her regiment in a review–was killed in action and her sculpture, showing her peaceful, about to go to sleep, is part of the regiment's monument at Gettysburg. Admirers frequently leave dog biscuits for Sallie on their visits to the battlefield.)

Sherman's army faced only token resistance. With John Bell Hood now in Tennessee, locked in a losing and costly campaign with Union Gen. George Thomas, the only regular army resistance was that of Joseph Wheeler's 3,500 cavalry. Wheeler would go on to serve in the United States Army during the Spanish-American War in 1898, commanding, among other units, Theodore Roosevelt's Rough Riders, and is credited, in the heat of battle, with mistakenly referring to the Spaniards he was fighting in Cuba as "Yankees," a sadly apocryphal anecdote. The Confederate cavalryman and his men were largely kept at bay by Sherman's cavalry commander, Judson Kilpatrick, a man noted for his alarming mutton-chop whiskers and his aggressiveness; he was regarded sourly by his own men, who had nicknamed him "Kill-cavalry." As they left Atlanta, Sherman ordered all communications with the rear of the army severed, including the telegraph, to keep his movements a secret. He was confident his men could live off some of the richest agricultural land in the South and just as confident that the next time he used the telegraph it would be with the Atlantic Ocean in sight, at Savannah.

The enthusiasm of Sherman's men literally would have been dampened almost immediately. It began to rain, and Sherman's troops became intimately acquainted with the singularity of the red clay mud of Georgia. The network of country roads that the two wings of the army used turned to

---

[170] Burke Davis, *Sherman's March*, Vintage Books, New York: 1988, p. 10.

viscous sludge. Fortunately, the army had traveled light—sixty-five artillery pieces and a herd of cattle among its most important baggage—and soon its soldiers established a steady pace of about fifteen miles a day. Historian John F. Marszalek provides a vivid description of a typical day on the march:

> Reveille came at daybreak and sometimes earlier. The 62,000-man army usually spent the night in tents, the campsites stretching in all directions. After a sparse breakfast, they formed the columns and began moving. Railroad tracks were upended and destroyed. Black and white pioneers cleared the path ahead, with Sherman himself sometimes joining in the physical labor. There was no lunch stop; instead, the men ate whenever and whatever they could. When they reached the assigned campsite in the evening, each man hooked his tent half to another's, pitched it, and then prepared the only full meal of the day over a fire. The soldiers entertained themselves by letter writing, card games and other such diversions, but the favorite activity was to hear the adventures of the foragers.

> As the main columns had been marching all day, organized soldiers and others fanned out in all directions, looking for food and booty. Very quickly, these foragers came to be called "bummers," and it was they who did the most damage to the countryside and provided the most food for the troops. They wandered out five or more miles from the main columns and became experts at finding hidden food, horses, wagons and even slaves. Operating under varying degrees of supervision, their exploits formed the foundation of Sherman's lasting reputation.[171]

The work the bummers did was thorough, and Sherman's vision of "total war" soon colored the thinking of his men, including a soldier, Edwin Levins, in Morris Denham's 12th Wisconsin Infantry:

> We took everything we could lay our hands upon and I will say never since I have been a soldier did we fare better, lived like princes in the eating line, flour, meal, rice, fresh pork, chickens, geese, turkeys, honey, fresh beef, sweet potatoes, pumpkins, turnips, sugar and molasses being plenty. But we took all and there is not enough left

---

[171] John F. Marszalek, "Scorched Earth: Sherman's March to the Sea," *Hallowed Ground Magazine*, Fall 2014, http://www.civilwar.org/hallowed-ground-magazine/fall-2014/scorched-earth.html

along the line of our march to save the people from starvation. They must go elsewhere or suffer with hunger.[172]

If there was a measure of justice in Sherman's "devils" looting the plantation of a wealthy slaveowner like Dolly Summers Lunt, there was none in the foraging these soldiers practiced in their drive to the sea. Theoretically forbidden from entering private homes, they did so anyway. They ransacked the homes of the humblest Georgians, black and white, as well as the wealthiest; W.B. Emmons, a soldier in John D. Brown's 34th Illinois, reported that civilians hid their livestock and food stores in swamps but that slaves frequently led them to those hiding places; hundreds, he added, began to follow the 34th and the rest of Sherman's army.[173]

A Union "bummer." From Major George Ward Nichols's *The Story of the Great March from the Diary of a Staff Officer, 1865.*

Sherman attempted to discourage the newly-liberated slaves, called "contrabands," from following the army. They

[172] "Letter from Edwin D. Levins," 12th Wisconsin Infantry, December 18, 1864, *Civil War Voices*, http://www.soldierstudies.org/index.php?action=view_letter&Letter=588
[173] W. B. Emmons, Diary, 1864-65, University of Iowa Special Collections, http://128.255.22.135/cdm/ref/collection/cwd/id/1688

were slowing the pace of his march and represented unwanted competition for the food that Georgia farmers were unwillingly providing his soldiers. One of his commanders, Jefferson C. Davis, finally lost his patience with the mass of contrabands at his division's rear. On December 9, 1864, in crossing deep-running Ebenezer Creek, the last of Davis's regiments across released the division's pontoon bridge. It floated away in the rushing water. The army's followers were stranded on the other bank, and, even worse, they were now vulnerable to the violence of Confederate troops, like Wheeler's cavalry, or the irregulars who wandered the countryside, and the irregulars were merciless. The 34th Illinois's W.B. Emmons reported that "bush whackers" had shot nine Union soldiers dead after they had surrendered; a tenth, the only survivor, lived long enough to tell the story.[174] So some of the justifiably terrified former slaves tried to cross the creek and were swept away; Davis's men attempted to rescue them, but hundreds may have drowned. The callousness of the incident at Ebenezer Creek led to calls for Davis's court-martial; he was protected by Sherman but, in a gesture of atonement, 400,000 acres of Savannah-area farmland were later distributed among local freedmen.[175]

Four days after Ebenezer Creek, Sherman's troops began to arrive at the outskirts of Savannah, where they were to link up with a Union fleet commanded by Admiral John Dalhgren and its supplies, anchored offshore. But between Dahlgren and Sherman lay Fort McAllister, and it would have to be taken if the two commands were to unite. That task fell to a division that included Vitalis Runels's 47th Ohio. Sherman was watching Runels and his comrades from a distance when they rushed the fort, widely spaced to minimize the killing power of the Confederates' heavy

---

[174] Emmons Diary, 11/24/1864.
[175] "March to the Sea: Ebenezer Creek," Georgia Historical Society, http://georgiahistory.com/ghmi_marker_updated/march-to-the-sea-ebenezer-creek/

artillery. Beyond that, Fort McAllister had little to impede Sherman's men. Its garrison was small and after only fifteen minutes of combat, it was in his hands: "They took it, Howard!" Sherman yelled to the nearby Gen. O. O. Howard. "I've got Savannah!"[176] He hadn't, not quite, but Sherman would enter and occupy the city itself on December 21, when he would present it, in a telegram to President Lincoln, as his Christmas gift. Sherman had reached the sea.

An illustration from *Harper's Weekly* shows the assault on Savannah's Fort McAllister.

Once Savannah was secured, the willful destruction of the previous five weeks abruptly stopped.[177] But when Sherman turned north early in 1865 and entered South Carolina, it resumed with a ferocity that eclipsed what had happened in Georgia. South Carolina was the cradle of secession and

---

176 Burke Davis, p. 106.
177 Marszalek, "Scorched Earth."

rebellion, and Sherman's soldiers, as they turned north along the Atlantic seaboard, did the kind of work they'd done in the March to the Sea with a sense of self-justification that was lubricated, in the case of Columbia, the state capital, by the generous amounts of liquor they seized. A Union general, Henry Slocum, drily observed of Columbia that "a drunken soldier with a musket in one hand and a match in the other is not a pleasant visitor to have about the house on a dark, windy night."[178] The winds Slocum cites carried the fires throughout the city; contemporary photographs show the kind of destruction that wouldn't be seen again until the siege guns of the First World War leveled cities in Belgium and northern France.

Charleston, South Carolina, in ruins, 1865. *Library of Congress.*

[178] "Sherman Sacks Columbia, South Carolina," http://www.history.com/this-day-in-history/sherman-sacks-columbia-south-carolina

A century and a half after Sherman's march, he remains one of the most controversial figures in American history, seen by many as a war criminal, seen by his defenders as the single figure most responsible for shortening the war that was consuming a generation of young men. While the latter view has merit, Sherman's legacy would continue to play out in wave of criminality of the immediate postwar period, and it was one that Arroyo Grande veterans somehow managed to escape. In *Marching Home,* Brian Matthew Jordan writes that

> According to the estimate of one historian, nearly three-quarters of the men who donned Union blue were under the age of thirty. Young and impulsive roughs suddenly unmoored from the drudgeries of war could hardly be expected to behave in a restrained way. After all, they had confiscated acres of cotton and thousands of slaves, torched southern cities, maimed enemies, and waged a more devastating kind of war from Virginia to Georgia to the Carolinas.[179]

Ultimately, Sherman would display the same generosity of spirit that Grant displayed toward Lee when he accepted the surrender of Joseph Johnston's forces two weeks after Appomattox. But when the time came for his "little devils" to go home, the terror that some of them would bring with them after the war as civilian lawbreakers resembled the terror they'd once brought to Confederate widows in little farmhouses during the March to the Sea. Former Confederates, like the James brothers in Missouri, would begin their careers as outlaws, too. The postwar increase in crime also brought profits to one Gilded Age industry: in 1875, gun manufacturers, intending to capitalize on already-burgeoning sales, published a popular pamphlet, *The Gun in Its Home and on the Road,* which argued that the revolver would be an indispensable tool in the new nation that had emerged from four years of war.

---

[179] Jordan, *Marching Home*, p. 43.

Chapter 9.
The Army that Marched in its Sleep
Appomattox, 1865

    The war's end came so swiftly that the four years before must have seemed a century. Arroyo Grande veterans Joseph Brewer, Austin Abbott, Adam Bair, William Strobridge, Charles Clark, Samuel McBane, and George Purdy were all involved, directly or indirectly, in the chase to Appomattox Court House and Lee's surrender, in fighting that lasted a little over two weeks. Lee ultimately lost because he could not overcome multiple enemies: the Army of the Potomac, Edward O. C. Ord's Army of the James, Sheridan's cavalry—all told more than 150,000 Union men, or triple Lee's numbers. Grant's strength did not include the imminent arrival of John Schofield's veterans of fighting in Tennessee, headed east to link up with either Grant or with Sherman as need dictated.

One more enemy, and perhaps the most telling, was hunger. By March of 1865, the proud men of the Army of Northern Virginia, hunched in their trenches, were reduced to pitiable daily rations, a pint of corn meal and an ounce or two of bacon.[180] That meant that Lee's strength—50,000 men—was dwindling every day, as hungry men left Petersburg and headed home, where they had fields to prepare and families to look after.

A Union Army "Dictator" mortar at Petersburg. In some cases, these were mounted on trains in a forerunner of German railroad guns of the First World War. This mortar could hurl a shell weighing over 200 pounds nearly a mile. *Library of Congress.*

---

[180] Shelby Foote, *The Civil War*, Volume III, p. 629.

In northern Virginia, spring meant mud. Horses, wagons, and even infantrymen could not move through Virginia mud, whose chief property, suction, made roads impassable. Grant's next offensive would have to wait for the roads to dry. When the roads were ready, Grant would resume the dance he'd led the previous spring. This time, he would continue to stretch Lee's Petersburg line to the Confederate right by sliding Union troops to the west. Eventually, the string would snap. Either Lee's dwindling army would be stretched so thin that a weak spot in the miles of trenchlines would present itself or, even better, Grant would finally force Lee to come out and fight on open ground. In the open, the Union numbers would crush Lee's army. In fact, since the only Southern supply line, the Weldon and Petersburg Railroad, was directly in the path of this westward shift, Lee would have to come out and make a run for it; without the railroad, he couldn't feed his hungry men.

And coming out of the trenches would prove to be Lee's only choice after a disappointing defeat on March 25, 1865. The last important offensive of the Army of Northern Virginia came on Lee's far left, when the seemingly indefatigable Georgian, John B. Gordon, led an assault on Fort Stedman, just inside the Union lines. Gordon had the same idea Grant had: if Gordon could punch a hole in his enemy's lines at this point, then it would be the Northerners' major supply line, the railroad link to City Point just beyond the fort, that would be severed and the Army of the Potomac would then be in serious trouble. Lee gave the talented Gordon his blessing, and on the morning of March 25, he launched the assault, which had been meticulously planned, down to teams of axemen to break up the abatises—the obstacles, made of sharpened wooden spikes, that prefigured barbed wire–that so impeded infantry. It was a stunning success, at first.

Adam Bair and his 60th Ohio regiment were part of the defenses nearby, and Hezekiah Bradds, a soldier in the 60th's Company C, recounted the morning of March twenty-vie years later:

Early that morning I was the first to give alarm, "Johnnies in our works!" They (the Johnnies) had taken about all of the 14th N. Y. regiment and had gotten all there were in the videt [sic] pits. They had also entered Fort Stedman.

I had chosen a place between two flankers. I ran to place and Sergt. Bulin furnished me with cartridges- -tossed them at my feet. Not a Johnnie got north of Fort Stedman. Five hundred of their bravest men were picked to take Romer's Battery, nearly a mile away on a hill, but they failed, for a Pennsylvanian regiment moved into the fort, and when their force came they were badly worsted and retreated.

Lee's reinforcement did not arrive in time and the retreating force was passing back, getting over our works. Their reinforcements arrived and the situation looked desperate to me.

A General on a gray horse got over their works and came in full tilt, waving sword to stop the fleeing force. At pull of trigger and crack of gun he fell. He always bore on my mind. That pull of trigger and crack of gun saved many lives - maybe 10,000.

Their reinforcements hadn't arrived in time. I was in plain sight of all reinforcements and of the fleeing rebels. There were many carried off the field, and my last shot was necessary there. I then went down into Fort Stedman and found two Johnnies there badly wounded and inquiring what we were going to do with them. I consoled them the best I could. Our colors and our flag were still waving over the fort.

I said, "Don't you like our colors better than your own?"

They said, "we are not talking now."[181]

In the attack on Fort Stedman, Lee lost 4,000 men he could not afford to lose: no amount of audacity could compensate for the numbers game that Grant had been

---

[181] Chris Volker, compiler, "With the 60th Ohio Around Petersburg," Washington D.C. *National Tribune*, April 8, 1926, http://archiver.rootsweb.ancestry.com/th/read/OHADAMS/1999-06/0928834176

playing since The Wilderness, and now it was a game that he was more clearly winning.

To Philip Sheridan, newly-arrived from the Shenandoah Valley, it seemed that it was the rain that was winning. Sheridan had left the now-secure Valley to link up with Grant at Petersburg; his army, largely stripped of the foot soldiers who had been transferred to Grant's control, now consisted mostly of the cavalry that he'd used so effectively to neutralize Jubal Early. By 1865, there was no commander, with the possible exception of Sherman, whom Grant so trusted. He wanted Sheridan's help to catalyze the Army of the Potomac, still saddled with a reputation for sluggishness that dated back to McClellan's temporizing in 1862. If Sheridan had a premonition of his own mortality—a massive heart attack would kill him at 57—then slowness was his worst enemy. Sheridan delivered such an impassioned soliloquy at Grant's headquarters, directed against the rain, the mud, and Robert Edward Lee, that Grant's chief assistant and sobriety manager, Gen. John Rawlins, ushered him into Grant's tent to repeat the speech, which he felt would be good for the boss's morale.[182] Grant, unusually indecisive about launching this final campaign, in large part because of the weather, was delighted. On March 31, he sent out Sheridan and his cavalry, with broad discretionary command power, which Sheridan would use to fire at least one corps commander for what he perceived as willful tardiness. The little general and his horse soldiers went darting across Lee's right and toward the railroad that supplied the Army of Northern Virginia.

Arroyo Grande's future baby doctor, Charles Clark, was already ahead of his commander, Sheridan, to the west. Clark was part of the 1st New Jersey Cavalry and so under the command of the twenty-five-year-old brigadier general who

---

[182] Bruce Catton, *A Stillness at Appomattox*, Doubleday & Co., New York: 1952, p. 345.

was Sheridan's match for aggressiveness: George Armstrong Custer. Clark's duty wasn't glamorous: Custer's division was busy felling trees and laying them down to make corduroy roads for the rest of Sheridan's force as it came up, and among those troopers now on the move was another future Arroyo Grande resident, William Strobridge, part of the 1st Michigan Cavalry. Strobridge fought under yet another subordinate reflective of Sheridan's aggressiveness: Brigadier Gen. Thomas Devins had come to be called "Sheridan's hard hitter."

Lee understood how dire the threat of Sheridan was, so he dispatched cavalry forces and George Pickett's division, which had suffered so terribly at Gettysburg, to a little crossroads, Five Forks, to block the cavalry's way to the Weldon and Petersburg, or Southside, Railroad. Meanwhile, Sheridan put 9,000 troopers on the road to Five Forks with William Strobridge and his commander, Devin, in the lead. So it was Devin, on March 31, who discovered that Pickett's 12,000 Confederates had gotten in the way and set up a blocking position just outside the hamlet of Dinwiddie Court House. Devin's cavalry and Pickett's infantry fell on each other.

Earlier in the war, the notion of cavalry even attempting to take on a force of this size was ludicrous, but by 1865 Northern industry had provided a measure of equity: Sheridan's troopers were armed with breech-loading weapons like the Spencer carbine. Some of them may have even have had Henry lever-action repeating rifles (many Illinois regiments had them, including the 11th Illinois Infantry, in the Army of the Potomac's II Corps, a unit that included Arroyo Grande settler Joseph Brewer); although this new weapon lacked the range of a Springfield or Enfield muzzle-loading rifle, a trooper with a Henry could fire 15 shots in the same time it took the best infantrymen to shoot three.[183]

The 71st Illinois, like Joseph Brewer's 11th Illinois, was armed with the Henry rifle. Here, members of the 71st's color guard, with the regiment's mascot asleep at center, brandish their revolutionary new weapons. *Library of Congress.*

Unfortunately, Pickett's men *were* the best infantrymen, and Devin realized he was in over his head, so he had to ask for Sheridan's support. In the meantime, his cavalry retreated, but held Pickett and his men at arm's length, giving up ground slowly. Sheridan arrived to bolster Devin's

---

[183] Andrew L. Bresnan, "The Henry Repeating Rifle: The Weapon of Choice!" 2011, http://44henryrifle.webs.com/civilwarusage.htm

division and, typically, ordered Custer to launch a charge, Custer's specialty. This one was unintentionally comical because Custer's division had to charge across a field of Virginia mud. Had motion-picture cameras been available in 1865, Custer's men could have been filmed in what would appear to be slow motion. An exasperated Sheridan called them off. When night fell, Pickett had driven the cavalrymen back into, but not out, of Dinwiddie.

Both William Strobridge and Charles Clark would have enjoyed the next day, April Fool's, because its victim was George Pickett. During the night, Gen. Governeur Warren's V Corps infantry came splashing into Dinwiddie, and in the early afternoon, Strobridge, Clark, and Sheridan's cavalry fell on Pickett's left, just outside Five Forks, while Warren's infantry, after a delay of two hours caused by what Sheridan thought to be Gen. Warren's fussiness, fell on the Confederate right. Sheridan, who would dismiss Warren after the battle, would not tolerate slackness of any kind: during the day, a Union skirmisher was hit in the throat and collapsed near Sheridan, moaning that he'd been killed. Sheridan disagreed. The stumpy little general, leaning sideways in his saddle, glowered down at the fallen infantryman and admonished him to pick himself up and keep moving, which the chastened young man did. He moved forward a full thirty feet before he collapsed again. He had been killed, after all.[184] Pickett had no antidote for Sheridan's determination, for the firepower of the cavalry or for the weight of Warren's V Corps infantry, and his command was driven back. Three thousand Confederates were taken prisoner—another precious and irreplaceable loss for Lee—and even worse, Sheridan had the railroad that supplied Petersburg at his fingertips. Five Forks was the turning point of a campaign of turning points. Now Lee had to come out of his trenches.

---

[184] Foote, p. 872.

A Confederate casualty in the Petersburg trenches; an *abatis* is in the foreground. *Library of Congress.*

Grant wasn't willing to wait for Lee to make a run for it. Soon after he heard of Sheridan's success against Pickett, he ordered a general offensive all along the Petersburg trenchlines. The Third Battle of Petersburg began in the pitch-black pre-dawn of April 2, 1865. A Union army surgeon, watching the assault from a federal fort, could see nothing until the combined muzzle flashes of thousands of Confederate rifles lit the horizon the way a brush fire will when it crowns a hilltop. When a line of flashes went black again, the doctor knew that the Union assault had carried the Confederate entrenchments. [185] Adam Bair's 60th Ohio hit the Confederate left, where John B. Gordon, who'd led the

---

[185] Catton, p.362.

assault on Fort Stedman, was in command; Samuel McBane, 123rd Ohio, and Capt. George Purdy, 11th West Virginia, assaulted the center with Gen. Edward O.C. Ord's Army of the James; in Gen. Andrew Humphreys' II Corps, Joseph Brewer of the 11th Illinois and Sgt. Austin Abbott of the 7th Michigan hit Henry Heth and his men—Heth had been the general whose troops brought on the general engagement at Gettysburg on July 1, 1863—on the Confederate right.

Richmond, in ruins, April 1865. *National Archives.*

The Union assault led to the collapse of the Confederate defense, and the rapidity of that disintegration, after months of stalemate, stunned Union soldiers even more than it did the Confederates, including Austin Abbott's brigade commander, Col. William Olmsted. He reported that he'd "advanced the Seventh Michigan...and about twenty men of [the] First Minnesota, with telescopic rifles, to attack the fort [assigned his brigade]...At 8 a.m. Lieutenant-Colonel La Point reported that he captured the fort, also the one in the rear, and kept advancing by the left." In fact,

Abbott's brigade would continue moving by the left, headed west, in the direction the Confederates were retreating.[186] Along the way, the 7th Michigan bypassed Petersburg and might have seen the glow of the fires set to destroy stores in Richmond, just beyond. The war cry at the war's heady beginning had been "On to Richmond!" Now the city was irrelevant. Lee's army was headed west, marching fast, so there Grant's army would go.

What Lee needed was time and space between his men and Grant's, but for that, he had to feed his troops to buy the energy they would need to stay ahead of the surging Union armies. So he angled west and south—to the west, there was an as-yet untouched branch of the Southside Railroad at Amelia Court House. If he could meet a trainload of rations said to be headed there, his men could draw enough strength to head south where, in Lee's mind, what was left of the Army of Northern Virginia still had a chance, if they kept moving, to join Joseph Johnston and his army in North Carolina. Johnston was backpedaling in the face of Sherman's relentless northward march, while Lee was desperately trying to keep ahead of Grant and Ord, marching just behind him, with Northern men that were well-fed, fit, and almost smelling peace in the springtime air.

But Grant wasn't satisfied. He was still behind Lee, and he wanted to get out ahead of him. So the Union commander cut Sheridan loose and sent him pushing hard to the northwest. Sooner or later, Sheridan would get ahead of Lee's men and he would wait for them, impatient at the chance to kill more Confederates, and then Grant and the bulk of his army would come up to crush Lee's forces from behind.

---

[186] "Appomattox Reports of Colonel William A. Olmsted, Fifty-ninth New York Infantry, Commanding First Brigade," *The War of the Rebellion: A Compilation of the Official Records of the Union and Confederate Armies*, Volume XLVI, Part 1 (Serial Number 95), pp. 759-763.

Gen. Philip Sheridan, center, and his staff, 1864. The diminutive Sheridan had perhaps the strongest killer instinct of all of Grant's subordinates; he was determined to finish the war. *National Archives.*

After coming out of the trenches with soldiers who were elated to leave them, Lee wasn't interested in providing entertainment for Phil Sheridan. And, as desperate as the situation was, he wasn't interested in the self-indulgence of despair. He had to move his army 140 miles to link up with Johnston, but that march would take place on roads that the Army of Northern Virginia knew and Grant's army didn't. And, even though he was now down to fewer than 50,000 men, Lee could still deliver stinging blows to the Union troops who'd been stalking him for ten months now. At two sharp skirmishes, at Sutherland Station on April 2 and at Namozine Church on April 3, the Southerners staggered their pursuers and kept the Northerners at a reasonably safe

227

distance.[187] But what Lee's army now needed was food, and 350,000 rations awaited them at Amelia Court House.

The train was waiting for Lee's men when they arrived on April 4. Details eagerly began sliding open the freight cars' doors and the cars were packed. There was ammunition, weapons, harnesses, and saddles.

There was no food.

A crestfallen Lee, careful not to show his disappointment, still was forced to take hat in hand and appeal to the little town's citizens: "The Army of Northern Virginia arrived here today," he told them, "expecting to find plenty of provisions. But to my surprise and regret, I find not a pound of subsistence for man or horse." He pleaded for help, and he sent foraging parties and wagons out to the countryside. But the larders of Amelia Court House, after four years of war, were empty. So were the supply wagons that the weary horse teams brought back from nearby farms. Lee wouldn't have appreciated the provenance of the saying, but this was the kind of cruelty that Sherman meant when he spoke of war "as all cruelty. There is no use trying to reform it." His men were issued horse feed and tried to work their jaws around kernels of corn that were impenetrable.[188] At least they had the chance to rest as more Confederates came up to Amelia–Lee was forced to wait the rest of April 4 to allow his army to regroup– to take their turn in hearing the bad news. Lee had meanwhile telegraphed his urgent need for food and the next day would head west for Farmville, where the railroad could bring up a trainload of rations instead of harnesses, and then strike out for Lynchburg.

---

[187] Jay Winik, *April 1865: The Month that Saved America,"* Harper Perennial Books, New York: 2001, pp. 124-25.
[188] Randy Kraft, "Tranquil Setting of Appomattox Belies its Stormy History," Allentown *Morning Call*, April 11, 1993, http://articles.mcall.com/1993-04-11/entertainment/2923796_1_appomattox-court-house-civil-war-site-historic-appomattox-county

For the Confederates, the Appomattox Campaign was a death of a thousand cuts, and now misfortune fell on even their meager line of supply. On the morning of April 5, Charles Clark's 1st New Jersey Cavalry found a trailing Confederate supply train and, like a pride of lions singling out a herd's straggler, they pounced. They were met by a mixture of infantry and cavalry and quickly overwhelmed them. Before getting away just ahead of newly-arrived rebel forces, the New Jersey regiment burned 180 supply wagons.[189] The force that Clark and his regiment had encountered remains a source of controversy. Although official reports don't mention it, some of the soldiers in the supply train may have been African Americans. Lee had issued General Order #14 on March 23, calling for the recruitment of slaves who would be freed in return for their military service. A Confederate officer who arrived on the scene as the cavalry began its attack reported the presence of black soldiers, in "good gray uniforms," attempting to throw up breastworks with their rifles stacked nearby.[190] If that officer's account is true—and it's a controversial point among historians—it would show that not only had the 1st New Jersey deprived Lee of his supply train, but that some of the Union cavalrymen may have seen evidence that if the Army of Northern Virginia was starved for food, its general-in-chief was starved for soldiers.

But Grant was still losing soldiers, as well. 8,000 of his men had been killed, wounded or taken prisoner since the breakout from Petersburg. Now, he would lose 800 more, and among them was another Arroyo Grande pioneer, the 123rd Ohio's Samuel McBane. Since northern Virginia is so cut up by streams and rivers, securing fords or bridges became critical to both sides during the Appomattox Campaign. As Lee moved out of Amelia Court House, he

---

[189] Henry J. Pyne, *The History of the First New Jersey Cavalry*, J.A. Beecher, Publisher, Trenton, NJ: 1871, p. 308.
[190] "Black Soldiers in the Appomattox Campaign," National Park Service, https://www.nps.gov/apco/black-soldiers.htm

decided to head for the Appomattox River crossings. If he could get his army across and then destroy the bridges behind them, it would buy the time and space that the Confederates needed. For Lee and his men, one vital bridge on the Appomattox was High Bridge, a towering steel-and-brick span that had been built in the mid-1850s; a smaller wooden span paralleled it. Grant wanted his troops at that crossing before Lee could use it; Gen. Edward O. C. Ord ordered about 900 men from Samuel McBane's 123rd Ohio, the 54th Pennsylvania Infantry, and the 4th Massachusetts Cavalry to destroy the bridges. The raid would not end well for the federal forces.

High Bridge in a pre-war painting. *Album of Virginia.*

It was Lee's steadiest subordinate, James Longstreet, who heard reports of a federal force headed for High Bridge, so he detailed cavalry commanded by Brig. Gen. Thomas Rosser to destroy the approaching enemy, and to emphasize the importance of the mission to Rosser, Longstreet used words that so many Civil War commanders had grown far too fond of: Rosser was to eliminate the threat "if it took the last man of his command."[191]

So what Rosser brought with him to High Bridge were both grave instructions and, for one of the last times in the Civil War, a command that outnumbered the Union force, the one that included McBane. Rosser hit them hard, backing them up the bridge they were to destroy, and in a protracted firefight, the 123rd Ohio and the 54th Massachusetts began to run low on ammunition. In a desperate bid to help the infantry, the little party of horse soldiers, fewer than 80 troopers from the 4th Massachusetts Cavalry, barreled into the Confederates with a saber charge. They were cut down, including their gallant young commander, Col. Francis Washburn. Washburn's saber and sash went home to his mother. The 123rd Ohio went into Confederate custody: Rosser had saved the crossing and captured 800 Yankees in the process.

If capture was a terrible way for Samuel McBane to end the Civil War, the Confederate victory was fleeting. The Confederates crossed the Appomattox at the two bridges, but Union troops, including Austin Abbott's 7th Michigan Infantry, drove the Confederates off before they could destroy them. Now Grant, too, had a way across the Appomattox River. On the other side, as Lee continued his march toward Farmville and rations, three generals—Richard Anderson, William Mahone, and John Gordon—began to talk quietly among themselves. Perhaps the time had come for surrender; their men had been asked to march and fight to the limits of their endurance and beyond. They were falling

---

[191] Richard F. Welch, "Burning High Bridge: The South's Last Hope," *Civil War Times* Magazine, March/April 2007, http://www.historynet.com/burning-high-bridge-the-souths-last-hope.htm

asleep in their ranks as they moved along the roads. They had nothing left to give. It was agreed among the three that Anderson should broach the subject with the next man up the command ladder: James Longstreet.[192] In the meantime, there would be food at Farmville. There were hams there, and tin-foil packets of French soup, and cornbread and slabs of bacon whose aroma on a frying pan was the best restorative a soldier could hope for.[193]

During the Appomattox Campaign, Lee was losing high-ranking officers, not just private soldiers. Gen. A.P. Hill (left) was killed in action April 2; Richard Ewell was captured four days later. *National Archives.*

But what some Confederates would be gnawing on instead of bacon was living human beings, in one of the last and most vicious battles of the war, at Sailor's Creek. Here, on April 6, George Custer's cavalry, including Charles Clark, fresh off his regiment's destruction of the supply train, attacked a gap in the retreating Confederate columns led by James Longstreet. As infantry from two Union corps began to arrive, their men cheering Philip Sheridan at his

---

[192] Ibid
[193] Winik, p. 133.

appearance, the battle became general and it was fought with a ferocity, on the Confederates' part, that had to be borne of exhaustion, hunger, frustration, and fury. They turned on their pursuers and fought them without mercy in hand-to-hand combat that included clubbed muskets and bayonets, but then the Confederates dropped even their rifles to come in close with their tormenters: they used knives, fists, bit noses and ears, wrapped their fingers around their enemies' throats to choke them. Sailor's Creek was savage and intimate, and, of course, once their adrenaline had been exhausted, the hungry rebels could fight no more. April 6 ended with the surrender of nearly 8,000 of Lee's men, including six generals, including the man who, after Chancellorsville, had taken command of Stonewall Jackson's old corps, Richard Ewell. Lee, watching the rout from a distance, for once let his emotions surface: "My God!" he cried. "Has the army been dissolved?"

Combat artist Alfred Waud sketched Confederates surrendering in the face of a cavalry attack during the Appomattox Campaign. *Library of Congress.*

It was close to dissolution. Historian Jay Winik's description of Lee's retreat in his book *April 1865: The Month That Saved America* is stunning and approaches poetry in several passages. The one element that could keep this army together was rations, and Winik writes that, in suffering remindful of Napoleon's retreat from Moscow, an entire army was literally starving to death:

> ...unless they ate, moving at this grueling pace, their life expectancies could be measured in days and, for some men, in mere hours. As they marched, the Army of Northern Virginia tore branches off trees, fitfully gnawed at wild buds, or even peeled and ate the bark itself. Every sudden halt saw a new round of men, like dim, purgatorial souls, pitifully sink to their knees or senselessly wander off in search of food or restful escape of a long, deep sleep. Artillery mules collapsed, forgotten in roads turned liquid by the rain; wagons slid into muddy ruts and abruptly halted, sunk axle-deep and waterlogged, too heavy for the malnourished horses to pull them. They were immediately abandoned. And weary men discarded their weapons so as to have only themselves to drag along. In every direction the dead—men, mules and horses—began to litter the roadside.[194]

Still, the army made it to Farmville. Another train was waiting, and this time it carried food. Men cooked bacon in what must have been a dreamlike state and began to stuff themselves with big mouthfuls of cornbread while waiting for the bacon to fry up. Adding to the surreal feeling of the day was the presence of the pretty young women of Farmville Female College, who must have regarded Lee's filthy men with a mixture of compassion and horror. But the sight of teenaged girls would have lifted the spirits of the soldiers, and then there was the food, and then, before some of them could finish eating, before many could even begin to eat, Union cavalry began to arrive.

Before he gave up the town—Grant would bed down that night in a Farmville hotel—Lee got the trainload of

---

[194] Ibid., p. 131.

rations moving and so out of federal hands. His disappointed men would have to follow it and its 300,000 issues of rations to the next stop at Appomattox Station.[195]

On April 8, Custer got there first.

Wilmer McLean's home, Appomattox Court House, Virginia. *National Archives.*

It's doubtful that two men suffered more in the next hours than Lee and Grant. The enormity of the situation finally seemed to shake Lee's will. As the Army of Northern Virginia went to sleep the night of April 8 for the last time as

---

[195] "The Best Part of the Civil War...The End," Virginia State Parks, http://bestpartofthecivilwar.org/best-part/

an army at the county seat, the little town of Appomattox Court House, on every horizon the Southerners could see the glow of Union campfires. "I would rather die a thousand deaths," Lee murmured, but perhaps the time had come to respond to the courtly letters Grant had been sending across the lines, calling for negotiations to end the bloodshed.

Lee's crisis was spiritual, and Grant's was physical. At what should have been the pinnacle of Grant's life–the man deemed a failure and a drunkard was now about to become the man who had defeated the greatest American general since Washington– but he was tormented by a migraine headache. An aide with a message slipped into the room where the general-in-chief was supposed to be sleeping, found it empty and then found Grant, pacing outside with his head in his hands, suffering. The young man suggested a cup of coffee. Grant assented. It helped, the migraine, just a little. The next day's news would cure it.

At daylight on Sunday, April 9, 1865, in a last desperate attempt to break through the ring that surrounded the Army of Northern Virginia, Gen. John B. Gordon's command attacked Sheridan's men and pushed them back, but then the exhausted Confederates could not sustain their momentum, and beyond Sheridan's cavalry there were two infantry corps, spoiling for their turn. When Lee received word that not even Gordon could break through, he knew that his war was over. He asked Grant for a truce and a meeting.

At about 3:45, the two men met in Wilmer McLean's neoclassic brick home. McLean was the man whom the war had followed, because he had moved his family after the First Battle of Bull Run, fought in part on his farmland, to distance them from the violence. Now the war was ending in his parlor. There, Grant worked out details the surrender in his daily order book, working over a little table that would be confiscated later by Custer, with his usual brashness, as a gift for his beloved wife, Libby, a woman destined for a lifetime of elegant widowhood. Custer's commander (and Charles Clark's, and William Strobridge's) Philip Sheridan was there in the parlor, looking on. So was Edward O. C. Ord, the commander of Capt. George Purdy and the temporarily captured Samuel McBane. At one point, in an attempt to break the tension, Grant told Lee that he remembered him from their days fighting in Mexico; Lee sadly replied that he could not recall Grant, sixteen years his junior and therefore, in that war, a supporting player far down in the cast.

Lee is flanked by his son, Custis, left, and his aide Walter Taylor in a photograph taken at the war's end. *Library of Congress.*

Lee looked up intently and with relief at Grant as he read the surrender terms the Illinois soldier had written out in his order book. They were mild. The Confederates were to surrender their weapons, give their parole that they would not again rebel against the government of the United States, and then they were free to go home. In the meantime, Grant saw to it that 50,000 rations would be issued to Lee's starving men. There was one catch. Officers were allowed to take their horses home with them, but Grant had omitted enlisted men.

Lee commended Grant but asked if this part of the terms could not be re-written. Grant wrote rapidly and amended the surrender: Lee's enlisted men would be allowed to take the Army of Northern Virginia's tired horses and mules home with them.[196] It was, after all, time for spring planting, time for the new start that every spring promises.

---

[196] Robert Guisepi, ed., "The American Civil War: The End," http://history-world.org/appomattox.htm

Epilogue.
Starting Over

Morris Denham, a veteran of Sherman's campaigns, built this home on Ide Street in Arroyo Grande. *Author photo.*

A news item from the El Dorado, Kansas, *Republican,* Aug. 10, 1894:

Arroyo Grande is a very nice town, five miles inland, in one of the richest valleys in the state. Here they grow apples, peaches, apricots, nectarines, prunes, plums and berries in all kinds of profusion, besides grain, beans, corn and most vegetables in great abundance. The hill lands, not suitable for agriculture, afford a very luxuriant growth of rich, juicy grass which is grown during the

rainy season and cures on the ground during the dry season, which
not only increases its fattening properties and obviates the
necessity of putting up hay for stock except a limited amount for
dairy cows and work horses. . .One [Kansan] whose acquaintance I
have made and in whose magnificent prune and apricot orchard I
have been, cleared over a thousand dollars last year and expects to
do much better this year. . . Mr. Carpenter, of Chase county, is on
the highway to wealth, and many more might be.[197]

Arroyo Grande farmer Thomas Hodges, a veteran of
the 45th Missouri Infantry, shows off some Arroyo
Grande Valley produce in the early 1900s. *Courtesy
Bennett-Loomis Archives.*

The writer, John Jones, came to Arroyo Grande for his
health, which was improving, as well; the Carpenter brothers,
Chauncey and Emery, had moved from Chase County,

---

[197] El Dorado (Kansas) *Republican,* Friday, August 10, 1984, p. 2, accessed at
Newspapers.com March 6, 2016.

Kansas and were just getting established as farmers in Arroyo Grande. Glowing accounts like this weren't rare, and they appeared even in former Confederate states. This one, from the Anderson, South Carolina *Intelligencer,* appeared in 1888, as its writer was being given a tour in a sulky:

> Half way between Nipomo and Arroyo Grande we had a beautiful view of the Pacific. It is about five miles away. We could see the steamers moving slowly along to the great city of San Francisco...We reached Arroyo Grande about 2 o'clock. It is about 16 miles from Santa Maria, and is a beautiful little place. The population is about 600. The soil is very fine, and produces a great variety of crops. About the first person you meet is a Real Estate agent with tickets containing the following: 'Arroyo Grande Valley produces 60 to 80 tons of carrots, per acre; 40 to 50 tons of squashes, per acre; 2 ½ tons of beans, per acre; 300 sacks potatoes, per acre; 270-pound squashes, 100-pound beets, 5-pound onions, 10-pound potatoes, Irish. We challenge the world to equal this record.
>
> [The] Arroyo Grande Valley is in the southwestern part of San Luis Obispo County. The climate is as nearly perfection as possible...[198]

Farm fields, foreground, and the Santa Lucia foothills to the east, Upper Arroyo Grande Valley. *Author photo.*

---

[198] Anderson, South Carolina *Intelligencer,* Thursday, February 23, 1888, p.2, accessed at Newspapers.com March 6, 2016.

241

Mr. Jones suggests that the Arroyo Grande Valley is so rich that area farmers are tempted to be less industrious than their Chase County, Kansas, counterparts, but if one can avoid the temptation to slacken, fortunes can be made, like the one being built by Mr. Carpenter. Local farmers might strenuously and fairly object to that characterization. Farming in Arroyo Grande could be just as hard as it was anywhere else, and sometimes as dangerous as the war that the veterans had fought. Samuel B. Miller of the 24th Iowa survived Vicksburg and the 1864 Shenandoah Valley campaign only to be killed in 1902 by a bean cutter. While bringing in a crop in the Huasna Valley, the machine hit a snag, threw Miller forward, under his horses, which dutifully kept moving, pulling the bean cutter over him[199] It was a death as horrific

Two of Sherman's veterans would settle in the Arroyo Grande area: John Henry Alcott and his wife, Christena; Vitalis Runels, seen here wearing his Grand Army of the Republic badge. *Photos courtesy Tom Alcott and Ken Harders.*

---

[199] "Mangled by Bean Cutter," Los Angeles *Herald*, Vol. XXX, NO. 18, October 20, 1902.

as any on the battlefield.

But Jones's account was correct in some ways: the soil was rich, the climate was mild, and Arroyo Grande represented a chance for Union veterans—in the decade after the war, eight had already moved to Arroyo Grande or to the Huasna Valley[200]— to start a new life. For some, like the 47th Ohio's Vitalis Runels, it represented redemption.

Runels was an ambitious man. After his time with Sherman's army in the Georgia and Carolina campaigns, he'd gone home, gotten married, started a family and started a town. Runelsburg, Ohio, was his real-estate dream. It had agricultural potential and it had something else going for it. The railroad was coming, and the little village of Runelsburg, with couple of shops and a few homes, had the chance to become the city of Runelsburg. And then, as so often happened to postwar real-estate investors, the railroad was built somewhere else.

Vitalis Runels's hotel, today a bed and breakfast on East Dana Street in Nipomo. *Courtesy Ken Harders.*

---

[200] 1880 Federal Census, Arroyo Grande Township and Huasna, ancestry.com

Runels's dream didn't evaporate. He simply moved it to Nipomo, south of Arroyo Grande. By the 1890s, he was farming and had built The Runnels House Hotel (the family has since dropped one "n" in their surname), today, a bed and breakfast, and would live for the next 43 years in Nipomo. His four daughters and two sons would continue to establish the roots Vitalis had planted here. One descendant, Donald, was a war hero, killed in the sinking of the USS *Northampton* off Guadalcanal in 1942. Ensign Runels would have a destroyer escort named for him. Another descendant, also a farmer, Tom Runels, would serve as an Arroyo Grande city councilman.

Erastus and Mary Emilie Fouch and family, taken at about the time of the First World War, exemplify the hard work and prosperity of two generations. Their children (l-r): Frank, Harley, Anthony, Lillie, Edwin and Elby. Erastus, like Vitalis Runels, is wearing his G.A.R. badge. *Courtesy Jack English.*

The veterans who settled in Arroyo Grande did so at an opportune time. In 1881, the railroad did come here: the narrow-gauge Pacific Coast Railway, which originally consisted only of a horse-drawn line from the wharf at Port Harford, or Avila Beach, into San Luis Obispo, was extended to Arroyo Grande. The track crossed the creek on a trestle bridge and ran along the base of Crown Hill, where the high school that Gettysburg veteran Erastus Fouch wanted so much would be built fifteen years later.

Arroyo Grande, 1894. The "Boots and Shoes" sign to the right likely indicates the shop of veteran Thomas Whiteley. *Courtesy South County Historical Society.*

The railroad was vital, as a 1937 special edition of the weekly newspaper, the Arroyo Grande *Herald-Recorder* noted, because the postwar influx of veterans generated both a real-estate boom and a boom in crop production with, as a later newspaper article noted, no real connection to markets:

The old "El Camino Real," connecting the California missions with wheeled traffic by "caretas," those clumsy looking wagons with solid wood wheels hauled by oxen at a speed of no more than a mile an hour, constituted the means of transportation . The road was merely a dirt trail. The beasts of burden hauled produce to the sailing vessels, returning with New England and European supplies.[201]

The railroad's completion made large-scale vegetable and tree crop cultivation practicable and it generated consumerism—of items as diverse as farm equipment and little girls' dolls—thanks to Midwestern mail-order entrepreneurs like R.W. Sears. No one knew his rural patrons better than Sears, who made his catalogue slightly smaller than his major competitor's, Montgomery Ward. This meant that on parlor tables in farm homes as far away as Arroyo Grande, the Sears catalogue would always be on top. And few places *were* farther away than Arroyo Grande, at the edge of the Pacific.

This home, the oldest in Arroyo Grande, was built by Gettysburg veteran Bela Clinton Ide in the late 1870s or early 1880s. Ide is seen at right at about that time. *Photo courtesy Luci Stickler Fitzsimmons.*

---

[201]"Pacific Coast Railroad was Begun in the Year 1869," Arroyo Grande Valley *Herald-Recorder*, Jan. 6, 1937, Anniversary section, p. 2

Arroyo Grande was so isolated that Fred Jones, the grandson of Francis Branch, born on his grandfather's Rancho Santa Manuela in 1871, had never seen a train. One childhood memory centered on his first sight of the Pacific Coast Railway. When Jones and some ten-year-old companions saw their first locomotive, a little narrow-gauge engine coming through Corbett Canyon, they watched from atop a split-rail fence as long as they could stand it. Convinced that the engine was coming straight for them, they leaped off the fence and continued to watch it pass from a safer, and more distant, location, hiding in some hillside brush.

Another sign of progress: Dr. Charles Clark, a cavalry veteran, was making his Arroyo Grande house calls by automobile by the time this photo was taken, about 1912. Behind the wheel is a young woman, probably Dr. Clark's daughter, Lenora. *Courtesy the Bennett-Loomis Archives*

The prosperity of Jones's childhood town was tempered by cycles of economic stagnation that marked the postwar American economy. This sometimes resulted in acts of violence, particularly in 1886, as the nation was emerging from three years of recession. The frustrations the slump had generated were expressed in another sad American phenomenon that also comes in cycles, in xenophobia. On February 11, two days after massive anti-Chinese riots in Seattle had ended, 300 men, including "all the leading citizens and business men [sic] of this place" descended on Arroyo Grande's nascent Chinatown. The 1870 census counted 25 Chinese residents, nearly all Cantonese. The mob ordered them to leave.[202] Six weeks later, mob violence claimed a Lopez Canyon farmer, another immigrant, from Switzerland, named Peter Hemmi, and his fifteen-year-old son, P.J. The two were lynched from the Pacific Coast Railway bridge that spanned Arroyo Grande Creek. They were accused of killing a neighbor and wounding his wife in a shooting that was the climax of a simmering property dispute. The second terrifying PCRR episode of Fred Jones's young life came when he saw P.J., a boy his age, hanging from the bridge.

Violence was an anomaly in a little town that valued interdependence and community spirit. Evidence for this kind of cooperation comes from ranch logs kept by David Newsom. Newsom, like veteran Erastus Fouch, was an advocate for public education and, as the son-in-law of pioneer Francis Branch, a man of substance. A September 1872 entry notes that "Shaw [Missionary Ridge veteran Edward Shaw] and Newsom agree to fix the price the butter between themselves @ 25¢ per lb the year round." Many farmers got their start by leasing land from Newsom and making payments with their labor. A January 1876 entry shows Newsom crediting Paul Riel, a regular army veteran, and his sons $14.50 for five days' work for clearing the *monte*,

---

[202] "Ordered to Leave," Reno *Gazette-Journal,* 13 February 1886, p. 1.

the thick scrub that tangled farmland adjacent to the creek, and another $2.50 for planting strawberries. Newsom did the same with the area's lone Navy veteran, Bill Ash, who sometimes took payment, like a real sailor, in whiskey.[203] John Rice, the Sioux Uprising veteran, was instrumental in forming the Arroyo Grande Valley Water Company, which diverted the waters of the creek, via a wooden flume, to irrigate crops in the upper valley.[204]

A dapper Navy veteran, Bill Ash, poses in a San Luis Obispo studio in the 1880s. *Courtesy the Bennett-Loomis Archives.*

[203] Shirley Bennett Gibson, compiler, Newsom Ranch logs, 1872-1878.
[204] Aileen Nygaard, Assistant Planner, City of Arroyo Grande, "Historical Resource Designation: 756 Myrtle St. (Rice House), December 13, 2013.

By the turn of the century, the little town was flourishing. The local weekly, the Arroyo Grande *Herald,* later the *Herald-Recorder,* busied itself in 1898 with praise for the annual sweet pea fair ("A wealth of bloom, a glory of color and a Sea of Fragrance," the headline proclaimed)[205], a call for sidewalks, for a town fair to show off the bounty of the valley, and published, on the front page, the Address of Welcome delivered by Miss Edna Conrad on behalf of the high school's graduating Class of 1898.[206]

Erastus Fouch's farmhouse was near what is today's Lopez Drive, east of Arroyo Grande. *Courtesy of Jack English.*

Sometimes the Arroyo Grande Creek, which nurtured the farmland below the high school, built in 1896 atop Crown Hill, disrupted the harmony of the town. In 1911, a week of March rains ended with five inches falling in twenty-four hours. The banks beneath a corner of the Pacific Railway freight house washed away, leaving it poised

[205] Arroyo Grande *Herald,* June 25, 1898, p. 1.
[206] Arroyo Grande *Herald,* July 3, 1898, p. 1

precariously over the new, deeper channel left behind. Stables owned by the Steele family plummeted into the creek. Louis Routzahn, whose flower seed farms were an economic mainstay in the Arroyo Grande Valley, lost a barn, machinery shed, and a warehouse where, for several hours, his sons and some of his employees were stranded, surrounded by rising waters. Fields farmed by veterans Erastus Fouch and by the sons of the 2nd Iowa Infantry's Henry Bakeman were "badly cut up," and their crops destroyed.

Worst of all, a 14-year-old boy, Sam Cundiff, was drowned when the debris that had blocked the creek in a narrow channel collapsed, and a massive wave of water fell on the Cundiff family, their wagon and their two-horse team as they were attempting to ford the creek. The Cundiffs, one son, one daughter and a family employee were rescued; Sam was swept away.[207] The Valley wouldn't experience a disaster so devastating until the Great Depression, when San Luis Obispo County farm prices were halved between 1929 and 1933, from $12.7 to $6.4 million.[208] If the war was long over, 1911 demonstrated that the veterans' lives were not marked by everlasting peace.

As has been the case in the twentieth and twenty-first centuries, the single most effective advocate for the veterans would be the veterans themselves. The organization that represented the Civil War generation, the Grand Army of the Republic, was founded in 1866 Illinois and by 1890 claimed more than 400,000 members and included an auxiliary, the Women's Relief Corps.[209] The G.A.R. became a powerful political force cultivated by presidential candidates and was dedicated to providing modest pensions for veterans and their widows—John Rice received $4 a month; Eliza Bakeman,

---

[207] Arroyo Grande *Herald-Recorder*, March 11, 1911, p.1
[208] http://www.slocounty.ca.gov/Assets/AG/croprep/HistoricCropReports/Crop+Report+1933.pdf
[209] "Grand Army of the Republic History," http://www.suvcw.org/?page_id=167

Henry Bakeman's widow, received $8—and to establishing veterans' homes.[210]

The G.A.R.'s most enduring contribution may have been the annual observance of Decoration Day—today's Memorial Day—beginning in 1868. In early 20th century Arroyo Grande, that day was observed by the Col. Harper Post of the G.A.R., founded in 1880, with a parade from downtown to the town cemetery, typically by led a flag-bearer who was the senior of his contemporaries—Paul Riel, born in 1810 Germany, would have been a fatherly sergeant during his regular army regiment's wartime service.

A member of the women's auxiliary, Katie Dieffenbacher, remembered in a 1937 interview that the parade and the patriotic observance at the cemetery would be followed by a chicken dinner at the Grand Army Hall—across from the I.O.O.F. Hall on Bridge Street—where up to 150 participants would be served, including the members of the town band and the schoolchildren who'd accompanied the veterans in their parade.[211] Arroyo Grande seems to have been singular in the way it honored its veterans, giving them the validation many other aging Union soldiers longed for.

While local veterans attended statewide encampments in San Francisco and a Los Angeles G.A.R. delegation put in at Port Harford in 1886 for a tour of the area, it wasn't until 1897 that a countywide G.A.R. organizational meeting was held at Arroyo Grande's Methodist Campground on Wesley Way. Annual meetings, called "encampments," would be held for the next decade or more in Arroyo Grande, Pismo Beach, and at Sycamore Springs, near Avila Beach.

---

[210] Shirley Bennett Gibson, compiler, Civil War veterans' pensions recorded in the Arroyo Grande *Herald*.
[211] "Mrs. Katie Dieffenbacher, Member of Col. Harper Relief Corps for 42 Years," Arroyo Grande *Herald-Recorder*, 1887-1937 Commemorative Edition,

A G.A.R. encampment at Pismo Beach in the early 1900s. *Courtesy the Bennett-Loomis Archives.*

A 1910 San Luis Obispo *Tribune* story records that year's encampment. Timothy Munger recounted his experience in Libby Prison, songs like "Marching Through Georgia" were sung, and there was a recitation of Whittier's "Barbara Fritchie,"[212] the narrative poem celebrating a legendary 95-year-old Marylander who refused to take down her American flag as Lee's army marched through Frederick during the Antietam campaign. (In a 1943 visit to what is today Camp David, the half-American Winston Churchill regaled FDR with a recitation of the poem from memory.) The encampment featured a cross-section of Arroyo Grande: Bela Clinton Ide was the postmaster; Erastus Fouch's family owned the local soda works; Thomas Whiteley, a bootmaker, had a shoe shop; Timothy Munger was a justice of the peace; Adam Bair and William Lane farmed in the Huasna Valley;

---

[212] "Veterans Enjoy Days at Camp Stevenson," San Luis Obispo *Tribune*, August 9, 1910, p. 1.

253

Henry Bouchard and Charles Bristol farmed in Nipomo. The encampment that year ended with a promise to meet the following year in Pismo Beach. Over time, promises like that couldn't be kept.

🦅

The English-born Thomas Whiteley—another veteran who gave his name to a local street–died in 1898; members of the Harper Post of the G.A.R. accompanied the body of a comrade who now "was in the presence of the great Commander-in-Chief." Bela C. Ide 's obituary in 1922 noted a man known for "his quiet, amiable manner, he was the friend of every man, woman and child." When Otis W. Smith died at the Sawtelle veterans' home in 1923, the death announcement didn't reveal his secret—the Medal of Honor. Erastus Fouch died at his Upper Valley ranch three years later, "after a life of honor and integrity." Fouch was remembered as "a heroic figure of a man, over 6 feet tall, with clear-cut aquiline features, [who] wore his hair and beard in the old style. Grave and conservative of speech, he was a person to be noted." Among the last to die, in 1933, was the 45th Missouri Infantry's Thomas Hodges, who came to Arroyo Grande in 1878, when "the valley was a wilderness, but Mr. Hodges worked hard to clear the land which was later set out to fine apricot and walnut trees, and he became one of our most prosperous ranchers." There were only two G.A.R. members remaining to attend Hodges' funeral. The hearse was preceded by a large group representing a new generation of veterans, from the First World War; they carried the American and the American Legion flags. At graveside, a bugler played "Taps."[213]

Five years later, there was one more Gettysburg reunion, in 1938, when organizers were prudent in distancing the Union and Confederate encampments. Five years after that, Arroyo Grande's last veteran, Henry Bouchard, would die in the midst of World War II. The national G.A.R. would meet one time more, in August 1949, in Indianapolis. That last encampment was comprised of six Union veterans; the youngest was 99 years old. In 1954, the last combat soldier of the war, James Albert Hard of the 37th New York Volunteer infantry, died at 109.

He was the last survivor of a war that, in many ways, has survived his generation and many since. It left a legacy of battles that still needed to be fought for the "new birth of freedom" that Lincoln identified in two transcendent minutes at Gettysburg. Many of those battles have been fought, in the last seventy-five years, in the Old Confederacy, at Central High School in Little Rock, Arkansas, and at the Edmund Pettus Bridge in Selma, Alabama. Some of the fallen in this cause wouldn't be buried with honors and speeches; three young voting-rights workers were buried in an earthen dam in Neshoba County, Mississippi. Other battles would need to be fought across two oceans.

That is because, seventy-five years ago, not all the forces of reaction were American in origin. In January 1941, Medal of Honor winner Otis W. Smith's grandson, Johnnie, would enter an army belatedly preparing to fight an even more terrible war, this one against fascism. Hitler declared war near the end of that year, though he had no obligation to do so after the Pearl Harbor attack that had claimed two Arroyo

---

[213] Arroyo Grande *Herald* and *Herald-Recorder;* March 5, 1898; September 7, 1922; March 15, 1923; February 4, 1926; February 17, 1933.

Grande sailors on U.S.S. *Arizona*. The dictator was jubilant, thinking America decadent and Americans, in his simplistic and misshapen worldview, a "mongrel people."

A new generation of patriots went to war after Pearl Harbor, including three Robison brothers, members of a longtime Arroyo Grande family, here, finally home in 1945. (Left to right) John, U.S. Navy; Bob, U.S. Army; Hubert, a Navy medical corpsman with the U.S. Marine Corps. *Photo courtesy John Robison.*

Prime Minister Winston Churchill was said at the time to have been nearly as pleased as the parochial Austrian dictator was. Unlike Hitler, Churchill knew about Grant and Sheridan, knew what the Iron Brigade had done at Gettysburg, and knew as well what Jackson and his "foot cavalry" had done at Chancellorsville. Churchill was an avid student of American history and he admired Americans. After all, his mother, Jennie, had been born in Brooklyn.

Three thousand miles from Brooklyn, on the Pacific Coast, the Huasna Valley's Johnnie Otis Smith was preparing to go to war. He was just one of over three hundred young men and women from southern San Luis Obispo County who would join the military in World War II, including the Gularte brothers, Manuel and Frank, whose family came from the Azores, and the Fuchiwaki brothers, Hilo and Ben, whose family came from Japan. Thelma Murray, from nearby Oceano, would become a Marine in 1943 to honor the memory of her younger brother, George, killed on Tarawa. The Robisons, another pioneering Arroyo Grande family, sent three sons off to fight the war. So this, too, was a brothers' war, but in this war American brothers fought on the same side and under the same flag.

On December 7, 1941, the first CBS news bulletin would be broadcast to Californians at about 11:30 a.m. On hearing the news of the burning wrecks along Battleship Row, Arroyo Grande's families would have been shocked and somber at Sunday lunch, pushing listlessly at plates of food for which they had no appetite. That wasn't the mood a continent and an ocean away. In the depth of an English winter night. Winston Churchill was filled with hope. In an instant of clarity, he understood that now democracy would not—*could* not—perish from the earth.

Appendix.
Erastus Fouch Goes to War,
1861-62

Erastus Fouch about 1886. *Photograph courtesy of Jack English.*

Erastus Fouch enlisted in the 75ᵗʰ Ohio in December 1861 with his brother, Leonidas; Erastus was sixteen years old and Leonidas was eighteen. Their father and another brother would fight later in the war, in Tennessee; Erastus was the only survivor of the four. He moved to Arroyo Grande in 1886—about the time this photograph was taken.

Monterey, Highland County, Ohio, December 1861

This is the private diary of Erastus Fouch. His post office address, Elk, Vinton Co. Ohio. Was born in Washington County in the year of our lord A.D. 1845 and at the age of 16 volunteered December the 4ᵗʰ at Vinton station under captain George Fry for the term of three years. On the following Thursday Dec. the 19ᵗʰ, took the train at Vinton Station at 8 o'clock P.M. for Camp Wool, Athens Co. Ohio and arrived safely at camp…

Volunteer regiments commonly elected their company officers, a fact noted by Fouch:

December 16

Politicks runs high. Great electioneering going on today…

December 17

Politicks runs higher than ever [uncertain] Caldwell the proposed candidate for 1ˢᵗ Lieut.

December 23

Today just before dinner we drew our haversacks and canteens. Before breaking ranks, the Lieut (Caldwell) ordered us to hurry and eat our dinners and then strike tents and prepare to move. All things being in perfect readiness, at 4 o'clock we started for the depot, passing through the principal streets of Athens [Ohio]. Music playing. We was greeted by the ladies and gentlemen from almost every corner. Winding our way to the depot, we was soon on the spot and speedily embarked in the special train provide for us...We was on our way to Camp McLean [Ohio, near Cincinnati, where the regiment would train as a unit]. Passing swiftly from one station to another, we soon found our selves in the fond embrace of sleep on the cushioned seats of the cars.

A Union Army camp kitchen. The meal that Erastus Pouch and his friends put together must've been far better than the fare served here. *Library of Congress.*

January 1, 1862

This morning out mess agreed with seven messmates to have a new years dinner to be partaken of on the ground accordingly…various sums were subscribed amounting in the aggrigate to $6.00. The bill of fare were completed, composing nearly everything the best markets could afford. Lieuts. R.W. Caldwell and Rannells were invited and by common consent of all interested, Rev. T.A. Wolf was invited to…officiate at the head of the table.

The note was handed to him and his excellency readily accepted the proffered invitation and was promptly on hand at the appointed time. He occupied the head of the table and Lieut. Caldwell the opposite end and W. Rannells the right center. After all being ready the Dr. asked gods blessing after which we then proceded to devour the prepared sustainance.

January 14

Expressively cold cold today. Co. drill this forenoon.

January 15

Still cold. We drew our arms and equipment today (Enfield rifle)

Enfield rifles, of British manufacture, among Confederates killed at Fredericksburg during the Chancellorsville campaign, 1863. *Library of Congress.*

January 16

...The order forward march was a command by the Col. and the music started up old Yankey doodle, and away we marched through the crowded streets led by the bugler...Untill we reached the port and embarked on the steamer Telegraph, said to be the largest boat that ever made its way up to Parkersburg.

February 20 (Shenandoah Valley, Virginia)

This morning opens up with a snow storm. Raw air bad weather for marching. At 9 o'clock the Col. ordered battalion to forward march. About an hour by sun we halted in a nice open field or meadow near the wood. We then pitched our tents for the night. Soon the teams were on hand and plenty of good hay to sleep on so we rested very well.

"Yankee Doodle" would've been a popular air for a Union fife and drum corps like this one. *Wikimedia Commons.*

February 23

...The col. gave us a few orders extraordinary or rather a word of caution. He said Fellow Soldiers: Up to this date our regiment has born a good reputation and I am sorry to announce to you that on yesterday that reputation was some what injured.

Now I wish it understood...that here after their shall be no foraging or pillaging what ever...and in the future if I hear of any one taking what does not belong to him he shall be severly punished...

...One thing more I wish to make mention of their shall be no straggling. You must necessarily keep in ranks for we are now getting into an enemies country and stragglers are liable at any time to be cut off. Now I wish those orders to be obeyed…

February 24

4 of our company is left in the Beverly hospital sick with the measles. Roads rather better today than formerly have been. For the first few miles we made very good time. Today we passed some of the finest country I have seen since I have been in via.

April 1

This is all fools day and the boys commenced to take advantage of it early. Today we got our pay for which we feel truly thankful…Talk of forward movement but believe it all to be gammon [gossip].

April 7

Early this morning the bugle sounded for us to get ready. The indications are that we have foul weather. Suffice it to say that this morning we ate a scanty breakfast, for our team has not yet come to hand. Soon we was on our way in persuit of the enemy. 3 miles up and we come to where the secesh had burned the bridge.

April 19

This morning we was awakened from our slumber by orders from our Lieut. To get up from our sleep and be ready to march in 5 minutes for the enemy was advancing toward

Monterey [in Highland County, Virginia]. Soon we was up and ready to march. Our knap sacks were left behind in the care of _____ so we had nothing to carry but our equipage. Without a bite of breakfast we soon was in to the line and of on a force march...

Some six miles were gained in about two hours and then into line of battle, so a stop be ready should the enemy appear in sight...Soon the rebels attacked our pickets and general firing ensued...Our men fought bravely and well deserve the name of praise for their honor and conduct while engaged. The contest lasted about two hours and a half. By this time the cannon opened fire on them and made them retreat in a hury...

May 8, 1862

The Battle of McDowell, Virginia, pitted two brigades commanded by John C. Fremont—as an explorer, Fremont and his party had camped near the site of John Rice's house, across the Arroyo Grande Creek from the old high school playing fields at the base of Crown Hill. The brigade that included Fouch's 75th Ohio attacked Thomas J. "Stonewall" Jackson's troops who held a position on a hillside.

...About 10 o'clock, the long roll was beat and soon we was into line of battle. About noon the rebels made their appearance on a distant hill perhaps a mile off. Our cannons opened fire on them and cannonaded them until 4 o'clock...[we] were ordered out on the field. Now the battle commenced. Volley after volley was fired in [rapid] succession of intervals of hardly a second at best. Bullets flew around our heads as thick as hail. The parties were about 200 yards to 900 apart. The force of the enemy was...strong and our force _____. The old 75th fought desperately as well as bravely with Gen. McIlroy in command. Gen Schenck and his men has arrived...the contest lasted about 4 hours and then the firing ceased.

Co. I one killed and two wounded. My Brother Leonidas fell to rise no more.

The regiment lost 87 killed, wounded and missing at the Battle of McDowell. Erastus does not mention his brother again.

Appendix II
Our Confederates

There are few things historians love more than learning new things, even if it might be at their own expense. This true of the book *Patriot Graves,* as well. Since its publication in 2016, local groups of Confederate descendants have researched and found the graves of at least six Confederate veterans who lie amid the graves of their one-time foes in the Arroyo Grande District Cemetery. Many thanks to historian Barron Smith, Robert Peak of the Sons of the Confederacy, Mary E. Hall of the United Daughters of the Confederacy, and, again, cemetery superintendent Mike Marsalek who, armed with this new information, has identified the graves of Confederate soldiers and potential Confederate soldiers.

Records from the National Park Service registry of Civil War veteran confirm the service of four of these soldiers:

- Thomas Melton Duke, Co. K, 32nd Arkansas Infantry, 1823-1902
- Russell R.R. Holmes, Co. A, Duckworth's Tennessee Cavalry, Unknown-1883
- James Anderson Johnson, Co. I, 16th Missouri Infantry, 1841-Unknown
- Lucius B. Nichols, Co. D. 24th Georgia Infantry, Unknown-1932

Nothing is more illustrative of the tragedy of the Civil War than the experience of Lucius B. Nichols. Born in North Carolina, his family moved to Georgia when Lucius was a toddler; he was fifteen years old when he enlisted in the 24th

Georgia Infantry in August, 1861—sadly, his mother would die less than a year later, at thirty-six. By that time, Pvt. Nichols and the 24th had been badly bloodied at the Seven Days Battles during McClellan's Peninsular Campaign and in the Antietam Campaign, where, at Crampon's Gap, they lost forty-three percent of the 292 men engaged. The 24th was among helping to block elements from the Army of the Potomac that were seeking to penetrate the gap, a pass in South Mountain, and then fall on the flanks of Lee's forces as they moved north. Lee would eventually gather his army at Sharpsburg, along Antietam Creek.

Two months later, what was left of the decimated 24th was behind a stone wall on Marye's Heights At Fredericksburg. The regiment's position was marked by its regimental flag, which bore a curious addition: sewn onto the red, white and blue Stars and Bars was a gold harp, reflective of a region in Georgia and a regiment with a significant population of Irish immigrants. Indeed, Lucius Nichols' regimental commander at Fredericksburg was County Antrim-born Col. Robert McMillan, a former state senator, who became brigade commander when his predecessor, Gen. Thomas Cobb, was killed on the heights by a shell fragment.

It would be the commander of the Union's Army of the Potomac who would do most of the killing at Fredericksburg. On Decemer 13, 1862, Ambrose Burnside ordered his men, organized into what he called "Grand Divisions," to advance on Lee's Confederates on their high ground atop Marye's Heights. The slaughter the Confederates inflicted would provoke one of the war's most famous quotes. On watching the Union soldiers falling in their ranks on the plain below, Lee was shocked. "It is well that war is so terrible," he said in aside to James Longstreet, "otherwise we would grow too fond of it."

Burnside's doomed assault on Marye's Heights, in the distance, at Fredericksburg. *Library of Congress.*

It was the 24th Georgia that inflicted much of the carnage that the two Confederate generals were witnessing, but it was also one of the Irish-born Robert McMillan's finest moments. He was later described as walking coolly up and down the ranks of his men as they crouched behind the stone wall, counseling patience, reminding them to hold their fire. At the last possible moment, McMillan ordered his men, including the 24th, to stand up and fire, virtually into the faces of their enemies. "Give it to them now, boys!" he shouted. "Now's the time! Give it to them!"

In many cases, their enemies were also their kinsmen. The unit closing in on McMillan's section of the stone wall was made up of soldiers from the Irish Brigade, made up almost entirely of Famine immigrants whose families had settled in New York, Pennsylvania, or Massachussets. McMillan knew it; he had seen, in a glance over the stone wall, the green battle flag of the 28th Massachusetts. The results were terrible:

every officer in the 69th New York, a regiment whose fame would extend into its service in World War I, was killed. But although the Brigade would continue to fight and would distinguish itself in the Wheatfield at Gettysburg, the Georgians had shattered it that day. Nearly 1400 of them went into battle at Fredericksburg; eight weeks later, only 340 were available for duty.

Troops, including McMillan's Georgians, fire from behind the stone wall at Fredericksburg in this 1894 illustration. *Library of Congress.*

The ordeal wasn't over for Nichols and the 24th Georgia, either. The regiment had only begun to see the worst of the war: Chancellorsville, Gettysburg, the terrible slaughter at The Wilderness, Spotsylvania, Cold Harbor, Petersburg and, finally, Appomatox lay before them. It was at Appomattox where the sixty survivors, four officers and fifty-six enlisted men, surrendered. Young Union officers cut pieces from their battle flag, with its Irish harp, for souvenirs.

Works Cited

"8th Ohio Cavalry," http://www.ohiocivilwar.com/cwc8.html

"25th Ohio, Company B."
http://freepages.history.rootsweb.ancestry.com/~cemeteryprojec
t/25th/CoB.html

"75th OVI Notes,"
http://www.cwrumblings.info/Articles/75OVINotes.pdf

"75th Regiment Ohio Volunteer Infantry, 1861-65," Ohio Civil War
Central,
http://www.ohiocivilwarcentral.com/entry.php?rec=1142

"95th Regiment Ohio Volunteer Infantry," Ohio Civil War Central,
2016, Ohio Civil War Central. 12 Feb 2016
http://www.www.ohiocivilwarcentral.com/entry.php?rec=890

"130th Pennsylvania Volunteer Infantry Monument"
.http://www.nps.gov/anti/learn/historyculture/mnt-pa-130.htm

"1862 Dakota War: Minnesota's Other Civil War,"
http://www.exploringoffthebeatenpath.com/Battlefields/Dakota
War/index.html

"1865 May 29: Edwin Levings on The Grand Review — 'The
moments of that day will long linger in the memories of our
boys,'" The Civil War and Northwest Wisconsin, May 29, 2015.
https://thecivilwarandnorthwestwisconsin.wordpress.com/

1870, 1880, 1900, 1910 Federal Census, Arroyo Grande Township and
Huasna, ancestry.com

Adam Bair obituary, posted May 2, 2013, Ancestry.com,
http://mv.ancestry.com/viewer/60b4d97b-28c8-4d1a-bdc1-
85c0fc9069dd/51511777/13212990675

Adams, Michael. *Living Hell: The Dark Side of the Civil War*, Johns
Hopkins University Press, Baltimore: 2014.

Adelman, Gary and Daniel Landsman, "East Cemetery Hill:
Confederates on the Crest," The Civil War Trust.
http://www.civilwar.org/battlefields/gettysburg/gettysburg-
history-articles/east-cemetery-
hill.html?referrer=https://www.google.com/2014.

Alberts, Don. "The Battle of Glorieta: Union Victory in the Far
West," The Civil War Trust,

http://www.civilwar.org/battlefields/glorietapass/glorieta-pass-history-articles/glorietaalberts.html

Alexander, Edward. "Life of the Civil War Soldier in Battle: And Then We Kill," *Hallowed Ground* Magazine, Winter 2013, http://www.civilwar.org/hallowed-ground-magazine/winter-2013/life-of-the-civil-war-soldier-battle.html?referrer=https://www.google.com/

Anderson, South Carolina *Intelligencer*, Thursday, February 23, 1888, p.2, accessed at Newspapers.com March 6, 2016.

Angel, Myron. *History of San Luis Obispo County*, Thompson and West, Oakland: 1883.

"Appomattox Reports of Colonel William A. Olmsted, Fifty-ninth New York Infantry, Commanding First Brigade," *The War of the Rebellion: A Compilation of the Official Records of the Union and Confederate Armies*, *Volume XLVI*, Part 1 (Serial Number 95).

Arnold, Ralph and Robert Anderson, *Geology and Oil Resources of the Santa Maria Oil District, Santa Barbara County, California*, United States Geological Survey, Government Printing Service, Washington D.C., 1907.

Arroyo Grande *Herald* and *Herald-Recorder;* March 5, 1898; June 25, 1898; July 3, 1898; March 1, 1911; September 7, 1922; March 15, 1923; February 4, 1926; February 17, 1933.

Bailey, Anne J. *The Chessboard of War: Sherman and Hood in the Fall Campaign of 1864*, University of Nebraska Press, Lincoln: 2000, p. 5.

Bailey, Donald S. and the Editors of Time-Life Books, *Battles for Atlanta: Sherman Moves East*, Time-Life Books, Alexandria, Virginia: 1985, p. 43.

Bartleson, Frederick A. *Letters from Libby Prison*, books.google.com/books/about/Letters_from_Libby_Prison.html?id=SF8fAQAAMAAJ

Basset, Thomas "Sherman's Southern Sympathies," New York *Times*, January 17, 2012, http://opinionator.blogs.nytimes.com/2012/01/17/shermans-southern-sympathies/?_r=0

Bengston, Wayne. "Sherman Loses his 'Right Bower,' About North Georgia, http://www.aboutnorthgeorgia.com/ang/James_Birdseye_McPherson

"Black Soldiers in the Appomattox Campaign," National Park Service, https://www.nps.gov/apco/black-soldiers.htm

Bollet, Alfred J. "The Truth about Civil War Surgery," *Civil War Times Magazine*, October 2004, http://www.historynet.com/the-truth-about-civil-war-surgery-2.htm

Bresnan, Alfred L. "The Henry Repeating Rifle: The Weapon of Choice!" 2011, http://44henryrifle.webs.com/civilwarusage.htm

Brigg, Greg. "The Battle of Nashville: The Crushing Blow of a Forlorn Hope," *Hallowed Ground* Magazine, Winter 2014, http://www.civilwar.org/hallowed-ground-magazine/winter-2014/the-battle-of-nashville.html

Brown, Alonzo. "Battle of Champion's Hill," *History Of The Fourth Regiment of Minnesota Infantry Volunteers During The Great Rebellion, 1861-1865*, St. Paul, Minn., The Pioneer Press Company, 1892, http://battleofchampionhill.org/brown.htm

Brown, Dee. *Bury My Heart at Wounded Knee*. Holt, Rinehart and Winston: New York: 1970.

Brumgardt, John R. ed. *Civil War Nurse: The Diary and Letters of Hannah Ropes*, The University of Tennessee Press, Knoxville: 1980.

Carpenter, Alfred. "Letter on the Battle of Gettysburg," A Civil War Journal: Company K, 1st Minnesota Volunteer Infantry Regiment at Gettysburg, July 1-4 1863. Winona County Historical Society, 1998.

Catton, Bruce. *The Army of the Potomac: A Stillness at Appomattox*, Doubleday, New York: 1953.

--. *The Army of the Potomac: Glory Road*. Doubleday & Co., Garden City, New York: 1952.

Cave, R.C. "Dedicatory Remarks, Soldiers' and Sailors' Monument, May 30, 1894," Southern Historical Society Papers, Volume 22. Reverend J. William Jones, Ed. http://www.perseus.tufts.edu/hopper/text?doc=Perseus%3Atext%3A2001.05.0280%3Achapter%3D1.27%3Asection%3Dc.1.27.198

"Civil War Defenses of Washington," National Park Service, http://www.nps.gov/cwdw/learn/historyculture/president-lincoln-under-direct-fire-at-fort-stevens.htm

"Civil War Diseases," http://www.civilwaracademy.com/civil-war-diseases.html

"Civil War Quotes," http://www.21stmichigan.us/quotes.htm

Clarke, Isaac. "Sand Creek Memoir—'All One-Sided,'" Colorado
College Special Collections.
https://sites.coloradocollege.edu/ccspecialcollections/2013/09/
11/isaac-clarkes-memoir-of-the-sand-creek-massacre/

Coen, Joel and Ethan. *True Grit*, Screen adaptation by based on the
book by Charles Portis, http://moviecultists.com/wp-
content/uploads/screenplays/true-grit.pdf

"Dan Sickles's Temporary Insanity,"
http://www.murderbygaslight.com/2009/10/dan-sickless-
temporary-insanity.html. November 2009

Davis, Burke. *Sherman's March*, Vintage Books, New York: 1988..

Davis, Stephen. "Cheatham Hill," The Civil War Trust,
http://www.civilwar.org/battlefields/kennesawmountain/kennes
aw-mountain-history-articles/cheatham-
hill.html?referrer=https://www.google.com/

"Death of Captain Charles H. Bruce," Montgomery County, Indiana,
Civil War History, June 12, 2015,
https://mccw.wordpress.com/category/58th-indiana-infantry/

"Death of E.S. Shaw," San Luis Obispo *Breeze*, Feb. 4, 1902.

"Did the Battle of Gettysburg really begin as a search for shoes?"
www.todayifoundout.com. March 9, 2015.

Drake, Rebecca Blackwell. "The Battle of Champion Hill,"
http://battleofraymond.org/history/chill1.htm

Drury, Bob and Tom Clavin. *The Heart of Everything That Is: The Untold
Story of Red Cloud, An American Legend*, Simon and Schuster, New
York: 2014.

El Dorado (Kansas) *Republican*, Friday, August 10, 1984, p. 2, accessed
at Newspapers.com March 6, 2016.

Ellis, John H. "History of the 60th O.V.I. of 1864," Sept. 1890,
http://freepages.genealogy.rootsweb.ancestry.com/~volker/hist
ory/civilwar/memoirs/60thmemellis.html

Emmons, W.B. Diary, 1864-65, University of Iowa Special
Collections,
http://128.255.22.135/cdm/ref/collection/cwd/id/1688

"Erastus Fouch," ancestry.com.
http://person.ancestry.com/tree/983870/person/549903464/fac
ts

"Faces of Friends," *The Temple Artisan*, Vol. X No. 3 August 1909.

Faust, Drew Gilbin. *This Republic of Suffering: Death and the American Civil War.* Vintage Books: New York, 2008.

"Fighting Tom Sweeney," http://www.aohdiv1.org/sweeney.html

Foote, Shelby. *The Civil War, A Narrative. Vol. III: Red River to Appomattox.* Vintage Books: New York, 1986.

Freeman, Douglass Southall. *Lee's Lieutenants, Volume 3: Gettysburg to Appomattox.* Charles Scribner's Sons: New York: 1972

Gary, Alex. "Military 'miracle' part of history of 74th Illinois," Rockford Register Star, Sept. 20, 2009, http://www.rrstar.com/article/20090920/News/309209925

"General Order No. 8, Army of the Potomac, July 29, 1864," *Record of the Court of Inquiry on the Mine Explosion during The Battle of the Crater, July 30, 1864,* http://www.beyondthecrater.com/resources/ors/vol-xl/part-1-sn-80/or-xl-p1-004-coi-mine-explosion-battle-of-the-crater-july-30-1864/

"General William Rosecrans' Report at the Battle of Chickamauga," https://historyengine.richmond.edu/episodes/view/5179

"George Henry Purdy," ancestry.com

"Gettysburg: The Correspondence From the Famous Story of Lieutenant Bayard Wilkeson, Killed at Gettysburg." http://www.raabcollection.com/civil-war-autograph/civil-war-signed-gettysburg-correspondence-famous-story-lieutenant-bayard#sthash.y7l08iUv.dpuf

Gibson, Shirley Bennett, compiler. Civil War veterans' pensions recorded in the Arroyo Grande *Herald.*

Gibson, Shirley Bennett, compiler. Newsom Ranch logs, 1872-1878.

Goodwin, Doris Kearns. *Team of Rivals: The Political Genius of Abraham Lincoln.* Simon and Schuster, New York: 2005, p. 654.

Goss, Troy B. "Pvt. Isaac Dennis Miller," Troy's Genealogue, http://genealogue.net/millcivwar.html

"Grand Army of the Republic History," http://www.suvcw.org/?page_id=167

Grinspan, Jon. "How Coffee Fueled the Civil War," New York *Times,* July 9, 2014, http://opinionator.blogs.nytimes.com/2014/07/09/how-coffee-fueled-the-civil-war/?_r=0

Guisepi, Robert, ed. "The American Civil War: The End," http://history-world.org/appomattox.htm

Hartwig, D. Scott. "I can't tell you what we suffered" Prisoners, Part 2 – A Union Story," From the Fields of Gettysburg: The Blog of Gettysburg National Military Park. November 29, 2012. https://npsgnmp.wordpress.com/2012/11/29/i-cant-tell-you-what-we-suffered-prisoners-part-2-a-union-story/

Haskew, Michael. "Bragg versus Rosecrans: Profiles in Generalship at Stones River," *America's Civil War* Magazine, January 1997, http://www.civilwar.org/battlefields/stonesriver/stones-river-history/bragg-rosecrans.html

Higham, Carol. *The Civil War and the West: The Frontier Transformed,* Praeger Books: Santa Barbara, California: 2013.

"Historic Crop Reports, San Luis Obispo County." http://www.slocounty.ca.gov/Assets/AG/croprep/HistoricCrop Reports/Crop+Report+1933.pdf

Hoig, Stan. *The Sand Creek Massacre,* University of Oklahoma Press, Norman: 1974.

Homstad, Daniel. "Abraham Lincoln: Deciding the Fate of 300 Indians Convicted of War Crimes in Minnesota's Great Sioux Uprising," *American History Magazine,* December 2001. http://www.historynet.com/abraham-lincoln-deciding-the-fate-of-300-indians-convicted-of-war-crimes-in-minnesotas-great-sioux-uprising.htm

"How it Started," The Sioux Uprising of 1862. http://www.d.umn.edu/~bart0412/project.htm

"How the Civil War Soldiers Marched," http://www.civilwarhome.com/soldiersmarch.html

"In Search of a Southern Manifest Destiny: Sibley's Brigade – The Confederate Army of New Mexico," Thoughts, Essays, and Musings on the Civil War: A Civil War Historian's Views on Various Aspects of the American Civil War, January 13, 2012, https://bobcivilwarhistory.wordpress.com/2012/01/13/in-search-of-a-southern-manifest-destiny-sibleys-brigade-the-confederate-army-of-new-mexico/

"James A. Dowell," Register, Sawtelle Home for Disabled Veterans, Los Angeles, CA, http://interactive.ancestry.com/1200/MIUSA1866_113910-00655?pid=249017&backurl=http://person.ancestry.com/tree/9 147826/person/-548408604/gallery&usePUB=true&_phsrc=uub9&usePUBJs=tr ue

"John B. Gordon," http://www.brotherswar.com/Antietam-Gordon.htm

"John M. Chivington." PBS *The West.*
https://www.pbs.org/weta/thewest/people/a_c/chivington.htm

"Joseph S. Brewer," Register of Officers and Men of New Jersey in the Civil War 1861-65.

Jordan, Brian Matthew. *Marching Home: Union Veterans and their Unending Civil War,* Liveright Publishing, New York: 2014.

Krick, Robert. "Like Chaff Before the Wind: Stonewall Jackson's Mighty Flank Attack at Chancellorsville," The Civil War Trust. http://www.civilwar.org/battlefields/chancellorsville/chancellors ville-history-articles/flankattackkrick.html

Krieger, Daniel, "Civil War-era postmaster helped keep California in the Union," San Luis Obispo *Tribune,* October 6, 2012. http://www.sanluisobispo.com/news/local/news-columns-blogs/times-past/article39425256.html

Lee, Chulhee. "Military Service and Economic Mobility: Evidence from the American Civil War," February 2010. http://www.sciencedirect.com/science/article/pii/S00144983120 00046

Leigh, Phil. "Who Burned Atlanta?" New York *Times,* November 13, 2014, http://opinionator.blogs.nytimes.com/2014/11/13/who-burned-atlanta/

"Letter from Edwin D. Levins," 12th Wisconsin Infantry, December 18, 1864, Civil War Voices, http://www.soldierstudies.org/index.php?action=view_letter&Le tter=588

Linder, Douglas O. "The Dakota Conflict Trials," http://law2.umkc.edu/faculty/projects/ftrials/dakota/Dak_acco unt.html

Loomis, Patricia and Mary Mueller, *The Settlers of Arroyo Grande,* California, CreateSpace Publishing, 2014.

Los Angeles *Herald,* Oct. 20, 1902; Feb. 28, 1908, p. 7; Sept. 24, 1906, p. 10; Oct. 15, 1905, p. 7, June 19, 1909.

Mangus, Mike. "The Fifty-Fifth Ohio Volunteer Infantry," January 17, 2014. http://www.ohiocivilwarcentral.com/entry.php?rec=1183

"March to the Sea: Ebenezer Creek," Georgia Historical Society, http://georgiahistory.com/ghmi_marker_updated/march-to-the-sea-ebenezer-creek/

Marszalek, John F. "Scorched Earth: Sherman's March to the Sea," *Hallowed Ground* Magazine, Fall 2014, http://www.civilwar.org/hallowed-ground-magazine/fall-2014/scorched-earth.html

Middlecamp, David. "Photos from the Vault," San Luis Obispo *Tribune*, May 8, 2001.

Morrison, Annie and John Haydon, "Erastus Fouch," *The History of San Luis Obispo County and Environs*. Historic Record Company, Los Angeles, CA: 1917, p. 573.

"My God! We are attacked! Disorganized surprise at Shiloh Church," Civil War *Daily Gazette*, April 6, 2012, http://civilwardailygazette.com/my-god-we-are-attacked-disorganized-surprise-at-shiloh-church/

Nygaard, Aileen, Assistant Planner, City of Arroyo Grande. "Historical Resource Designation: 756 Myrtle St." (Rice House), December 13, 2013.

"No Man Can Take Those Colors and Live." The Civil War Trust, http://www.civilwar.org/battlefields/gettysburg/gettysburg-2011/the-battle-for-herbst-woods.html

Oxley, James. "A History of Company H 24th Iowa Volunteer Infantry" http://battleofchampionhill.org/oxley.htm

"Pacific Coast Railroad was Begun in the Year 1869," Arroyo Grande *Herald-Recorder*, Jan. 6, 1937, Anniversary section, p. 2

Parker, L.N. *History and Genealogy of the Ancestors and Descendants of Captain Israel Jones who removed from Enfield to Barkhamstead, Conn., in the year 1759*. Laning Co, Norwalk, Ohio: 1902, Ancestry.com.

Pfanz, Harry. *Gettysburg—Culp's Hill and Cemetery Hill*. University of North Carolina Press, 2011.

Prezelski, Tom. "California and the Civil War: 1st Battalion of Native Cavalry, California Volunteers," California State Military Museum, http://californiamilitaryhistory.org/1stNatCavCV.html

"Private Erastus Fouch," http://www.findagrave.com/cgi-bin/fg.cgi?page=gr&GRid=55097035&ref=acom. July 18, 2010.

Pyne, Henry J. *The History of the First New Jersey Cavalry*, J.A. Beecher, Publisher, Trenton, NJ: 1871.

"Reconstructed comparative time table for the day of 25 Nov. 1863," The Battles for Chattanooga 23, 24, and 25 Nov. 1863, http://www.aotc.net/Chattanooga.htm#timetable

Rector, Matthew. "Lost by Co E 58th Indiana at Chickamauga," Aug 7, 2009, http://www.authentic-campaigner.com/forum/archive/index.php/t-24215.html

Reeves, Frank. "The Burning of Atlanta, Seared into America's Memory," Pittsburg *Post-Gazette*, August 31, 2014, http://www.post-gazette.com/local/city/2014/08/31/The-burning-of-Atlanta-seared-into-America-s-memory/stories/201408310090

Reno *Gazette-Journal*, 13 February 1886.

"Report of John Maxwell, Secret Service, Confederate States, of explosion at City Point, December 16, 1864," The Siege of Petersburg Online, http://www.beyondthecrater.com/resources/ors/vol-xlii/part-1-sn-87/number-375-petersburg-campaign-report-of-john-maxwell-secret-service-confederate-states-of-explosion-at-city-point/

"Reports of Colonel Andrew L. Harris, Seventy-fifth Ohio Infantry, commanding regiment and Second Brigade," July 5, 1863. http://www.civilwarhome.com/harrisgettysburgor.html

"Richard P. Merrill," http://opinionator.blogs.nytimes.com/2014/07/09/how-coffee-fueled-the-civil-war/?_r=0

Roster of the 75th Ohio Volunteer Infantry Regiment, http://www.civilwarindex.com/armyoh/rosters/75th_oh_infantry_roster.pdf

San Francisco *Chronicle*, Dec. 12, 1912.

San Luis Obispo *Breeze*, October 28, 1901, Oct. 7, 1911.

Schultz, Duane. *Over the Earth I Come: The Great Sioux Uprising of 1862.* St. Martin's Press, New York, 1992.

Scott, Douglas. *Uncovering History: The Legacy of Archaeological Investigations at the Little Bighorn Battlefield National Monument*, United States Department of the Interior; Lincoln, Nebraska: 2010.

Sears, Stephen W. *Chancellorsville*, Mariner Books, New York: 1996.

-- *Gettysburg*. Houghton-Mifflin Co., Boston and New York: 2003, p. 189.

"Sgt. Thomas Brown Provides His Mother with an Eyewitness Account of the Disastrous Battle of the Crater," Aug. 1, 1864,

http://www.rhinelander.k12.wi.us/faculty/rhslibrary/globalstudi
es/Letter%202%20-%20Civil%20War.pdf

"Sherman Sacks Columbia, South Carolina,"
http://www.history.com/this-day-in-history/sherman-sacks-
columbia-south-carolina

Silver, Nate. "What is Driving Growth in Government Spending?"
New York *Times*, January 16, 2013,
http://fivethirtyeight.blogs.nytimes.com/2013/01/16/what-is-
driving-growth-in-government-spending/?_r=0

Skilton, Alvah. "Account of the Battle of Kennesaw Mountain," from
the blog *The Battle of Kennesaw Mountain: June 27, 1864*,
https://kennesawmountain.wordpress.com/accounts/union-
accounts/57th-ohio-captain-alvah-skilton/

Slotkin, Richard. "The Battle of the Crater," New York *Times*, July 29,
2014, http://opinionator.blogs.nytimes.com/2014/07/29/the-
battle-of-the-crater/?_r=0

Spangler, Edward. *My Little War Experience*. York Daily Publishing
Co., York PA: 1904.

Stephenson, John. "Battle of Champion's Hill," *America's Civil War*,
Sept. 1999,
http://www.civilwar.org/battlefields/championhill/champion-
hill-history-articles/battle-of-champions-hill.htm

Stillwell, Leander. *The Story of a Common Soldier of Army Life in the Civil
War, 1861-1865*. Project Gutenberg, September 8, 2008..
http://www.gutenberg.org/files/26561/26561-h/26561-h.htm

Suderow, Bryce. "The Battle of the Crater: The Civil War's Worst
Massacre,"
http://www.goordnance.army.mil/history/Staff%20Ride/ADDI
TIONAL%20READING/BATTLE%20OF%20THE%20CRA
TER

"Sylvanus Ullom," ancestry.com
http://person.ancestry.com/tree/7953517/person/24031195449
/facts

Teague, Chaplain Chuck. "Barlow's Knoll Revisited,"
http://www.militaryhistoryonline.com/gettysburg/articles/barlo
wsknoll.aspx. 2001

"The Battle of Shiloh, 1862" Eyewitness to History,
www.eyewitnesstohistory.com, 2004.

"The Battle of Shiloh: An Iowa Perspective,"
http://www.iowacivilwarhistory.com/uploads/1/3/0/6/130624

52/item_6_-_shiloh_-
_an_iowa_perspective_meyer_with_study_questions.pdf

"The Best Part of the Civil War...The End," Virginia State Parks,
http://bestpartofthecivilwar.org/best-part/

"The Indian Executions: An Interesting Account, from our Special
Correspondent." New York *Times*, Dec. 26, 1862.
http://www.startribune.com/dec-26-1862-38-dakota-men-
executed-in-mankato/138273909/

"The Life of Silas Soule," Sand Creek Massacre National Historic
Site, National Park Service,
http://www.nps.gov/sand/learn/historyculture/the-life-of-silas-
soule.htm

Thompson, Robert. "Battle of Cold Harbor: The Folly and Horror,"
The Civil War Trust.
http://www.civilwar.org/battlefields/coldharbor/cold-harbor-history-articles

Toombs, Samuel. *New Jersey Troops in the Gettysburg Campaign from June 5
to July 31, 1863*. The Evening Mail Publishing House, Orange, NJ:
1888.

Townshend, Timothy. "Lincoln, Grant and the 1864 Election,"
National Park Service,
http://www.nps.gov/liho/learn/historyculture/lincolngrant.htm

Van Buren, James Lyman. "Diary of a General from the Battle of the
Wilderness and Fortifications at Petersburg,"
http://www.raabcollection.com/james-lyman-van-buren-
autograph/general-jl-van-burens-battle-journal-person-
effects#sthash.6PzmoQMt.dpuf

Volker, Chris, compiler. "With the 60th Ohio Around Petersburg,"
Washington D.C. *National Tribune*, April 8, 1926,
http://archiver.rootsweb.ancestry.com/th/read/OHADAMS/19
99-06/0928834176

Welch, Richard F. "Burning High Bridge: The South's Last Hope,"
Civil War Times Magazine, March/April 2007,
http://www.historynet.com/burning-high-bridge-the-souths-last-
hope.htm

Wert, Jeffrey. "Closing the Back Door: The Shenandoah Campaign of
1864," *Hallowed Ground* Magazine, Winter 2004,
http://www.civilwar.org/battlefields/cedarcreek/cedar-creek-
history-articles/shenandoah1864wert.html

West, Mike. "CSA scout Dewitt Jobe died horrible death,"
Murfreesboro *Post*, October 7, 2007

http://www.murfreesboropost.com/csa-scout-dewitt-jobe-died-horrible-death-cms-6850

Wheeler, Linda. "Flames consume Shenandoah Valley in Union campaign," Washington *Post*, September 11, 2014, https://www.washingtonpost.com/lifestyle/style/flames-consume-shenandoah-valley-in-union-campaign/2014/09/11/cc7ec46c-349b-11e4-9e92-0899b306bbea_story.html

White, Lt. Col. Edward. "Cedar Creek Report, Commander, 24th Iowa, 4th Brigade, 2d Division, 19th Corps," http://www.history.army.mil/books/Staff-Rides/CedarCreek/24IA.htm

Whitehorne, Lt. Col. Joseph. "The Battle of Cedar Creek: A Self-Guided Tour," Center of Military History, United States Army, April 1991.

William, Jeff. "This Week in the American Civil War," July 22, 2013. http://mncivilwar150.com/this-week-in-the-american-civil-war-july-22-28-1863/

Wilson, James Harrison. *The Campaign of Chancellorsville, April 27-May 5, 1863*. Charles L Story, Printer: Wilmington, Delaware, 1911,

Winik, Jay. *April 1865: The Month that Saved America*, Harper Perennial Books, New York: 2001.

Wood, Thomas J. "The Battle of Missionary Ridge," Oct. 1, 1890, http://www.aotc.net/TJ%20Wood.htm

Zimmermann, S. "Michael Silver Killed In Action during Civil War," Wayne County Historical Society, October 11, 2012, http://waynehistoricalohio.org/2012/10/11/michael-silver-killed-in-action-during-civil-war/

Index

X

About the Author

The author with one of his best friends,
Irish setter puppy Brigid.

Jim Gregory grew up in the Upper Arroyo Grande Valley of San Luis Obispo County, California. He attended a two-room country school and graduated from Arroyo Grande High School. He studied history and journalism at Cuesta College and at the University of Missouri and later received his teaching credential from California Polytechnic State University. He was an editor and reporter before he began a thirty-year career teaching high school history. Gregory lives in Arroyo Grande with his wife, Elizabeth, a teacher at St. Joseph High School in nearby Santa Maria, and his sons John and Thomas. The family also includes a Basset hound, two Irish Setters, a platoon of cats, and one tortoise named Lucy.